Palms Won't Grow Here and Other Myths

Warm-Climate Plants for Cooler Areas

DAVID A. FRANCKO

TIMBER PRESS
PORTLAND · CAMBRIDGE

W

Published in 2003 by
Timber Press, Inc.
The Haseltine Building
133 S.W. Second Avenue, Suite 450
Portland, Oregon 97204, U.S.A.

Timber Press
2 Station Road
Swavesey
Cambridge CB4 5QJ, U.K.

Printed in Hong Kong

Library of Congress Cataloging-in-Publication Data

Francko, David A.
    Palms won't grow here and other myths : warm-climate plants
for cooler areas / David A. Francko.
        p. cm.
    Includes bibliographical references (p.).
    ISBN 0-88192-575-6
        1. Landscape gardening. 2. Landscape plants--Sunbelt States.
3. Landscape plants--Snowbelt States. I. Title

SB473.F815 2003
635.9--dc21
                                                    2002029149

Palms Won't Grow Here
and Other Myths

To Diana, Tyler, and Amy—
what a wonderful journey it has been.

Contents

Preface 9

Part I North-by-South Landscape Basics

Chapter 1 Introduction 15
Challenging Myths: "Everyone Knows Those Things
Won't Grow Here" ◆ Subtropical Gardening ◆ Planning
for Climate Change ◆ My Orientation and Conventions
Used in the Book

Chapter 2 A Primer on North-by-South Gardening, or Botany for Poets 29
Why Do Palms Grow in Florida? ◆ Cold Hardiness ◆
Cold Hardiness as a Function of the Plant Body ◆
Cold-Tolerance Mechanisms and Limits: The Importance
of Acclimation ◆ Plant Hardiness-Zone Maps and the
Geographic Scope of the Book ◆ The Ever-Changing
Face of Zone Maps ◆ What Is Microclimate?

Chapter 3 Microclimate-Based Landscape Planning and Design 49
Determining Your Garden's Microclimates and
Microhabitats ◆ Design Elements for a North-by-South
Landscape ◆ Companion Plants to Complement
a Warm-Climate Design ◆ Preparing Planting Beds
for Specimen and Companion Plants

Chapter 4 Four-Season Care for Warm-Climate Plants 73
Care of Warm-Climate Plants during the Growing Season
◆ Winter Care Principles ◆ Minimalist Techniques for
Winter Care and Protection ◆ Active Winter Protection
Techniques

Contents

Part II   Warm-Climate Plants for Temperate Landscapes

Chapter 5   Cold-Hardy Palms   101
            Clump Palms for the Temperate Landscape ◆
            Clump Palms as Die-Back Perennials ◆ Arborescent
            Palms for the Temperate Landscape

Chapter 6   Broadleaved Evergreen Trees and Shrubs   144
            Evergreen Magnolias ◆ Evergreen Hollies ◆
            Other Evergreen Trees and Shrubs

Chapter 7   Crape Myrtles and Other Deciduous Trees and Shrubs   183
            Crape Myrtles ◆ Other Important Deciduous Trees
            and Shrubs

Chapter 8   Bamboos, Bananas, Yuccas, Cacti, and Other Exotic
            Temperate Plants   213
            Bamboos ◆ Temperate Bananas ◆ Yuccas, Cacti,
            and Agaves

            Appendix: Additional Resources   247
            Bibliography   254
            Index   257

Color plates follow page 48

Preface

This book is about adventurous landscaping and gardening: growing warm-climate species and varieties in areas where they are not supposed to grow. It is about creating a synergistic landscape that combines the best of the northern and southern flora into a cohesive whole. Indeed, you can grow palms in Birmingham, Michigan, as well as in Birmingham, Alabama, and there are varieties of banana trees that do as well in Dayton, Ohio, as in Daytona Beach, Florida.

Obviously, this book challenges conventional landscaping wisdom, but I base this challenge on scientific experiments and data and, most importantly, on the experiences of temperate gardeners who have been growing these plants for years. Without this broad-based dataset and the many unpublished, yet important, observations made by people in the trenches, this book would not have been possible. As such, I am pleased to acknowledge the support, encouragement, and information that I received from many, many people as this book progressed from concept to reality.

I am indebted to Louis B. Anella of Oklahoma State University in Stillwater; Fred S. Breeden of Brentwood, Tennessee; Rich Goohs of

9

Streetsboro, Ohio; Sean Hogan of Portland, Oregon; Kevin McCartney of Cookeville, Tennessee; Lucy M. Repper of Middletown, Ohio; and Bryan Swinney of Oklahoma City, Oklahoma, for supplying photographs for this book. Thanks are also due to many friends and neighbors in Oxford, Ohio, and other nearby areas who graciously allowed me to photograph plants in their yards. To protect their privacy, I will not list them by name, but they have my sincere gratitude.

Robert Ogletree and Michael Prairie of Tennessee provided insights, comprehensive long-term datasets, and encouragement throughout the writing process. I especially thank Robert for helping to set up an unforgettable palm safari to Quebeck, Tennessee, where my colleague Ken Wilson and I had a chance to meet Charles and Diane Cole. Mr. Cole is one of the true hardy palm pioneers, whose experimental approach to growing palms and other warm-climate plants in east-central Tennessee dates to the early 1960s. The Coles' amazing landscape was the source of many photographs in this book, as well as insights on cultivation techniques and long-term winter hardiness.

Bryan Swinney, Don Moorhead, and John Lodes of Oklahoma brought me up to speed on exciting warm-climate plant developments in that state and nearby areas, and they reminded me why I still have so many fond memories of life in the Sooner State. John also provided me with specimens of *Sabal* 'Birmingham' from his Tulsa garden. Robert Wallace of Iowa State University helped with *Opuntia* identification and other insights on hardy cactus biology. Mike Heim, a science teacher in zone 3b northern Wisconsin, was kind enough to share information and photographs of plants that even *I* was surprised he was successful with. These data provided a firm context for extending the hardiness rating for numerous trees, shrubs, and herbaceous plants. Similarly, Kiril Donov of Bulgaria was kind enough to share his perspectives on growing trunked palms in rigorous climates. Betty Shor provided a preprint copy of an unpublished article as well as invaluable information on bamboo flowering cycles and survival data. Eddy Krifcher of Pittsburgh, Pennsylvania; Leland Lindauer of Grand Junction, Colorado; Robert Morris and John Hetzler of Colorado Springs, Colorado; and Billy DeVincentes of Mount Vernon, New York, provided data and ideas about plant successes in those areas. J. D. Roswell of California and Nick Parker of British Columbia awakened me to the wonderful world of adventurous gardening in the Pacific Northwest. Kyle Brown, a long-time palm enthusiast from northern Florida, shared insights and several rare, experimental palms that are now growing in Ohio.

I extend a special thanks to Tamar Myers of South Carolina, who has been a source of inspiration to so many adventurous gardeners. She was kind enough to send me a set of *Palm Quarterly* from the mid-1980s; from these I learned about her early experiments on palm cultivation in Franklin, Ohio—this was a revelation to me. And she did not laugh at me when I told her what I was attempting here in Oxford, Ohio. Similarly, Jeff Stevens of Apison, Tennessee, and other officers and members of the Southeastern Palm and Exotic Plant Society have been extremely helpful and encouraging.

Through my work on the Miami University Hardy Palm Project, I learned much from several incredibly knowledgeable nursery folks who not only sell the species and varieties covered in this book, but provided me with guidance and encouragement. Jerry Burton, owner of Burton's Bamboo Garden in Morrow, Ohio; Rick Goohs, owner of Buckeye Bamboo Company in Streetsboro, Ohio; and Ned Jaquith of the Bamboo Garden in Portland, Oregon, provided enormously valuable information on bamboo biology. Steve and Diane Galehouse, owners of Plant Crafters Garden Center in Westlake, Ohio, provided me with a business perspective on warm-climate plant sales in northern Ohio. Doug Cepluch, owner of Eagle Creek Nature Center in Colerain Township, Ohio, shared valuable insights and specimens and was a source of photographs for yuccas, succulents, and other plants. Ken Willeford of Ken's Nursery in Columbia, Tennessee, gave tips on plant selection and cultivation and helped me locate specimens in that state.

Gerry McKiness, owner of Gerry's Jungle at the Neotropic Nursery in McDonough, Georgia, deserves special thanks. Gerry sold Miami University many of the palms and other plants we are experimenting with in Ohio, and he spent many hours counseling me on the ins and outs of growing these species in temperate areas. He was not formally trained in botany, but there are few people who know more about palm biology than Gerry McKiness. He is a gold mine of information, and he and his family are truly wonderful people. I especially acknowledge his work as an expert reader in examining my entire manuscript for errors and omissions.

I also acknowledge the efforts of Ken Wilson, professor of botany at Miami University, my colleague on the Miami University Hardy Palm Project, and coprincipal investigator on the grants that support our work. He and members of our research group, including graduate students Stepanie Roberts, Lu Li, and Meepa Lokuge and undergraduate researchers Alison Boutin, Mike Glueckert, Todd Gorman, Eva Hager, Katie Kettler, Robin Lewis, Eric Nagy, Sarah Wilhoite, Michele Wilkerson, and Janelle Yarina, contributed to this book in many ways. They are helping to pave the way for more cold-hardy palms and other ornamentals. Ken and I gratefully acknowledge the financial support of the Ohio Plant Biotechnology Consortium and the Department of Botany, which provided funding for plants, experimental materials, travel, and other items, and the Miami University Campus Services Department, which provided funds for plants as well as horticultural assistance.

Diana, my wife and best friend, is totally responsible for any redeeming qualities I may have, and she was a constant source of encouragement during this project. Our children, Tyler and Amy, have been good sports over the years, allowing their father to enjoy plant forays on innumerable family trips.

Finally, I thank Carolyn Keiffer, assistant professor of botany at Miami University, for serving (in Stephen King's parlance) as the ideal reader for this book. Carolyn is an excellent botanist and a fellow plant geek—an unbeatable combination in a critical reviewer of this book. I especially thank Neal Maillet, executive editor of Timber Press, who believed in this project, offered extremely helpful comments on the original proposal, and was responsible for getting this book into the Timber Press family. Special thanks also to Lisa DiDonato, the project editor, who was a joy to work with and who corrected innumerable faux pas and misuses of the English language. All remaining errors are mine alone.

North-by-South Landscape Basics

Chapter 1

Introduction

All really new ideas have a certain aspect of foolishness when they are first proposed.

—Alfred North Whitehead

Nothing is so useless as a general maxim.

—Lord Thomas Macauley

I will bet there are as many gardening and landscaping books on the market as there are plant species available at your local nursery. Well, that may be an exaggeration—but not by much. So why should you read *this* book? If you have read this far, it is safe to say that you are already an avid, accomplished gardener or an aspiring gardener; you are interested in trying something different from the run-of-the-mill landscapes in your neighborhood; you live in an area with cold winters but have coveted the types of plants in warm-climate areas; and you are willing to be adventurous and try some of these plants, but you lack the knowledge base needed to act on your ambitions. This book is addressed to you.

North-by-South landscaping seeks to bridge the botanically unnecessary but often hard-and-fast distinction between southern and northern plants in the temperate landscape. This is not subtropical gardening per se, although North-by-South landscaping is rooted in the traditions and philosophy of subtropical gardening. Rather, it is about integrating warm-climate plants into an existing temperate landscape and creating a cohesive whole that is greater than the sum of the parts. North-by-South landscaping challenges myths about where plants *should* grow and replaces those myths with evidence on where they *can* and *do* grow.

Gardening is as much about personal outlook as it is about technique. For many of us, gardening provides our primary means of artistic expression, as well as the challenges and joys of creating a landscape that makes a personal and emotionally satisfying statement. Adventurous gardeners do not simply dig holes and drop in plants. Rather, they creatively assemble a palette of plants and structural features through which they can wander and be refreshed in mind and body. There are as many ways to do this successfully as there are individual preferences. Most gardeners living in cold-winter areas have been conditioned to believe that their palette is limited to only a few colors: the eight-crayon box of cold-hardy species in the landscape trade. This book, quite simply, is designed to expand your palette, to give you a sixty-four-crayon box of plant choices to work with. Although there is nothing wrong with blue or red, sometimes the landscape plan you want to implement needs aquamarine or scarlet.

Regardless of where you travel in the world, you'll find that the typical household, civic, and industrial gardens in a given region share certain characteristics. Local climatic and soil conditions, common native plant species, ornamental plant availability, and tradition dictate that for every region there is, for lack of a better term, a default garden style. For example, to complement native maples, oaks, and other deciduous tree species, developers in the northern half of the United States typically install yews and needle-leaved conifers as foundation plantings and add color with flowering bulbs and summer annuals. In the southern states, we associate southern magnolias, flowering crape myrtles, oleander, towering pines, and live oaks with a look and feel that is traditionally "southern." In Florida and the coastal South, palm trees define the landscape.

In this book, I challenge the notion that tradition (or perhaps better stated, landscaping inertia) alone is a valid reason for restricting yourself to default gardening in temperate parts of the United States, Canada, and Europe. Specifically, I challenge the notion that southern plants cannot (and should not) be grown in temperate gardens. At the outset, I want to emphasize that I am not against native plants or regional conventional wisdom in plant selection per se. Rather, this book is about challenging conventional wisdom in your garden—about being an adventurous gardener. By adventurous, I do not mean ignoring common sense and expecting miracles. Instead you must be willing to take some chances, make some mistakes, and invest a little more effort.

I use the term *southern* to denote those plants that are considered by most people to be subtropical or tropical in their distribution and growth requirements (for example, most palm trees), as well as those traditional mainstays of the southern U.S. garden (for example, southern magnolias and crape myrtles) that are actually adaptable to temperate conditions. The term *temperate* is often incorrectly used to denote northern climates. In fact, much of the southeastern United States features a temperate climate, and many areas in the lower Midwest are climatically similar to the upper South. In the field of vegetation ecology, scientists denote temperate biomes as those major ecosystem types (deciduous forest, grassland, desert) lying between roughly 30° and 60° latitude both north and south of the equator. That includes southern Canada and all of the United States except the Florida peninsula, the immediate coast of the Gulf of Mexico, and southern Texas. In this book, I use *temperate* to describe regions with true four-seasons climates and cold winters with regular, significant bouts of subfreezing weather. Temperate plants, then, are species that can grow and thrive under such broadly defined conditions. Warm-temperate plants are species native to warmer parts of the temperate zone; I will use the qualifier *warm-climate* to denote plants that are typically found in areas without cold winters, even though many of these species are in fact hardy in cold-winter areas. By presenting specific examples and hard data, I hope to convince you that the conventional wisdom and distinctions between so-called temperate versus tropical plants and northern versus southern gardens are at best confused and very often flat wrong.

Challenging Myths:
"Everyone Knows Those Things Won't Grow Here"

Gardeners living in the temperate areas of the United States and Canada have long returned from trips to Florida, the coastal Deep South, or California yearning to grow some of the plants that make these areas so botanically interesting. A group of palms, banana trees, and flowering crape myrtles evokes something elemental in the human psyche—a lush, exotic look most people think is impossible to achieve back home in Ohio, Missouri, Maryland, or Pennsylvania. This desire is not confined to more northerly gardeners, however. Even gardeners in decidedly southern metropolitan areas such as Atlanta or Raleigh might expect bemused scorn from neighbors if they plant a palm tree in their front yards. After all, "Everyone knows those things won't grow here."

Until very recently, most people would have put the smart money on the neighbors. But sometimes the smart money backs a losing hand. Most amateur gardeners and even most gardening professionals are conservative by nature, and it takes a while before long-held notions, even incorrect ones, pass away. "Everyone knows," for instance, that newly planted trees should be placed in a planting hole amended with lots of peat and a handful of fertilizer and then staked to prevent wind stress from damaging delicate roots. This method sounds pretty logical and seems to make botanical sense, but like many common-sense notions about nature, actual data brings us in another direction. When horticulturists challenged the conventional wisdom and did controlled experiments, most trees actually established themselves faster and showed more vigor if they were planted in well-tilled, reasonably fertile native soil without being staked. Why? It turns out that a tree planted in a hole containing enriched soil tends to take the easy way out, rooting well only in the loose, amended, and fertilizer-rich soil and refusing to extend its roots into the parent soil. This is especially true in heavy clay soils—the kind many of us garden in. The roots grow round and round the planting hole and in a few years the tree can become root-bound, just as if it had been growing in a clay pot all along, because in essence it has. Most gardening guides now suggest that you stake a newly planted tree only in the most windswept sites and only when the root ball is small relative to the height and profile of the tree. The evidence suggests that unstaked trees allowed to move back and forth with the wind and forced to deal with moderate wind stress actually develop stronger root systems and stronger trunks compared with staked trees. And so it has been with the notion of growing warm-temperate and subtropical plants in temperate parts of the United States, Canada, and Europe. Everyone assumed that it could not be done, and therefore few people even tried to generate the objective data needed to evaluate specific plants under specific conditions.

Sometimes it is not lack of information, but the overextension of data, that leads to erroneous conclusions. One the most valuable lessons I learned early in my scientific training came from my master's degree advisor, Bob Heath at Kent State University: Make sure that you distinguish between the *real* conclusions that can be drawn from scientific data and the *extended* conclusions that the data suggest. Mark Twain said it well: "We should be careful to get out of an experiment only the wisdom that is in it—and stop there—lest we be like the cat that sits down on a hot stove lid. She will never sit down on a hot stove lid again; and that is well; but also she will not sit down on a cold one."

Twain's admonition directly applies to gardening, especially to the scientifically informed plant choices based on regional climatic factors. When the U.S. Department of Agriculture (USDA) updated its plant hardiness-zone map in 1990 and made vigorous and successful efforts to promote its use in the gardening industry and the public arena, they performed a valuable public service. In chapter 2, I discuss this and other zone maps. For now, let me simply note that the USDA hardiness-zone map divides the United States into ten broad geographic regions, or hardiness zones, based on the average annual minimum temperature. The 1990 map uses data from 1974 to 1986, a period of time that contains some of the coldest winters in the past century. And the next update of the USDA hardiness-zone map, due to be released in fall 2002, will incorporate data from the 1990s, one of the warmest decades on record. The American Horticultural Society heat-zone map is based on another climatic variable: the average number of days over 86°F (30°C) in a given area. Such zone maps are very useful in helping gardeners identify plants that have a good chance of success in the typical climatic conditions found within fairly broad geographic areas.

Zone maps are not absolute guides to plant survivorship, however, and should never restrict the informed gardener from experimentation. An informed gardener can easily squeeze a full USDA zone out of the microclimatic variations that exist in a typical home garden. With minimal winter protection, plants can be grown up to two hardiness zones colder than their generally accepted zonal limits. Furthermore, a lot of garden plant zonal information is simply wrong—many popular plants grown in the South are much more cold hardy than generally believed. It is simply that, until recently, too few people actually grew those plants outside the accepted range to document a range extension. A good example is the common bald cypress tree, a native of southern swamps and wetlands that is now planted successfully as far north as Minnesota, in upland as well as wetland conditions.

If the tag on a shrub says that the plant is hardy in USDA zones 7–9, usually local home centers or discount garden centers only within those zones will sell the plant. Most gardeners in the Deep South (and many plant suppliers and retailers in those environs) honestly believe that only an adventurous and perhaps misguided gardener would purchase a local shrub to take back to their zone 6 garden in Cincinnati and only an outright fool would carry it back to zone 5 Indianapolis or Kansas City and try to grow it. Never mind that Nashville, Tennessee, is also in zone 6 and the high mountains of North Carolina lie within zones 5b through 6a.

The fact is, plants cannot read the information on their tags. As long as their needs are met, they do not know whether they are planted in Florida, Georgia, or Ohio. This is *not* to say that you can dig up a queen palm tree in Orlando and stick it in your yard in Pittsburgh and expect it to survive and grow. However, a needle palm will do quite nicely in either the Steel City or in Orlando, provided that you know how to plant it, how to take care of it until it becomes established, and how to troubleshoot problems.

Subtropical Gardening

Since the mid-1990s, we have seen an explosion of interest in what may be termed *subtropical gardening*. I list many of the newer general reference books on this topic in the bibliography, and mainstream gardening periodicals such as *Fine Gardening* have featured articles dealing with similar themes. The term *subtropical gardening* needs to be qualified here, especially as it applies to this book. Subtropical or tropical gardening generally denotes a style in which the temperate gardener attempts to create a tropical feel through the use of tropical and subtropical plants and plants that are actually temperate but mimic the lush tropical look. There is absolutely nothing wrong with this type of adventurous gardening, and this book will show you how to create a true subtropical look in your temperate garden, if that is your desire.

One of the major objections (and misunderstandings) people have with this kind of gardening, however, is that they do not want their yard to look weird. Most gardeners simply want to integrate interesting plants such as palms, crape myrtles, and tree hollies into the framework of their temperate garden. (Notice I did not use the terms *southern* and *northern* here; as we will see, such terms are botanically meaningless.) You do not have to have a backyard that looks like a 1940s Hollywood movie set to incorporate subtropical themes into your garden. But, these days it is certainly possible to create a cohesive subtropical theme garden in climatic zones heretofore thought impossible. And in a nutshell, that's what this book is all about: giving you the tools and information you need to create a full-blown subtropical paradise in Nashville or simply to add a group of palms to your existing hosta and fern patio garden in Philadelphia. Both are examples of North-by-South landscapes—the incorporation of warm-climate species into a temperate landscape in a cohesive and aesthetically pleasing way.

Of course, the notion of growing exotic plants in unlikely places is not new. Those interested in the long history of subtropical gardening, especially in Victorian England, will find interesting treatments of this subject in Reynolds (1997a, 1997b). In a real sense, the history of exotic gardening in temperate climes is a story of two periods: Victorian England and the modern Internet era.

Robert Fortune, the intrepid English plant collector, saw and acquired his first Chusan palm (named *Trachycarpus fortunei*) in 1849 on the Zhoushan (formerly Chusan) Islands off the coast of eastern China. He had some plants shipped back to the Royal Botanic Gardens, Kew, and the success of these palms in the English climate helped ignite a passion for palm and exotic plant cultivation in Victorian England that persisted well into the twentieth century. As Reynolds notes, the Victorian passion for plants provided middle- and upper-class subjects of the British Empire with tangible links to the far-flung tropical and subtropical lands within the empire.

In the United States, outside of the truly subtropical areas, interest in growing subtropical plants in temperate climes never reached the fever pitch of Victorian England. Reynolds notes, however, that by the 1950s some individuals were experimenting successfully with palms in Virginia, southern Pennsylvania, interior Georgia, Tennessee, and the Pacific Northwest. The agreeable Mediterranean and subtropical climates of southern California and southern Florida, respectively, have long supported extensive interest in palm and tropical plant cultivation, and the best contemporary gardens of this kind are still found there. However, even in California and Florida (as well as the subtropical climates of the Gulf of Mexico coast and the Atlantic coastal plain of the Deep South) interest has increased in recent years as more and more plant species are being tried and found to be successful.

The modern era in subtropical-themed temperate gardening may be dated to the 1983 birth of the famous *Palm Quarterly* newsletter by editor and hardy-palm pioneer Tamar Myers. Myers experimented with growing palms in Franklin, Ohio (roughly 35 mi [56 km] north of Cincinnati in southwestern Ohio). She and contributors to the newsletter regaled each other with the trials, tribulations, and surprising successes of growing palms, bananas, and other seemingly impossible plants in temperate regions with true four-seasons climates and real winters. Authors hailed from all over the United States, Canada, and Europe.

Publication of the *Palm Quarterly* ceased in 1990. But by that time, *Hardy Palm International*, the journal of the Pacific Northwest chapter of the International Palm Society, plus other journals and newsletters of regional palm and exotic plant societies (for example, the Southeastern Palm and Exotic Plant Society and its newsletter *Rhapidophyllum*) had filled the void for their respective memberships. Advances in palm cultivation and experimental gardening were reaching large audiences on a regular basis, and the interest snowballed.

Palm societies notwithstanding, perhaps the greatest impetus to challenging the zone in recent years has come via the Internet. If you type in key terms such as "hardy palms" or "cold-hardy bananas" on any search engine, you will get literally hundreds of web sites around the world offering plants, seeds, and other materials for sale and information on personal gardening experiences. Professional and semiprofessional societies devoted to growing palms and other exotic plants, such as the aforementioned International Palm Society, the Southeastern Palm and Exotic Plant Society, and the Pacific Northwest Palm and Exotic Plant Society, now feature extremely popular web sites with chat rooms and message boards. Information that used to take years to percolate through the gardening world now reaches vast audiences instantly.

Most importantly, plants that used to be almost impossible to find (and some even previously unknown to science) are now accessible at the click of a mouse from anywhere in the world. The plant biotechnology explosion of the 1990s and early 2000s—not just genetic engineering, but more prosaic commercial methods such as plant tissue culture propagation and rapid hybridization techniques—have led to the introduction of numerous plant varieties that have vastly greater vigor in colder climates. In chapter 6 I will introduce you to hardy camellias and citrus varieties, readily available plants that are hardy in temperatures below 0°F (–18°C) and that were literally only a pipe dream ten years ago.

Planning for Climate Change

If you are a practical sort who wants to think about what your garden should look like ten, twenty, or more years down the road, it is prudent to consider the effects of global warming on the sorts of plants you install now. I realize that this whole concept, tied up as it is in controversy and politics, is a real hot-button issue for most people. But as a trained environmental scientist, my interpretation of the evidence is in concert with the great majority of the scientific community. The average global temperature is almost certainly rising and probably has been doing so for at least a few decades. There is strong evidence that the carbon dioxide content in the atmosphere has been on the rise as well. What remain open questions are how much and how fast temperatures are rising, the relative contributions of human activities and natural events, and what countermeasures might be used.

Conservative estimates suggest that in many parts of the United States, Canada, and Europe, the mean annual temperature will increase at least a couple of degrees in the next three to four decades and perhaps 6°F (3.5°C) by 2100. That does not sound like too much until you consider that 5°F (3°C) is about the difference in annual mean temperature between Cincinnati and Knoxville or Aberdeen and London. Put another way, a 5°F increase in mean temperature is equivalent to a half USDA hardiness-zone change, or about 150–200 mi (240–320 km) in latitude.

As I write this chapter, I have just given interviews to reporters from several newspapers who published articles on our palm work here at Miami University. One of the hooks they built into the palm story was the report by U.S. Forest Service scientists Louis Iverson and Anantha Prasad that sugar maples, beeches, and other Midwestern forest trees may vanish from all but the extreme northern United States by 2050, being replaced by northward-migrating loblolly pines and other southern species. I was asked whether I believed that we could not have grown palms in Oxford, Ohio, in 1990—in other words, did I believe that the climate warmed up enough around here in ten years to make the impossible possible. Of course not. Ours are not the first Ohio palms and are certainly not the only ones. (Besides, it is not possible to draw definitive conclusions about climatic change on the basis of ten years' worth of data.)

Still, it does make sense for gardeners to push the envelope a little bit in favor of more rather than less heat-tolerant plants in temperate parts of the world. In other words, a dwarf palmetto, which even skeptics accept as marginally hardy in zone 6, is probably a better long-term choice for a planting in Cincinnati, Nashville, or St. Louis, at least on the basis of climate, than an Alberta spruce, which is already at the southern limits of heat tolerance in a zone 6 garden.

My Orientation and Conventions Used in the Book

Before we move on to specifics, I want to share a bit about my background and some conventions I employ in this book. Although I have a doctorate in botany, I am not a horticulturist by formal training. My formal botanical training was in the field of limnology (the study of freshwater systems) and aquatic plant ecology, and my students and I still conduct research in this field. What I have learned about general gardening and growing specific plants, I have picked up by reading, talking with botanical colleagues and nursery owners, attending scientific conferences, and, most important, experimenting, failing, and then applying what I have learned to design new experiments.

This last point is critical. When I first got interested in horticulture, I naturally approached my new avocation as a gardener in the same spirit as my scientific work. Good science almost always challenges conventional wisdom. And, as famed nineteenth-century biologist Thomas Huxley said, "Irrationally held truths may be more harmful than reasoned errors." I have never felt constrained by gardening conventional wisdom that lacks a solid empirical basis. In fact, when someone tells me that something is impossible my immediate, almost visceral reaction is to challenge that statement and have a great deal of fun in the process.

As a scientist, I know that all facts about how nature operates are subject to revision if new evidence surfaces. My background in plant biology has certainly helped me, and as you will see later I believe that every successful gardener needs a firm grounding in botanical fundamentals (for example, Capon 1990). But I am also of the opinion that actual experimental evidence is much more important than dogma, especially when many of the commonly held beliefs about plant hardiness and suitability for one climatic zone or another are either incorrect or supported by meager evidence. I also believe that the journey is at least as important as the destination. Therefore, I try to present evidence for statements I make and then leave it to you to make your own judgements on real and extended conclusions of that evidence. And, I hope that I can convey to you, the reader, just how much fun this kind of landscaping can be.

I did not always see gardening as fun. As a child, I had the chore of weeding and tending our family's small, typical suburban garden in Garfield Heights, Ohio, near Cleveland. I hated it. I remember doing absolutely the quickest job I could, the minimum that would satisfy my mother and get me out of that dreaded parental injunction, "No playing with your friends until you're done weeding the garden, and that's final!" Now that I reflect on what my mother had planted in her garden, I realize she had some neat stuff—yuccas, mock orange, hydrangeas, and numerous perennials. But at the time it was just a green blur and a real pain.

When my wife, Diana, and I purchased our first house near Battle Creek, Michigan, we planted a small vegetable garden and put in some perennials. I also remember planting some kind of little shrubs along the foundation. I have no idea what they were. At that point in my life (and by this time I already had my Ph.D.), I did not know a yew from a box-wood and was perfectly happy in my ignorance. Even when we moved to Stillwater, Oklahoma, with its much longer growing season and plethora of southern plants, I was a barely literate gardener. I did, however, develop an appreciation and affinity for magnolias, crape myrtles, Burford hollies, and other plants that stood me in good stead later. I also participated in the trips of the field botany class to various parts of Oklahoma, and, to my surprise and glee, I learned that both alligators and dwarf palmettos are native to the extreme southeastern part of the state.

In the late 1980s I found a scraggly potted palm for sale at one of the local Stillwater nurseries. The salesperson did not know what kind of palm it was, and neither did I, but it was his opinion that "Those things won't grow here." Of course, after he said that I had to have it. I planted the poor thing, which I now realize was a small windmill palm, in some gritty soil on the south side of our house right next to the foundation. My reasoning was that it would be warmer there during the winter. True enough, but I neglected to think about summer conditions along a south-facing brick foundation in Oklahoma. My abortive experiment in palm cultivation quickly ended when the palm predictably fried during the first spell of normal Oklahoma summer heat and then succumbed altogether during the next winter. But that failure and my exposure to the myriad interesting plants that could be grown under borderline southern conditions in zone 6b and 7a Stillwater got me started.

The gardening bug finally bit, by necessity as much as anything else, when in 1990 we relocated to Miami University and Oxford, Ohio, just northwest of Cincinnati. After renting a university house for a few months, we purchased a newly constructed home in a subdivision. The lots had a fair number of native trees, but we elected to save money on the house by doing all of the landscaping ourselves. That meant designing planting beds, preparing soil, selecting plants, putting in a lawn, etcetera. Needless to say, I made lots of mistakes, some of them costly not only in terms of time but also money. My wife still teases me about our $200 stick, a tree I bought without a guarantee that, of course, promptly died.

Still, I was hooked. One of the things that intrigued me when we first moved to southern Ohio was that the Miami University campus and homes in Oxford featured several mature southern magnolias, willow oaks, and bald cypress trees. During a family trip to the Cincinnati Zoo a few months after we arrived, I saw a little shrubby thing called *Rhapidophyllum hystrix* (needle palm), which the plaque said was the most cold-hardy palm in the world. A palm in Cincinnati? Even though I was now living north of the Mason-Dixon line, maybe I didn't have to give up the southern plants I had come to appreciate. I began wondering what kinds of exotic plants I could try in our new landscape. At this time it was still difficult to find local sources for magnolias and other southern plants, but I found some things and purchased (or dug up) other plants during family trips. One of these plants was a 3-gallon windmill palm I bought in Tifton, Georgia, on the way home from Disney World. That windmill palm, unlike its short-lived cousin in Oklahoma, survived and was relocated to our present home in Oxford.

Tony Avent, noted horticulturist and owner of Plant Delights Nursery in North Carolina, has a motto that I have learned to accept and trust. He considers a type of plant hardy until he has personally killed it three times. As I noted earlier, the information on a plant identification tag at your local nursery is a *guide* to expected performance, not a dictate about what is possible. In many cases, that information is suspect due to insufficient data. So, let's disregard conventional wisdom and rely instead on modern, field-tested data. Yes, that southern magnolia you have dreamed of planting in your St. Louis yard *will* grow there and, chances are, you will now be able to find local trees if you know what to look for. Want to grow a hardy banana tree in Portland or Leeds? You bet. Just pick the right species and varieties, plant and take care of them properly, and be prepared for the neighbors to do double-takes when they walk past your yard.

I caution, however, that disregarding conventional wisdom is not the same thing as a blind leap of faith. I present useful, pragmatic information that you can employ to make informed decisions about landscape design and plant selection. I want to raise your consciousness a bit about choices you have, but I do not promise magic. After all, who wants to invest significant time, energy, and money on concepts that are scientifically untenable? As I said earlier, I will not tell you that you can grow all palm species in Tennessee or Missouri, but I can introduce you to several palm species and varieties that you are likely to have success with.

Accordingly, some ground rules and conventions are in order:

◆ Information I present in this book will, unless clearly noted, be based on personal experiences and reliable first-hand data of trusted professionals and expert amateurs. Any speculation, informed or otherwise, will be clearly noted as such.

◆ The term *hardy* will be fully explored so that you will not have to guess what it means in regard to specific plants. After all, a plant can be foliage hardy only to 20°F (–7°C) but shoot hardy to –5°F (–21°C) and root hardy to –20°F (–29°C). Which of these temperatures is the most important depends on the specific plant and one's own tastes, willingness to engage in winter-protection strategies, and tolerance of winter damage.

◆ Unless clearly noted otherwise, a key requirement for any plant that I discuss is that, once established, the plant must be able to survive at least 0°F (–18°C) with minimal damage and with minimal winter protection.

◆ Finally, terms such as *subtropical, tropical,* and *warm-temperate* can be confusing when applied to plants, gardening techniques, and such. Unless otherwise noted, I will use the qualifier *warm-climate* to refer to those plants or gardening styles that are found in the tropics or subtropics but also are adaptable to truly temperate climates.

Chapter 2

A Primer on North-by-South Gardening, or Botany for Poets

Some are weather-wise, some are otherwise.

—*Poor Richard's Almanack,* 1735

Many palms and other warm-climate plants will do perfectly well in a temperate garden. If the plant's needs are being met, it cares not whether it's growing in the Rust Belt or the Sun Belt. That is a very big *if* though. What sorts of needs are critical and why? What makes some plants cold hardy and others not, and for that matter, what does the term *cold hardy* really mean? What is all this USDA hardiness-zone business, and where does my garden fall in various plant hardiness classification systems? Before covering methods used to grow warm-climate plants in temperate areas, it is useful to spend some time on basic botany for non-scientists, or botany for poets, if you will.

Why Do Palms Grow in Florida?

This is not a trick or trivial question. The simple answer is that the climatic and soil conditions palms need to grow and thrive are ideal or nearly so on the Florida peninsula. But let's look a little deeper. The key to understanding subjective concepts such as cold hardiness and drought tolerance lies in understanding plants as biological organisms. If you want to know how to grow palms in Tennessee or Colorado, you need to understand what makes these plants tick.

Contrary to what many of my first-year general botany students believe at the start of fall term, plants are indeed alive—they metabolize, sense and respond to their environment, reproduce, and feature every other biological process common to animals. Like animals, plants rely on their environment to provide them with the basic necessities of life. Plants need adequate—but not too much—light as an energy source for photosynthesis. They need adequate water to carry on metabolic reactions, to transport materials, and for structural support. They require lots of nitrogen and phosphorus to manufacture proteins, sugars, fats, genetic material, and energy-storage molecules. Plants also need a host of other mineral nutrients that must be dissolved in the soil moisture so that they can be taken up by roots.

When you feed a plant with fertilizer, you are not feeding it in the sense that you feed yourself or a pet. We animals require food materials rich in presynthesized organic nutrients such as amino acids, fats, carbohydrates, and vitamins. Plants can manufacture these from glucose they fix during photosynthesis, but to do this they need a carbon source (carbon dioxide from the air), an oxygen source (again from the air, but also a by-product of photosynthesis), water, and inorganic nutrients—nitrogen, phosphorus, calcium, iron, and many other mineral nutrients typically found in rich soil but frequently lacking in garden soils. It is these inorganic nutrients that one finds, in ideal balances, in good fertilizers.

So, in this context, palms do well in Florida because the environment there provides them with adequate sunlight, water, and mineral nutrients. But that cannot be the whole story. Most people in Florida actually have to fertilize their palms several times per year because the sandy soils are poor in nutrients. During the late 1990s drought conditions were created in much of the peninsula by explosive population growth coupled with several dry years in a row, and palms and other plants were consequently stressed. Perhaps the more central question, then, is why arctic cold fronts that sweep down into north-central Florida every few years decimate citrus groves and burn the foliage of queen palms, but leave the more common cabbage palms unscathed.

Cold Hardiness

The simple answer to the question above is that cabbage palms are very cold hardy and queen palms and citrus trees are not. Cold hardiness is *the* central factor of importance in this book. In the United States the term *plant hardiness* has almost become synonymous with cold hardiness, and to a large extent that is a biologically accurate view. But it is critical for experimental gardeners to realize that cold hardiness—the ability of a given plant to survive winter conditions in a given area—is the culmination of environmental stress events and plant responses to those events that plays out over the entire year and not just the winter season. As such, hardiness classification systems based solely on winter temperature minima must be taken with a very large grain of salt.

We are used to thinking about stress in human terms: work stress, financial problems, and so on. And it is difficult to pick up a newspaper or watch the evening news and not see some reference to another environmental pollutant that has been linked to human disease. Psychological pressures and environmental pollutants both induce stress responses in the human body. We can adapt to a certain amount of stress, but if the immune or other body system is overwhelmed, illness or even death can result. Plants also suffer stress, and there is a entire branch of botany that deals specifically with plant responses to environmental stress. The extremes of winter cold represent a key environmental stress factor that plants must deal with to survive. However, winter temperatures alone do not begin to tell the full story. Let's look at why plants are damaged or killed by winter cold and the adaptations some plants have that permit them to deal with cold stress.

First, most of a plant's body is water. Herbaceous (nonwoody) plants contain relatively more water and woody plants somewhat less. Unlike humans and other warm-blooded animals, however, plants cannot metabolize sufficiently to maintain a stable body temperature and, if temperatures drop below the freezing point of water (32°F, 0°C), that water can freeze. The formation of ice crystals within plant tissues can rupture living cells, causing cell death and tissue damage. If damage is superficial or localized (say just the leaf margins or tips), the plant can recover by sloughing off damaged leaves or stems. But if most or all of the plant is frozen, the entire plant dies. You see this syndrome in tender garden plants the morning after a hard freeze.

All plants have a genetically programmed minimum temperature below which their cells will always freeze and die. That is why, no matter how well you take care of your *Impatiens* and other herbaceous annuals during the growing season, they cannot survive unprotected outside in areas that receive annual killing frosts. These sorts of plants, by definition, are not cold hardy. Cold-hardy plants can and do adapt to freezing temperatures, but the mechanisms they use, the genetically programmed minimum temperature for survival, and the temperatures at which damage to major plant structures occur vary greatly between plant species and even varieties of the same species.

All cold-hardy perennials, both herbaceous and woody, that survive freezing temperatures make use of freeze-avoidance mechanisms and/or physiological freeze-tolerance mechanisms. For example, deciduous trees shed their leaves and other freeze-vulnerable plant parts in autumn to avoid having to deal with winter temperatures. In contrast, the woody stems of deciduous trees and both the stems and leaves of evergreen perennials use freeze-tolerance mechanisms. Plant physiologists consider these latter mechanisms to be of more generalized importance because, with the possible exception of die-back perennials that are killed completely to the soil line each year and regrow from underground structures, some form of physiological tolerance mechanism must be used lest the plant lose persistent aboveground structures. In a later section of this chapter, I discuss cold-tolerance mechanisms in depth.

Cold Hardiness as a Function of the Plant Body

First, let's consider aboveground versus underground plant tissues as they relate specifically to the term *cold hardiness*. One of the things I like best about Michael Dirr's splendid books on woody shrubs and trees and other landscape plants (for example, Dirr 1997, 1998, 2002) is that he always tells the reader exactly what he means when he uses the term *hardy* in relation to a specific plant or cultivar (cultivated variety). For example, under the general description section for his excellent treatment of the numerous crape myrtle cultivars on the market (Dirr 1998, 538–546), he noted the critical distinction between wood hardiness and root hardiness—the former usually somewhere around –5°F (–21°C) but the latter as low as –24°F (–31°C). This kind of information, which is lacking from most gardening books, is absolutely essential in my view. It allows the prospective gardener to make an informed decision about how much damage he or she is willing to live with on a yearly basis as a function of the landscape value of that specific plant.

Crape myrtles are grown as small to medium-sized trees in the southern and southwestern United States. They have extremely beautiful exfoliating bark and a wonderfully sinuous branching pattern. Crape myrtles are deciduous, but they exhibit decent autumn color and their beautiful trunks and branches provide winter interest. If you live in a climate where winter temperatures routinely drop much below –5°F (–21°C), you know from Dirr's information that it may be difficult (but not impossible) to grow that particular cultivar as a tree-form crape myrtle in your area, which is extremely valuable information. (Note, however, that in chapter 7 I will challenge this view with tips on winter protection and introduce you to tree-form crape myrtle cultivars that are cold hardy to much lower temperatures.)

But, recall Mark Twain's admonition quoted in chapter 1 about the pitfalls of overextending the conclusions of experimental data. That some crape myrtles are not especially wood hardy below about –5°F (–21°C) does *not* mean that you cannot and should not try to grow these wonderful plants in colder areas. This is a trap many gardeners, even experienced ones, often fall into. In the process they reject out of hand many exciting plant possibilities. They make two incorrect overextensions when assuming that the plant hardiness-zone information in a landscaping book or on a plant identification tag is absolute and applies to mortality of the whole plant. For many of the North-by-South landscaping plants discussed in this book, there is a large and quite fluid hardiness range, both in terms of critical temperature and the parts of the plant that are affected.

Let's return to the developmental biology of crape myrtle plants to see how this works. A well-mulched and well-watered crape myrtle sited in a favorable microclimate will likely be about 5°F (3°C) more cold hardy that the average figure quoted for the cultivar. But more important, even though the plant may be killed to the ground if the temperature drops to, say −12°F (−24°C), it is not dead. It will regrow from buds near or below the soil line and flower during the next growing season on new wood (that is, woody stems produced during the current growing season). Thus, if you want to grow a 4- to 6-ft (1.2- to 1.8-m) crape myrtle *shrub* (and some varieties grow even larger in a single season) that will reliably flower from late June through the first frost and take lots of heat and drought, do not pay heed to overextended conventional wisdom that ignores the distinction between wood hardiness and root hardiness.

In this next example the issue is even more complex. In broadleaved evergreens cold damage (as well as drought damage) first manifests itself as minor tip or margin burn on leaves facing the wind and sun. Sometimes spots of dead tissue appear randomly in the leaf. When temperatures get a bit colder, some leaves are totally killed. When colder still, most or all of the leaves and some branches are killed, resulting in defoliation in late winter or early spring. In palms, the primary (or spear) leaf often is killed due to freeze damage in the embryonic stem tissue. However, defoliated broadleaved evergreen trees, shrubs, and most palms that lose their spears will survive and recover the next growing season. Even in cases when extreme cold kills a southern magnolia or tree holly to the ground, it will usually regrow rapidly from lateral buds near or just below the soil line.

The temperature range that induces the above sequence of events is very broad. A hardy dwarf palmetto palm may experience minor leaf-tip burn at 10°F (−12°C) and major leaf damage at 0 to −5°F (−18 to −21°C), be completely defoliated at −15°F (−26°C), but survive and regrow from its underground bud tissue even after exposure to air temperatures of −20°F (−29°C) or lower. Thus, a decision on whether to plant dwarf palmettos in your landscape is governed not just by the likelihood that the palm will survive in your climate but also on how much damage you are willing to accept and how fast the plant regenerates after winter passes. To aid you in arriving at such decisions, I provide the full range of hardiness information relative to important breakpoints such as leaf hardiness, stem hardiness, and root hardiness.

Cold-Tolerance Mechanisms and Limits:
The Importance of Acclimation

It is beyond the scope of this book to provide an in-depth look at all plant cold-tolerance mechanisms. Suffice it to say that advances in cryobiology, the study of cold and cold-tolerance mechanisms, has provided us with some amazing insights in recent years. Did you know, for example, that frogs can survive the winter even if their ponds freeze solid? Even if you are a trivia buff and *do* know that factoid, you probably do not know that the same little trick is also shared by cold-hardy plants.

Although the specific mechanisms are still being worked out, frogs and many other animals survive freezing temperatures by producing antifreeze proteins and other compounds that lower the freezing point of cellular fluids and prevent ice crystals from forming within cells and rupturing delicate cell membranes. Many animals also produce ice nucleating proteins that limit crystal formation to the spaces between cells. Environmental cues signal the organism's metabolism that winter is approaching and it is time to gear up for antifreeze production. Thus, it's necessary for the animal to go through a process of acclimation to survive winter freezes. Should a frog be exposed to a hard freeze without having a period of acclimation, it will be unable to survive.

This is almost exactly what happens in cold-hardy plants. Many cold-tolerant plants share with animals the ability to lower their cellular freezing points via antifreeze compounds. In some plants, leaf tissues actually do freeze, but without destructive ice-crystal damage because crystals form outside the cells rather than within. Recent progress in genetic analysis suggests that many of the same genes are involved in both plants and animals. Even more interesting, research indicates that the suite of genes responsible for cold tolerance are also linked to drought tolerance (see, for example, Thomashow 1999; I discuss more on the linkage between drought and cold a bit later). But the responsible genes are not always active; they are turned on and off in response to environmental cues.

As days grow shorter and nighttime temperatures decrease in autumn, genetically induced physiological changes occur in plant tissues that gradually shift metabolism from an active growth mode to a dormant state. In common terms, the plant *hardens off* for winter. A hardened-off plant does not produce tender new grow that can easily freeze. Its cells contain a full complement of antifreeze compounds, and, in many evergreens, the leaf surfaces are covered with a thickened waxy cuticle to cut down on water loss and wind injury. As winter gives way to spring, these physiological changes are reversed, breaking dormancy when conditions are favorable for growth.

Should the acclimation process be interrupted by a prolonged period of unseasonably warm weather, a subsequent plunge in the mercury can be devastating. The temperate gardener who attempts to green up his or her marginally cold-hardy plants by fertilizing them very late in summer or autumn may be committing a botanical faux pas—such treatment often prevents or breaks dormancy. Some palm authorities, such as Henry Donselman (G. McKiness, personal communication), suggest that a midautumn fertilizer application may help palms overwinter, but I have seen no data on this effect in colder climates (zone 7a or colder). Likewise, the springlike weather in late winter that is almost a yearly occurrence in the middle latitudes of the United States wreak havoc on early-season flowering plants by causing them to break dormancy too early. Now we can understand a bit better why a cold snap is usually devastating to plants in Florida. Most plants, especially the evergreen flora typical of zones 8 and 9, rarely become completely dormant. Thus, even temperatures only moderately below freezing can cause severe freeze injury.

Each plant species has a genetically programmed lower temperature threshold. In principle, *that* is the information conveyed by the USDA hardiness-zone rating of a given species or variety. As I noted earlier, no amount of hocus pocus or number crunching will change the fact that a true tropical species is genetically incapable of surviving in a cold-winter climate. But in fact, the USDA hardiness-zone rating is only an *approximation* of the genetic minimum. In many cases, not enough people have attempted to grow the plant in colder climates. In other cases, because considerable genetic variability exists within a given species, some varieties turn out to be much more cold hardy that others. I will revisit both of these points as we consider specific plant groups in part 2. However, when considering the USDA hardiness-zone classification, recognize that the cold-tolerance limit for a *specific* plant that you purchase and install in your yard is very plastic and is conditional on several factors.

The specific genetic constitution of the individual plant. Some plants, like some people, are simply better able to shrug off disease and stressful environmental conditions due to their individual genetic constitution. Moreover, horticultural plant breeders have developed many cultivars of popular ornamental plants. Cultivars often exhibit enhanced cold hardiness compared with the natural (that is, wild-type) version of the species. For example, the cultivation of camellias outside the Deep South was almost unknown until the development in the 1990s of hardy hybrid varieties, some fully two USDA zones more cold hardy than traditional standard cultivars.

How the plant was grown during the preceding growing season and how long the plant has been growing in its present location. Any gardener knows that mortality is highest in the first year or two after you install a plant. It takes a minimum of three or four growing seasons for a woody tree or shrub, for example, to develop a large and deep enough root system to sustain itself through droughts and cold winter temperatures. So, a first- or second-year palm tree is vastly less cold hardy than it will be after growing in the same location for several years. Cold-hardiness data in the literature and on plant tags are usually reported for mature, established plants only. In this book, I give you my best estimate on hardiness ratings for juvenile specimens and for the first few years in the ground.

Whether a plant is newly installed or well established, the better shape it's in when it enters winter, the better it will be able to deal with cold. Warm temperatures and abundant water, nutrients, and sunshine during the growing season optimize photosynthesis and the production and storage of carbohydrates. These energy reserves nourish the plant during the colder, darker months of winter and are necessary for the production of antifreeze compounds. Thus, it stands to reason that a plant that has suffered through a prolonged summer drought will not be able to stand as much cold as a plant that enters winter in prime condition. This fact also explains why many warm-climate plants—southern magnolias and crape myrtles, to name two well-known examples—do well in the lower Midwest with its long, hot summers and winters with temperatures below 0°F (–18°C), yet languish in zone 8 England, where summers are relatively short, cool, and often cloudy and winters rarely drop below 10°F (–12°C).

How well the plant has become acclimated to winter conditions that include not only low temperature but also high wind, low moisture availability, bright sunshine, and other variables. Extremely low temperatures can literally freeze plant tissues, but plants can also be damaged or killed whenever the combination of cold temperatures, wind, and sun act together to dry out the leaves and stems. As chill winds blow across living tissue (plant or animal), the evaporative cooling effect creates a wind-chill factor—how cold it actually feels on the tissue surface due to the combination of wind speed and air temperature. Even though acclimated evergreen plant leaves have a waxy cuticle to minimize water loss from leaf surfaces, the leaves are still supercooled by winter winds. To make matters worse, a bright sunny day in midwinter heats the leaves and stimulates photosynthesis, which causes enhanced water loss from the leaves. During the growing season this water loss is quickly replaced by water brought up through the roots, but when the ground is frozen roots cannot access liquid water. The effect on evergreen leaves and stems is called *winterburn*: the leaves have been freeze-dried by a combination of cold, wind, sun, and water loss. I cannot emphasize enough how centrally important wind and sun exposure are to the extent of winter damage in warm-climate plants. In my experience and that of others growing marginally leaf-hardy evergreens, siting makes all the difference.

From late December 2000 through mid-January 2001, my landscape and others in southwestern Ohio experienced an all-time record span of consecutive days below freezing (eighteen) for this area. On several days during this cold spell, the sun was shining brightly in a cloudless sky and the wind howled, driving wind-chill temperatures well below 0°F (–18°C). As a consequence, the ground was frozen more deeply and for much longer than normal and even established evergreens suffered winter drought stress. Without exception, those plants exposed to full afternoon sun and the full force of wind suffered the most, even though the actual air temperatures were not abnormally low for this area.

The pattern of damage provided evidence that winter temperatures alone were a poor predictor of winter damage. In large established evergreen trees and shrubs that were somewhat wind-sheltered but exposed to full sun, the sun-facing leaves suffered perhaps 20–50 percent winterburn, but the shady side of the tree or shrub was almost undamaged. Established specimens of the same species growing in wind-sheltered sites with little afternoon sun had much less damage overall. Plants that were growing out in the open with no protection from either wind or sun were damaged on all sides. In small recently planted evergreen shrubs, most of the green leaves were completely burned—these leaves were dropped in spring and replaced with new growth.

There are many things you can do to minimize and even prevent winterburn and thus extend the zone for warm-climate plants. By using such methods, which will be discussed in depth in chapter 4, my plants were far less severely damaged than those in the area that were not actively winter protected.

The timing and duration of extreme winter events. The extraordinarily long, early-season winter cold in 2000–2001 affected most areas of the eastern United States. As a consequence, palm enthusiasts as far south as northern Florida reported that winter damage was the worst they had seen in years—due to prolonged duration and early arrival of cold, rather than absolute minimum temperatures. In general, a midwinter cold snap is less damaging than an early-winter one because plants have had time to harden off. A late freeze in spring is similarly damaging because plants have broken dormancy. It is not just how low the minimum winter temperature reaches in your area (that is, the USDA hardiness zone), but how long these extreme cold events last and when they occur. A given plant may be able to survive several hours at temperatures that would kill it if the same cold remains for a day or two. And a hardened-off plant can take much more cold than an actively growing specimen.

How well the plant is cared for before, during, and after especially cold weather conditions. Damage prevention and damage control are the two central themes underlying successful adventurous gardening. A freeze may or may not be fatal to a marginally hardy plant, depending on how it was prepared immediately before the extreme weather event and what sort of care it receives after the cold has passed—in some cases, within hours and in other cases what you can do early in spring.

Some of these conditions are seemingly beyond your control—you cannot dictate the weather, after all. But as I discuss in the next chapter, you can dictate to surprising extent the effects of weather on your plants and optimize their transition into, through, and out of winter. If you are interested in challenging the zone, your goal is to navigate your plants as optimally as possible through all five of these cold-hardiness factors above. To do that well, you need to know your plant hardiness zone and how the generalized information above might apply to you specifically.

Plant Hardiness-Zone Maps and the Geographic Scope of the Book

The USDA plant hardiness-zone map of North America has become virtually *the* gold standard in the nursery industry and among the gardening public to rate plants for use in various locales. Counterparts to the USDA map are also available for Europe. In any gardening book or at any plant seller, you absolutely cannot get away from this hardiness rating. Therefore, it is important to know where your garden lies in this classification scheme and, more importantly, what that means and does *not* mean in terms of actual gardening success or failure.

At this writing, the 1990 USDA hardiness-zone map is the most current version available and thus forms the underpinning for all zone-related plant discussions in this book (plate 1). The ten hardiness zones (zones 2–11) within North America were determined by average minimum winter temperature readings based on available data from 1974 to 1986. The USDA has awarded a contract to the American Horticultural Society to create a new, completely digital plant hardiness-zone map by late 2002, including updated temperature data for the past decade. This map will add four newly designated zones, calibrated for subtropical and tropical plants, to the existing eleven zones. Because the 1990s and early 2000s have been among the warmest periods in recent history, it is likely that many areas will be classified as warmer than they were in the 1990 map. (An interactive version of the 1990 map is available from the U.S.

National Arboretum via http://www.usna.usda.gov/Hardzone/. Although the URL for the 2002 map is not yet available, it will likely be accessible from the same government site.) Regardless of which version of the USDA map you use, however, the basics are similar.

Each zone represents a 10°F (6°C) range in winter minimum; because this is quite large, zones are further subdivided into two 5°F (3°C) intervals (a and b). Thus, in an average winter USDA zone 6b has an average minimum temperature somewhere between 0 and –5°F (–18 and –21°C), whereas zone 6a has a winter minimum between –5 and –10°F (–21 and –23°C). The higher the number, the warmer the zone, so zone 7 is 10°F warmer than zone 6, and so on.

In this book I follow general convention by including all of USDA zones 5–7 (about the middle two-thirds of the continental United States east of the Rocky Mountains as well as southern Canada), most of zone 4, and the colder parts of zone 8 (in the Southeast) within the scope of temperate climate zones. In the case of a few extremely cold-tolerant warm-climate species, coverage will extend into zone 3. USDA zones really do not work as well for the western United States and Canada, due to extreme elevational variation, but areas in the Pacific Northwest and Southwest in USDA zones 7 and 8 are also within the scope of this book, as are European zones analogous to those above. This definition of temperate incorporates an extremely large and geographically diverse area. It includes the metropolitan areas of Atlanta, Raleigh, Washington, Boston, Kansas City, Seattle, Detroit, Toronto, and Albuquerque. Obviously, not every plant that thrives in zone 8a Macon, Georgia, will thrive in Seattle, Washington (also zone 8). And the reason for this fact points up one of the major limitations of the USDA hardiness-zone map.

Based as it is on a single environmental variable—areas with similar average winter minimum temperatures where, in theory, the same groups of plants should be equally viable—the USDA hardiness-zone map cannot quantify the myriad other environmental and biological variables that collectively contribute to cold hardiness. Although Macon, Georgia; Seattle, Washington; and London, England, have similar mild winter temperatures, rainfall patterns, and soils, prevailing winds and, most importantly, summer heat and total yearly solar radiation vary greatly between locations. All of these factors influence a given plant's ability to survive

winter cold. A needle palm that is perfectly capable of surviving a –15°F
(–9°C) cold snap in zone 6 St. Louis might be killed by 10°F (–12°C) temperatures in cool and damp England, where mean summer temperatures
are about 15°F (9°C) lower than in St. Louis. Hardiness-zone maps that
quantify the amount of summer heat and yearly incoming solar radiation
(for example, the American Horticultural Society's heat-zone map published in 1997) may be used in concert with the USDA hardiness-zone
map to help sort things out.

Perhaps the most useful approach for the average informed gardener,
at least in my view and that of many horticultural professionals, is the
system developed by Sunset Books, first for the western United States and
then extended to the entire United States and Canada. The *Sunset
National Garden Book* (1997) divided the United States and Canada into
forty-five climate zones—twenty-four zones for the western United States
and Canada and twenty-one zones for the eastern United States and
Canada—based on similarities in major climatic indicators. In addition to
temperature means and extremes, these indicators included latitude; elevation; prevailing wind patterns; precipitation amounts and seasonal patterns; proximity to the oceans, the Gulf of Mexico, or the Laurentian
Great Lakes; ocean currents; mountain ranges; and several other climatic
patterns. As you might imagine, a map with this much detail is almost
impossible to reproduce in a single-page illustration, so I have not
attempted to do so here. To really appreciate how well this approach fine-
tunes the concept of climatic variation on a small geographic scale, I urge
you to obtain a copy of this book and view the multipage maps contained
therein. (In 2001 Sunset Books suspended publication of its *National
Garden Book,* publishing instead a new edition of the *Sunset Western
Garden Book* [2001], *Sunset Northeastern Garden Book* [2001], and *Sunset
Midwestern Landscaping Book* [2002]. I am not aware of a southeastern U.S.
version of this excellent series.)

Having so many zones could get confusing, but to me it simplifies
things a great deal. By considering all major environmental and climatic
factors together, gardeners in the same or similar Sunset zones have a
much better chance of sharing success with a given group of plants.
Following the convention of plant suppliers and most gardening publica-
tions, I will not use Sunset zone designations in the classification of

specific plants, instead providing only the USDA hardiness zones. For cross-referencing purposes, however, eastern United States temperate areas generally include the colder parts of Sunset zone 31 through the warmer parts of zone 43, with some exceptions both north and south. Subdividing the West is still a lot trickier, with its extremely complex climate patterns, but the plants I focus on are suitable for Sunset zone 2 through approximately zone 7 in the Pacific Northwest and zones 2, 3, and 10 in the rest of the West. I will note exceptions to these Sunset zones.

If you live in the southeastern and south-central United States, you are probably familiar with another climate-based map that has proven very useful over the years, the *Southern Living* magazine plant zone map. This map is published regularly in the magazine and is available online (http://www.southernliving.com/garden/zone.asp); it divides the South (quite properly) into what are scientifically termed phytogeographic regions, that is, geographic areas that are climatically similar and possess similar vegetation patterns. Thus, southern Ohio, Indiana, and Illinois are included as part of the upper South region along with much of Kentucky, West Virginia, Maryland, and northern Oklahoma. Similarly, *Southern Living* recognizes the essential differences in climate between the coastal South, which is warmed by the Gulf Stream and lies in the wind shadow of the Appalachians, and the interior upland South. I find it convenient to use these phytogeographic regions as descriptors of various plants and plant vegetation types.

The Ever-Changing Face of Zone Maps

USDA hardiness-zone maps, and for that matter all contemporary zone maps, are based on discrete datasets, and it is critical for the informed adventurous gardener to appreciate the limitations therein. The 1990 USDA map was based on 1974–1986, its predecessor covered 1930–1960, and the yet-unreleased 2002 map will include post-1986 data. One of the controversies that immediately arose with the publication of the 1990 update was that the new map moved the northern limits of each zone considerably further south, especially in the eastern United States and Canada. For example, Atlanta used to be in USDA zone 8 and was now in zone 7b. Southern Kentucky and parts of northern Tennessee, which used to be in zone 7, were now in zone 6a or 6b. Even the Florida Panhandle was moved from subtropical zone 9 to zones 8a and 8b. The 2002 USDA map will surely generate its share of controversies as well, even if the net effect is to show certain areas as warmer than they were in the 1990 version. Which of these maps is right? The answers are "both" and "neither." I belabor this point for several important reasons that directly affect later discussions in this book.

Regional climate maps represent statistical average conditions. There is considerable climatic variation from year to year. For example, table 2.1 contains winter minimum temperature data I collected in the forested area behind our home in rural Oxford for the 1990s.

Table 2.1

Yearly minimum winter temperature data from Oxford, Ohio.

Winter of	Minimum temperature (°F)	Minimum temperature (°C)
1990–1991	–6	–21
1991–1992	–2	–19
1992–1993	0	–18
1993–1994	–2	–19
1994–1995	–24	–31
1995–1996	–14	–26
1996–1997	–1	–18
1997–1998	+7	–14
1998–1999	–14	–26
1999–2000	–12	–24

The decade-long mean minimum temperature was –7°F (–22°C), right in the middle of USDA zone 6a, as the regional map suggests it should be. However, note the huge year-to-year variation, which includes the all-time record low for any date in Oxford in 1994–1995 and a zone 7b winter in the El Niño year of 1997–1998. In fact, only *one* winter during the 1990s fell within the range of zone 6a (–5 to –10°F, –21 to –23°C): Five of the ten winters were warmer than the zone 6a range and four others were colder.

Regional climate does change and will continue to do so in the future, perhaps at an accelerated rate. The earlier and later versions of the USDA map are likely both right. But, it is also likely that since 1990 most regions in the continental United States and Canada have been warming somewhat, and that trend should continue. My opinion mirrors that of numerous climate watchers who have been reporting 1990–2000 data on nationwide local winter minima—the 1990 USDA map is too conservative, a view that should be addressed in the 2002 update. Winter conditions in the 1990s through the present and resultant hardiness-zone classifications appear to more closely resemble those in the 1960 USDA zone map. You can have some fun with this topic if you like. The web site for the Southeastern Palm and Exotic Plant Society (the URL is provided in the appendix) and its newsletter *Rhapidophyllum* list member-generated zone maps for several of the southeastern states, usually based on hybrid datasets that span parts of both time periods (e.g., North Carolina, 1948–1999; Tennessee, 1970–1999) used to create the two versions of the USDA maps. These hybrid maps are much less conservative than the 1990 USDA map and are probably more accurate for the locations covered. The National Climatic Data Center of the National Oceanographic and Atmospheric Administration also publishes comparative winter temperature data for 1895 through the present on its web site (the URL is in bibliography), and you can get accurate longer-term insights into weather patterns in your specific area.

Large-scale climatic maps can never do more than present the average conditions over a large geographic area. The 1990 USDA map does a better job than the 1960 map of fine-tuning zonal information to account for urbanization, topography, and other local conditions, but the actual microclimatic variation in a typical home garden can vary over a full USDA zone. I will discuss more on this in a moment.

Reporting stations where map data are collected have changed through time and will continue to do so in the future, making it difficult or impossible to compare historical data directly. The National Weather Service (NWS) has been collecting official climatic data for Cincinnati since the 1860s. For most of this period, the official weather station was in the city proper, at Lunken Airfield, in a low-lying area near the Ohio River that has become strongly influenced by urbanization. In the 1970s the official reporting station was relocated to the new Greater Cincinnati–Northern Kentucky International Airport, located across the Ohio River in a rural area of northern Kentucky perhaps 10 mi (16 km) west of Lunken Airfield. Not only is Hebron, Kentucky, away from the heat island of downtown Cincinnati (although an airport is itself a heat island), the airport is sited on an exposed plateau rather than a sheltered lowland. It should not be surprising, then, that numerous temperature records have been set for Cincinnati recently. The microclimate in Hebron is considerably different from that of downtown Cincinnati, both in summer and winter. It is invalid to conclude anything from such record temperatures when they actually reflect different sites.

What Is Microclimate?

For all of the above reasons, a successful North-by-South landscape is best developed when a gardener pays heed to the garden's microclimates as well as what USDA or Sunset zone he or she lives in. The term *microclimate,* localized climatic conditions in a small geographic area, is somewhat operator-defined. That is, I can speak about the microclimate in a large urban area differing from that of the surrounding rural countryside, or I can rightly be referring to the dramatic differences between an exposed area on the north side of a home versus the sheltered area next to a porch on the southeastern side of that same home. Both of these applications are important to the prospective temperate-zone gardener interested in challenging the zone. An excellent and comprehensive overview of this subject can be found in Jane Taylor's essential book *Weather in the Garden* (1996).

Just as large-scale regional climate, or macroclimate, is determined by factors such as the amount of incoming solar radiation, prevailing winds, and elevation, so too is microclimatic variation a function of the same factors. But in the latter, it is localized differences, often over the space of feet, that dramatically change conditions. And as I have emphasized again and again (and will continue to do so), the conditions a given plant experiences are largely a function of microclimate, not macroclimate.

In chapter 3, using my home as an example, I outline ways for you to map your own garden area and create a zone map that is unique to your garden. For now, let me illustrate just how profound these differences can be with winter temperature minima data from thirty sampling sites in and around Oxford, Ohio, that I have collected over the past several years as part of the Miami University Hardy Palm Project. Rural areas within the city limits but away from concentrations of houses have consistently been about 5°F (3°C) colder than readings in more densely populated parts of town and 8–12°F (5–7°C) colder than sheltered areas near large buildings on the Miami University campus. My data suggest that our home in rural Oxford is in fact a zone 6a location, areas in town generally have zone 6b characteristics, and the campus microclimates are functionally zone 7a sites in terms of winter minima (Francko 2000). Not surprisingly, we can grow things on campus that are more difficult to grow in my home landscape. But even at our home site, there is about a 3°F (1.8°C) spread from coldest to warmest microclimate, so that the warm areas near our house are effectively borderline zone 6b. Thus, even though Oxford is a small city with a correspondingly small heat-island effect, the data suggest that the actual winter minimum temperatures vary by more than 10°F—more than a full USDA zone—over just a few miles and by several degrees even within the same garden.

Not only the winter temperature minimum is affected by local microclimatic conditions. Virtually every major factor responsible for regulating plant growth differs by microclimate. One of the most important temperature-related climatic factors, the length of the frost-free growing season, is dramatically variable depending on elevation, proximity to buildings, and other small-scale factors. The agricultural extension folks tell us that the growing season in rural southwestern Ohio averages about 185 days. Low-lying areas in our neighborhood (cold air sinks) frost at about the same time as do rural agricultural fields nearby, so that 185-day figure is fairly accurate. But anywhere within about 5 ft (1.5 m) of our house has a frost-free period about 10 to 14 days longer in both spring and autumn. Even more dramatic differences exist on the Miami University campus, where bananas growing in sheltered courtyards of large buildings often last until early December (in 2001, December 24), compared with the mid-October to early November demise of their brethren at our rural home.

The bottom line is this: As far as the banana plant is concerned, there is no appreciable difference in climate between the sheltered courtyard of Upham Hall on the Miami University campus and the exposed front yard of a rural home near Chattanooga, Tennessee, or Norman, Oklahoma. A southern magnolia will be exposed to similar annual temperature regimes on the southeastern side of a home in Cleveland, Ohio, and in the high mountains of North Carolina. A sheltered courtyard garden in Atlanta can support a hardy citrus tree that bears edible fruit.

Although it is important to know your zone, it is equally important to know that such information is at best a guide, not a prohibition. Many biotic and abiotic factors act in concert to produce that variable we call cold hardiness—winter minimum temperature is simply one of these factors. But as we have seen, the USDA hardiness-zone view of winter minimum, or for that matter any large-scale zone map, is at best an approximation of local conditions. *Your* garden almost certainly ranges over several degrees on either side of the average for your zone, and there is much you can do to optimize your local microclimatic regimes.

In many cases nursery plants are not rated for colder zones simply because traditionally they have not been grown there. In other cases, some varieties are markedly more cold hardy than others, even within the same species. Just because a plant species has a cold-hardiness range, that does not necessarily mean that the plant will die if exposed to lower temperatures. The key, as we will explore in the next chapter, is to choose the right plants, site them properly, plant them with attention to their needs, and care for them until they are well established and afterward. Then sit back and let the neighbors gawk.

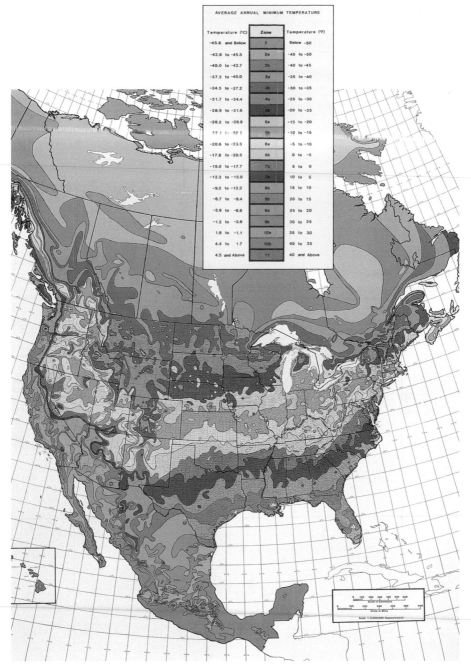

Plate 1 U.S. Department of Agriculture hardiness map of North America showing zones in 5°F (3°C) increments. Zones are based on temperature data from 1974 to 1986.

Plate 2 Shade bed design elements, Secrest Arboretum, Wooster, Ohio (zone 5b)

Plate 3 Water feature with *Hosta*, bamboo (*Bambusa multiplex*), and small windmill palm (*Trachycarpus*), Oxford, Ohio (zone 6a)

Plate 4 Dwarf palmetto (*Sabal minor*), azalea, and mondo grass (*Ophiopogon japonicus*), Tulsa, Oklahoma (zone 6b; photograph © Bryan Swinney)

Plate 5 Hardy sugar cane (*Saccharum arundinaceum*, right foreground) and *Musa paradisiaca* 'Mysore' (left foreground), Miami University campus, Oxford, Ohio (zone 6a)

Plate 6 Hardy *Hibiscus* cultivar, Oxford, Ohio (zone 6a)

Plate 7 Chameleon plant (*Houttuynia cordata*), Oxford, Ohio (zone 6a)

Plate 8 Canna lily (*Canna* 'Pretoria'), Portland, Oregon (zone 8; photograph © Sean Hogan, Cistus Design)

Plate 9 Castor bean (*Ricinus communis*, right) with *Musa* 'Dwarf Orinoco' and other hardy banana species in the garden of Doug Cepluch (pictured), Colerain Township, southwestern Ohio (zone 6a)

Plate 10 Chinese windmill palm (*Trachycarpus fortunei*) and Louisiana dwarf palmetto (*Sabal* 'Louisiana') covered with snow, Oxford, Ohio (zone 6a)

Plate 11 Needle palm (*Rhapidophyllum hystrix*) specimen planted in 1963, Quebeck, Tennessee (zone 6b)

Plate 12 Dwarf palmetto (*Sabal minor*, right) in a naturalized setting with needle palm (*Rhapidophyllum hystrix*, left), Quebeck, Tennessee (zone 6b)

Plate 13 Louisiana dwarf palmetto (*Sabal* 'Louisiana') grouped with black bamboo (*Phyllostachys nigra*) and gold dust plants (*Aucuba japonica*), Miami University campus, Oxford, Ohio (zone 6a)

Plate 14 Grouping of dwarf palmetto (*Sabal minor*) and golden bamboo (*Phyllostachys aurea*), Oklahoma City Zoo (zone 7a; photograph © Bryan Swinney)

Plate 15 Chinese fan palm (*Livistona chinensis*) at the end of the growing season, Oxford, Ohio (zone 6a)

Plate 16 Summer regrowth of an overwintered Chinese fan palm (*Livistona chinensis*), Miami University campus, Oxford, Ohio (zone 6a)

Plate 17 Dwarf bamboo palm (*Chamaedorea radicalis*), Miami University campus, Oxford, Ohio (zone 6a)

Plate 18 Grouping of untrunked cabbage palmettos (*Sabal palmetto*), Miami University campus, Oxford, Ohio (zone 6a)

Plate 19 *Sabal* 'Birmingham', Tulsa, Oklahoma (zone 6b; photograph © Bryan Swinney)

Plate 20 California fan palm (*Washingtonia filifera*), Tulsa, Oklahoma (zone 6b; photograph © Bryan Swinney)

Plate 21 Mexican fan palm (*Washingtonia robusta*), Livingston, Tennessee (zone 6a/6b)

Plate 22 Mature southern magnolia (*Magnolia grandiflora*) specimen in Spring Grove Cemetery, Cincinnati, Ohio (zone 6a/6b)

Plate 23 *Magnolia grandiflora* 'Bracken's Brown Beauty' foliage and flowers, Oxford, Ohio (zone 6a)

Plate 24 *Magnolia grandiflora* 'Little Gem' foliage and flowers, Miami University campus, Oxford, Ohio (zone 6a)

Plate 25 Sweet bay magnolia (*Magnolia virginiana*) foliage and flowers, Oxford, Ohio (zone 6a)

Plate 26 *Ilex ×attenuata* 'Foster's #2' foliage, Huron, Ohio (zone 5b/6a)

Plate 27 Burford holly
(*Ilex cornuta* 'Burfordii'),
Quebeck, Tennessee
(zone 6b)

Plate 28 *Ilex cornuta* 'Dwarf Burford', Oxford, Ohio (zone 6a)

Plate 29 *Ilex cornuta* 'Carissa', Oxford, Ohio (zone 6a)

Plate 30 American holly (*Ilex opaca*), Oxford, Ohio (zone 6a)

Plate 31 Gold dust plant (*Aucuba japonica* 'Variegata'), Miami University campus, Oxford, Ohio (zone 6a)

Plate 32 *Camellia* 'Winter's Charm', Oxford, Ohio (zone 6a)

Plate 33 A cape jasmine flower (*Gardenia jasminoides* 'Kleim's Hardy'), Portland, Oregon (zone 8; photograph © Sean Hogan, Cistus Design)

Plate 34 The winter flowering of winter jasmine (*Jasminum nudiflorum*) before leaf expansion, Oklahoma State University campus, Stillwater, Oklahoma (zone 6b/7a; photograph © Louis B. Anella)

Plate 35 The sporadic flowering of winter jasmine (*Jasminum nudiflorum*) after foliage has emerged, near Stillwater, Oklahoma (zone 6b/7a; photograph © Louis B. Anella)

Plate 36 Leatherleaf
mahonia (*Mahonia bealei*),
Middletown, Ohio
(zone 6a; photograph
© Lucy M. Repper)

Plate 37 Heavenly bamboo (*Nandina domestica*) has fuller growth and reddish
foliage in sun, Middletown, Ohio (zone 6a; photograph © Lucy M. Repper)

Plate 38 Oleander (*Nerium oleander* 'Hardy Double Yellow'), Miami University campus, Oxford, Ohio (zone 6a)

Plate 39 Red tip photinia (*Photinia ×fraseri*), Oxford, Ohio (zone 6a)

Plate 40 Japanese tobira (*Pittosporum tobira* 'Variegata'), Portland, Oregon (zone 8; photograph © Sean Hogan, Cistus Design)

Plate 41 India hawthorn (*Rhaphiolepis indica*), Miami University campus, Oxford, Ohio (zone 6a)

Plate 42 Monkey puzzle tree (*Araucaria araucana*), Quebeck, Tennessee (zone 6b)

Plate 43 *Daphniphyllum macropodum*, Miami University campus, Oxford, Ohio (zone 6a)

Plate 44 Japanese umbrella pine (*Sciadopitys verticillata*), Secrest Arboretum, Wooster, Ohio (zone 5b)

Plate 45 Japanese ternstroemia (*Ternstroemia gymnanthera*), Oxford, Ohio (zone 6a)

Plate 46 *Lagerstroemia indica* 'Carolina Beauty', Miami University campus, Oxford, Ohio (zone 6a)

Plate 47 *Lagerstroemia indica* 'Dallas Red', Streetsboro, Ohio (zone 5b; photograph © Rick Goohs)

Plate 48 *Lagerstroemia indica* 'Victor', Miami University Middletown campus, Middletown, Ohio (zone 6a; photograph © Lucy M. Repper)

Plate 49 *Lagerstroemia* 'Acoma', Oxford, Ohio (zone 6a)

Plate 50 Tree-form *Lagerstroemia* 'Hopi' in flower, Oxford, Ohio (zone 6a)

Plate 51 Exfoliating bark of *Lagerstroemia* 'Hopi', Oxford, Ohio (zone 6a)

Plate 52 Autumn color of *Lagerstroemia* 'Muskogee', Oxford, Ohio (zone 6a)

Plate 53 *Lagerstroemia* 'Natchez', near Static, Tennessee (zone 6a)

Plate 54 *Lagerstroemia* 'Tonto', Millville, Ohio (zone 6a)

Plate 55 Flower and foliage of a mimosa tree (*Albizia julibrissin*), Oxford, Ohio (zone 6a)

Plate 56 Katsuratree (*Cercidiphyllum japonicum*), Miami University campus, Oxford, Ohio (zone 6a)

Plate 57 Bigleaf hydrangea (*Hydrangea macrophylla*), Oxford, Ohio (zone 6a)

Plate 58 Bigleaf magnolia (*Magnolia macrophylla*), Secrest Arboretum, Wooster, Ohio (zone 5b)

Plate 59 Spring inflorescence of an empress tree (*Paulownia tomentosa*) Oxford, Ohio (zone 6a)

Plate 60 Willow oak (*Quercus phellos*) foliage, Miami University campus, Oxford, Ohio (zone 6a)

Plate 61 Bald cypress (*Taxodium distichum*), Miami University campus, Oxford, Ohio (zone 6a)

Plate 62 Fountain bamboo
(*Fargesia nitida* 'Ems River'), Miami
University campus, Oxford, Ohio
(zone 6a)

Plate 63 Canebrake bamboo
(*Arundinaria gigantea*), Miami
University campus, Oxford, Ohio
(zone 6a)

Plate 64 *Indocalamus tessellatus,* Streetsboro, Ohio (zone 5b; photograph © Rick Goohs)

Plate 65 Mature grove of yellow-groove bamboo (*Phyllostachys aureosulcata*), Burton's Bamboo Garden, near Morrow, Ohio (zone 6a)

Plate 66 *Phyllostachys rubromarginata,* Streetsboro, Ohio (zone 5b; photograph ©
Rick Goohs)

Plate 67 Dwarf variegated
bamboo (*Pleioblastus
variegatus*), Oxford, Ohio
(zone 6a)

Plate 68 *Semiarundinaria okuboi*, Streetsboro, Ohio (zone 5b; photograph © Rick Goohs)

Plate 69 *Musa acuminata* 'Rajapuri' grouping, Miami University campus, Oxford, Ohio (zone 6a)

Plate 70 Japanese fiber banana (*Musa basjoo*), Oxford, Ohio (zone 6a)

Plate 71 Japanese fiber banana (*Musa basjoo*) as part of a mixed border with palms, Tulsa, Oklahoma (zone 6b; photograph © Bryan Swinney)

Plate 72 Chinese yellow banana (*Musella lasiocarpa*), Miami University campus, Oxford, Ohio (zone 6a)

Plate 73 Adam's needle (*Yucca glauca*), Oxford, Ohio (zone 6a)

Plate 74 Naturalized Spanish dagger (*Yucca gloriosa*), Livingston, Tennessee (zone 6a/6b)

Plate 75 Beaked blue yucca (*Yucca rostrata*), Oklahoma City, Oklahoma (zone 7a; photograph © Bryan Swinney)

Plate 76 *Yucca smalliana* 'Bright Edge', Oxford, Ohio (zone 6a)

Plate 77 Eastern prickly pear cactus (*Opuntia humifusa*), Oxford, Ohio (zone 6a)

Plate 78 Prickly pear cacti and other succulents in a raised gravel bed, Colerain Township, southwestern Ohio (zone 6a)

Plate 79 Hardy century plant (*Agave parryi*), Colerain Township, southwestern Ohio (zone 6a)

Chapter 3

Microclimate-Based Landscape Planning and Design

> To have a garden where nature and climate do everything
> and man is called upon to do little more than scratch the
> ground and gather flowers and fruit might be very pleasant
> from one point of view, but it would take away all that to me
> constitutes the real interest of gardening, in its difficulties, and
> even its disappointments.
>
> —Canon Ellacombe

In real estate, the key to success is location, location, location. And so it is when planning your North-by-South landscape. Selecting the right plants for the right cultural conditions is especially crucial when you are challenging the hardiness zone. Equally important is the aesthetics involved in integrating tropical-looking plants into an existing temperate landscape. Your current landscape likely contains many desirable specimen trees, shrubs, and herbaceous species that would function well as companion plants for new warm-climate species. The effective North-by-South landscape integrates these floras into a cohesive whole.

As discussed in chapter 2, regional climatic maps can only approximate the local growing conditions in your garden. Moreover, *within* your garden are numerous microclimates that are easily one-half to a full USDA zone warmer (or colder) than the norm for your area. In most gardens, soil conditions, drainage, and other physical features of the habitat also vary, often over only a few feet of space. Whether you are starting a landscape from scratch or simply adding a few plants to an existing landscape, time spent on characterizing (and even modifying) the microclimatic and microhabitat regimes on your property is time well spent. But before you turn a single spade full of dirt or install your first plant, you should know what you want to accomplish. What look are you trying to achieve?

Garden plans need not be elaborate and they are always subject to change. But I have yet to meet a successful gardener who lacked an overall plan for his or her garden. I advise you to look at the many approaches to successful landscape design that are presented in every issue of top gardening magazines. Although I am reticent to single out any individual magazine, I personally learn the most on an issue-to-issue basis from *Fine Gardening*. An especially useful overview of basic and advanced concepts can be found in a recent issue of this magazine (White 2000).

Two other references come to mind. If you live in the Pacific Northwest or another temperate area with fairly mild winters, you will enjoy Jana Meiser's (2001) article on subtropical landscape planning in Oregon. For those who, like me, live in the lower Midwest or upper South, I urge you to obtain a copy of Diane Heilenman's excellent book *Gardening in the Lower Midwest* (1994). Her information on coping with the challenges of gardening in zones 5 and 6, what she calls the "zombie zones," is both enjoyable to read and right on target botanically. Even if you live in zone 7a you will find this a useful book because your climate too is quixotic, with rapid temperature fluctuations in spring, autumn, and winter common and damaging events.

Determining Your Garden's Microclimates and Microhabitats

The first step in designing a viable garden plan for the placement of marginally cold-hardy plants is to grid out your property in terms of microclimatic regimes. Many useful tips on this subject can be found in Jane Taylor's *Weather in the Garden* (1996) and articles by Beaulieu (1996) and Balistrieri (2001). Depending on how elaborate your garden plan will be, a microclimate grid can be as simple as a crude drawing or as detailed as a landscape architect's blueprint. You should look for the places on your property that are sheltered from the winter wind, have the proper compass orientation to maximize winter heat gain, and are not situated in low spots. In short, you are trying to identify those places within your garden that are heat islands—places with warmer-than-average conditions for your geographic area. The following factors influence microclimate.

Proximity to a large building or other source of heat. Even well-insulated homes and other modern buildings leak heat during the winter. In late autumn and early spring, you can identify how far away from your home and other buildings these warm spots extend simply by viewing the pattern of frost formation. You will note that on wind-exposed parts of your house, a light frost may extend almost to the foundation, but near more sheltered parts of your home and adjacent to overhanging structures such as porches and eaves, the frost-free line can extend several feet from the foundation. Similarly, if your home is near a large river or other water body, you will note a heat-island effect near the water's edge. A stone or brick wall will also create a heat island by absorbing solar heat during the day and radiating it at night. If you live in a neighborhood where houses are relatively close together—no more than 100 ft (30 m) or so—you will also observe that the area between the houses is a few degrees warmer that more open areas regardless of compass orientation.

Compass orientation. The compass orientation your house and/or outbuildings face profoundly affects microclimate. The warmest areas in the winter are generally along the south- and southeastern-facing walls, both due to the angle of the winter sun and the blocking of cold western and northwestern winds that prevail during the winter months. One caution is in order here, however: When you consider where to plant broadleaved evergreens, for instance a southern magnolia or a windmill palm, keep in mind that the drying effects of the afternoon winter sun in a southern exposure can cancel out the beneficial effects of warmer temperatures. I discuss more on how to ameliorate winterburn in the next chapter, but if you have a sheltered area with a northwestern or northeastern exposure, you may find this a better location for tender evergreens. In general, however, the warmest parts of your property will be along the south and southeastern walls, and the coldest and most exposed areas will be on the northern and western sides of structures.

Elevation. Cold air is denser than warm air and will sink to the lowest elevation in your garden. Thus, low-lying depressions and swales will frost first in autumn and last in spring. Avoid siting warm-climate plants in these low spots if possible—even a few feet of height above surrounding terrain will cause cold air to flow away from tender plants. A south-facing hillside is ideal.

Existing landscape features. Something as simple as a row of tall evergreen shrubs can block the wind and retain heat enough to create a significant heat island. Knowing this, you can plant a windbreak of fast-growing pines or cedars to create a safe haven for more tender plants in the foreground. At our home, for example, there is a small creek and bluff just to the northwest of our property line. Even though the vegetation cover is mostly deciduous, together the bluff and tree limbs form a fairly effective windbreak for the lower-lying garden areas on the northwestern side of our home.

Although you can gather useful information on where your warm microclimates are located simply by observing frost patterns, I strongly advise you to measure some temperatures as well. First, it is advantageous to know *exactly* how much warmer a given heat island is compared with the colder areas of your yard. You cannot get that kind of information from frost coverage alone. Also, there are so many variables involved that the differences from one garden to the next in the same neighborhood and even different parts of the same garden can and do range over several degrees. Second, you need actual temperature measurements to determine where your garden really stands with respect to USDA plant hardiness zones. Recall from chapter 2 that winter minimum temperatures (and thus the actual USDA zone rating) varies greatly between rural areas of Oxford, Ohio, and areas within the city and campus itself—enough to constitute a one-zone shift irrespective of microclimatic factors within a given home or campus garden. Because nearly all relevant plant hardiness information is given in terms of USDA zones, it is a real advantage for a gardener to possess hard, reliable data on his or her individual site.

The best way to gather these data is with a series of inexpensive thermometers that you can purchase from a home center or hardware store. Before placing them in your yard, make sure that they all read the same temperature under the same conditions and, if there is variation, make sure you note this when comparing actual field temperatures. It is easiest to do this inside your home; just lay them out on the kitchen table for about fifteen minutes and take readings. Attach thermometers to stakes. or dowel rods so that they are about 1–2 ft (0.3–0.6 m) above the ground. Place these in various areas of your property: open areas away from the house; low spots; right next to the foundation and at various distances away on northern, southern, eastern, and western exposures; and near any unique features (for example, a stone wall or grouping of evergreens) that might affect microclimate. By taking readings in the minutes immediately before sunrise and just as the sun is beginning to rise (generally the coldest time of the night) over several nights at all stations you should note a predictable pattern of temperatures.

There is generally more variation in microclimatic regimes during the cold winter months, and a dedicated gardener will probably want to gather several years of data on site-specific winter temperature minima for his or her own garden areas. But you can get a pretty good idea of your actual USDA zone classification with a single year of data. Just compare your temperatures with those of your local NWS reporting station, which is almost always the source of official highs and lows reported locally. If you know what the official winter minimum was for your general area, and you know what USDA zone that reporting station is located in, the difference between your minimum reading and the official one can tell you how much warmer or colder your particular location is.

For example, consider winter minima data for our area during 1998–1999. The official winter minima for both Cincinnati and Hamilton that year was –8°F (–22.2°C). The coldest and warmest parts of our rural garden were –14 and –11°F (–25.6 and –23.9°C), respectively. How can such a set of numbers be used to determine the effective zone of our home garden? The Greater Cincinnati–Northern Kentucky International Airport (the official NWS site in my area) is located in zone 6b on the 1990 USDA map. A query at our local library showed that the mean winter minimum for 1974–1986 was around –2°F (–18.9°C) at that location. That means that the winter of 1998–1999 was approximately 6°F (3.3°C) colder than the statistical norm on which the USDA hardiness map was based. It is reasonable to assume that my Oxford station data were also about 6°F colder than normal, and if you do the math, that would put the predicted mean in rural Oxford at around –8°F (–22.2°C), in agreement with the actual zone 6a classification for this area and very close to the –7°F (21.7°C) mean I actually measured for the decade of the 1990s (table 2.1). Because the warmest areas of our landscape are about 3°F (1.7°C) warmer than the areas away from our house, these warmer microclimates are effectively borderline zone 6b.

Design Elements for a North-by-South Landscape

Once you have a handle on your landscape's microclimates, it is time to start planning where you will site plants to take advantage of what you learned. First, you need to create an effective garden plan that maximizes the utility and beauty of your property. You will be considering how best to use existing trees and shrubs, in combination with new warm-climate specimen plants and appropriate companion plants, to create a pleasing visual statement. Finally, you will want to prepare planting areas so that your new landscape has the best chance of weathering the heat of summer and the cold of winter.

The desire to create a garden with a tropical look in a temperate climate does not necessarily imply that you want your yard to look like something out of a movie set. Although it is indeed possible to create a full-scale, lush tropical garden theme in a zone 6 or 7 climate, this requires the extensive use of potted plants and tropical perennials grown as annuals. Instead, I focus on a more conservative approach based on warm-climate plants that can become permanent parts of the temperate landscape. However, feel free to indulge your own dreams here. If a little bit of the Caribbean is what you want, you can easily incorporate potted plants and exotic annuals into the tried-and-true basic design strategies below.

A garden plan is an individualistic expression, as unique as the person who creates it, but there are certain constants that can help in your planning. Again, it is beyond the scope of this book to cover the topic of landscape design in depth, but let's examine some of the guiding principles involved in integrating tropical plants into the temperate landscape.

Work with your property and not against it. Is your lot flat or hilly? Is there a pronounced slope from one part of the property to another? Are there prominent physical features or especially attractive existing trees and shrubs that you would like to highlight? Alternatively, are there undesirable views that you would like to screen from sight? Is your house basically a square or rectangle, or does it possess courtyards, extended decking, or other architectural features? These sorts of considerations are the first step in designing an *integrated* landscape, that is, a harmonious, well-structured design that accentuates positives and minimizes negatives.

An adventurous temperate gardener faces two challenges: maximizing the opportunities afforded by existing vegetation and interesting physical features of the property and effectively integrating new warm-climate plants into the landscape in such a way as to create synergy—the new whole being greater than the sum of the parts. This turns out to be less difficult than you might think.

Recognize plants as architectural features that make a visual statement. Individual plants have several architectural properties: color, texture, form, and height. When plants are grouped together and integrated into the landscape, they also create an architectural synergy: contrasts in color or form, patterns of light and dark, movement, and seasonal change. The key to effective landscape design is developing effective combinations of plants in harmony with the physical surroundings.

When a museum visitor walks through an effectively designed art gallery, the journey is choreographed to tell a story and convey a central theme. The exhibit's curator not only wants the visitor to appreciate each individual painting or sculpture on its own merits, but displays the works in such a way as to create a mood and a unifying theme. A single sculpture makes a statement, but a body of related work tells a story that is revealed as the visitor journeys through the entire exhibit.

Now take that same concept and apply it to your landscape. Begin visualizing your property not as an ill-defined whole, but rather as a series of discrete island beds that are each anchored by existing or newly installed specimen plants. Each bed should make a visual statement, and the plants and other features within the bed should contribute to that statement. A journey through the planting beds in your yard should convey a mood and tell a story—and when you think about what story you want your landscape to tell, the first step is effective bed design.

The branching structure and pattern of a large tree, the unique shape of a palm leaf, and the bold silhouette of a banana plant each make an architectural statement, drawing your eye much as would a piece of sculpture. Such specimen plants provide a visual anchor for a portion of your garden. Branch shape and pattern, leaf texture and shape, and leaf and flower color provide the major architectural elements of individual plants, and the key to successful garden design is to create a harmonious tapestry of form, texture, and color.

When you plan a new bed, think curves rather than straight edges and right angles. Design curved island planting beds that incorporate specimen plants strategically within the borders of the bed and add plants that accent and complement the form, texture, and color of the specimen plants. A flowing, curving bed that follows the contours of the property is visually attractive and makes for easier maintenance. Curved beds that cross over structural features such as walkways and drives make the property seem larger by drawing the eye across these barriers. Work with, rather than against, your property. For example, let's say that you have a sugar maple in the middle of your front lawn currently surrounded by a sea of grass. Imagine how you might enclose this tree in a new island bed that extends and flows toward one of the margins of your property or toward and across a walkway or driveway. Then imagine how other newly installed warm-climate plants could complement the maple and each other, as well as the natural focal points of your home.

The easiest way to lay out the border of a new bed is to use a garden hose, heavy rope, or extension cord as a template. Work in strong sweeping curves that have a sense of natural flow. After you have laid out a potential pattern, step back and look at the pattern as seen from the street, front porch, and other vantage points. It is especially good to look from above, for instance, from a second-floor window. Make adjustments and reexamine it from all vantage points. The key is to make sure that the finished bed, with all installed plant material, will look appealing from all angles.

When you have a shape that works, mark the outline with a line of agricultural lime or a can of landscape spray paint—I prefer a paint line because it lasts longer and is easier to lay out. I always suggest leaving the bed at this stage and laying out the other beds before digging the first trench line because it's important that all the beds complement each other.

Tie beds together by creating visual lines of sight. Draw the eye forward and beckon the visitor to move through the garden. There should be a sense of mystery and flow tying all of your plant beds together. A person walking through your garden should always be wondering what is around the next corner. Plants of similar height that lead the eye to a taller specimen plant create sight lines, as does strategic placement of garden art, a pond, or other prominent feature. By using plants as screens at the bends of paths, garden visitors cannot see around the bend, compelling them deeper into the garden.

Create focal points along the journey. A well-told story has hooks—passages that jump out at readers when they move through the narrative. In your landscape, design in appropriate features that do the same thing. When visitors stroll through your garden and round a bend, provide a sculpture or an arbor that surprises them. Beckon visitors onward by placing a bench or water feature at the end of a path, compelling the visitor to complete the journey and enter this special sense of place and time that you have created.

These focal points and secret garden spaces should reflect your own unique style. Be creative. Your garden design should first and foremost make *you* happy. Even in a small yard it is possible to create a series of integrated planting beds connected with paths and use effective focal points and quiet retreat spaces that will allow you to wander and forget about the outside world for a while.

Use your full-sun areas and shady areas. One of the critical aspects of landscape design is the effective use of sun versus shade habitats. Of course, the plants you use to create a full-sun planting bed should be those species that thrive in full sun. Similarly, a shade bed uses shade-loving species. Although the species differ, the concept is the same: Anchor the bed around specimen plants and other major architectural features and create a tapestry of form and function with other plants and elements (plate 2).

Install a pond or other water feature. To my mind, a landscape without a water feature is incomplete. This is especially true in a North-by-South landscape design. Few landscape elements better complement the architecture of palms, evergreens, bamboos, and other warm-climate plants than the reflective surface of a pond. The sound of water splashing, the physical movement of water from a small waterfall or fountain, and the visual interest of aquatic plants and fish delight the senses (plate 3).

Every garden and home supply center carries a variety of inexpensive but durable ornamental pond kits and how-to manuals. Small garden ponds are easy to install in a single day, and the physical labor, although not inconsiderable, is satisfying. If you balance your pond with aquatic plants and fish, you will find that maintenance is minimal—usually just cleaning out leaves and debris in autumn and early spring and adding water occasionally if natural precipitation is insufficient.

Create vertical layers in your planting beds and integrate existing temperate woody species, new warm-climate species, and effective companion plants. A visually effective planting bed is vertically layered. The tallest specimen species are in the center of an island bed or at the back of a bed that is next to a building or other structure. Increasingly shorter trees and shrubs surround the taller species as you move to the edge of the bed, and the entire bed is edged with very short herbaceous or woody plants. If you have desirable mature trees or other native plants on your property, integrate your new plantings around them; an existing deciduous tree can be an effective specimen tree in a bed that also contains warm-climate trees, shrubs, and ornamentals. In a large planting bed there can be several tall specimens, just as there are many peaks in a chain of mountains. Regardless of bed design or numbers of specimen plants and structural shrubs, plan for the installation of appropriate companion plants to tie everything together.

Don't forget to consider those very cold-hardy broadleaved evergreen shrubs that you probably already have in your temperate landscape. Rhododendrons, azaleas, boxwoods, and similar evergreens species are essential features of Deep South gardens because they provide structure, form, and color and integrate well with more exotic trees and shrubs. But these plants are not just for southern gardeners. Many readily available varieties are fully hardy through zone 5 and even zone 4 in some cases. A few tips: For boxwoods, azaleas, and rhododendrons the zone rating and other cultural information on the plant label alone is a pretty good indicator of success in your area. But many veteran gardeners in the Midwest insist that balled-and-burlapped rhododendrons are far superior to plants in containers because the latter often do not grow roots into surrounding soil rapidly enough to prevent first- and second-year drought mortality. Also, when purchasing azaleas for tough Midwestern conditions, look for Gable or Girard hybrids, which were developed specifically for vigor in both summer heat and drought and winter cold. These acid-loving plants demand soil rich in organic matter. Rhododendrons, azaleas, and boxwoods will not perform well in heavy alkaline clay or in areas with poor drainage, so amend soil with humus, leaf litter, and other organic material; if drainage is a problem, create a raised bed.

Companion Plants to Complement a Warm-Climate Design

In chapters 5–8, I discuss the many warm-climate plant species and varieties that function as specimen plants or major architectural elements in your landscape design. Here, let's briefly consider the design concept of companion plants, the species that play off the specimen species. Palms, southern magnolias, and crape myrtles make strong visual statements in the landscape. Specimen plants are the stars of your landscape. But for maximal effect, these stars need to be surrounded by an effective supporting cast of low-maintenance, reliable companion species (plate 4). I cover some of these plants here, rather that later in the book, because in many cases you may already grow many, if not most, of these.

Of course, virtually all potted tropical plants make excellent companion plants. If the pots bother you, place them—pot and all—right into the ground, removing the plants before the first autumn frost. Species with large dramatic foliage and showy flowers are especially effective. I have used bird of paradise (*Strelitzia reginae*) as an in-ground tropical for several years, along with potted citrus and tender palm species—all purchased from local discount stores. If you use enough of these species, you can literally create a true tropical paradise in your yard during the warm months of the year.

But I want to focus on companion plants that are, for the most part, perennial in temperate areas. An amazing number of hardy plants dramatically heighten the tropical look but require little or no special winter care. A comprehensive listing of these species would require a whole book; instead, I focus here on some of the best choices for overall effectiveness and low maintenance.

Grasses and Grasslike Species

Perennial grasses come in a variety of sizes and can be used as hardy specimens as well as companions. Even the species that die back during the cold months have a visually interesting winter habit. Unless otherwise noted, all of the species described below are hardy at least through zone 5 and grow in full to partial sun.

***Arundo donax* (giant reed).** This species is a large bunch grass that can reach 15 ft (4.5 m) in height, with canelike stems and massive brown flower plumes. Giant reed can be invasive, but it is very tropical looking and works well with palms, bamboos, and crape myrtles. Both green and variegated forms exist.

***Hakonechloa macra* (Japanese forest grass).** This grass makes an excellent shrub border in shady areas, with delicate bamboolike stems and deep green leaves with bright gold strips.

***Liriope muscari* (lily turf or monkey grass).** This short bunch grass from the lily family (Liliaceae) spreads by rhizomes to form dense mats. Both dark green and variegated forms exist, with purple flower spikes in summer. Lily turf is excellent for edging along a bed or walkway, and is evergreen or nearly so in zone 6 and south.

***Miscanthus sinensis* (maiden grass).** Many forms of maiden grass are available, ranging in size as well as leaf shape, width, and coloration. In my view, this grass is unmatched for creating a lush tropical look and four-season interest with minimal maintenance (figure 1).

***Ophiopogon japonicus* (mondo grass) and related species.** This groundcover or edge species has a finer textured leaf than lily turf but is used in much the same way. Although mondo grass spreads slowly, it makes an excellent underplanting for palms and other dramatic plants (plate 4). Earlier references considered this a zone 7 or even zone 8 species, but this rating is incorrect. Mondo grass will thrive through at least zone 6, and some cultivars are now rated as hardy in zone 5. Cultivars include green forms, variegated forms, and perhaps the most dramatic of all, black mondo grass, with shiny black foliage tinged with green. Evergreen giant liriope (*Ophiopogon jaburan*, often sold as *Liriope gigantea*) is very similar to lily turf but grows much larger. Common in the Deep South, this excellent species is generally considered hardy through zone 7, but I've had specimens for years that perform almost as well as lily turf in our zone 6a winters (see figure 2).

Figure 1 Maiden grass (*Miscanthus sinensis*) defines a pathway, Colerain Township, southwestern Ohio (zone 6a)

Figure 2 Evergreen giant liriope (*Ophiopogon jaburan*), Oxford, Ohio (zone 6a)

Saccharum arundinaceum (**hardy sugar cane**). Relatively new to the marketplace, hardy sugar cane is spectacular and very tropical in form and habit. It is rated as hardy in zone 6 and can form massive clumps up to 10 ft (3 m) high and broad (plate 5).

Herbaceous Perennials

Among the best choices for companion plants are the herbaceous perennials, with their wide range of forms, dramatic foliage, showy flowers, and ease of care. There are literally hundreds of choices here, some of which are actually woody plants in the warmest parts of their range, and many of these companion species are evergreen throughout the winter.

Acorus gramineus (**sweet flag**). Suitable for full sun through light shade, sweet flag resembles a large clump of tufted grass with thicker, bright yellowish green leaves. It is evergreen through the winter even in zone 6 and brightens a shrub border. Sweet flag spreads via aboveground rhizomes. Several cultivars exist, and this perennial can even be planted in a pond or stream.

Aspidistra elatior (**cast-iron plant**). Do you have a deep-shade area that needs some structure and color? This plant is an excellent choice. Cast-iron plant grows in any soil and in conditions that are too dark for virtually any other plant. Several varieties exist, but the species has 1.0- to 2.5-ft (0.30- to 0.75-m) long and 3- to 4-in (7.5- to 10.0-cm) wide dark green leaves supported by 6- to 8-in (15- to 20-cm) leafstalks. Some closely related *Aspidistra* species with variegated or spotted leaves are now on the market. Leaf hardy through zone 7, cast-iron plant grows as a die-back perennial in colder areas (figure 3).

Bergenia cordifolia (**heartleaf bergenia**). This low-growing evergreen species has broad, heart-shaped, glossy, deep green leaves with toothed edges. The spring flower stalks have pinkish blooms. This plant makes a very strong architectural statement for a border, especially with hostas, hellebores, clump bamboos, and clump palms in shady areas. Heartleaf bergenia is hardy probably through zone 4, at least as a die-back perennial.

Buddleja davidii (**butterfly bush**). This deciduous shrub is usually killed to the ground in zone 6 and north, but it blooms profusely on new wood all through the summer. Flower clusters range from white to pink to lavender to deep purple, and all *Buddleja* species and varieties look very tropical in habit and form. The flowers will attract every butterfly in the area.

***Clematis* species.** This genus includes more than two hundred species of deciduous and evergreen vines. All have attractive spring to summer flowers and a vining habit that together produce the temperate equivalent of *Bougainvillea* in subtropical areas. Most varieties require at least partial sun, but some shade-loving cultivars also can be found. *Clematis* is wonderful for producing dense masses of vertical color (see Mikolajski 1997).

Gunnera tinctoria. I admit that I have been unsuccessful growing this plant in southwestern Ohio, but I am tempted to try again. *Gunnera tinctoria* looks prehistoric, with its massive 4- to 8-ft (1.2- to 2.4-m), deeply lobed leaves and similar height. It prefers wet, cool-summer climates, making it an ideal companion plant (or even specimen) in the

Figure 3 Cast-iron plant (*Aspidistra elatior*), Miami University campus, Oxford, Ohio (zone 6a)

Pacific Northwest. Glasshouse Works in southeastern Ohio, which markets this species, says that by planting in a sunken tub (to retain root zone moisture) in partial shade this species can be grown in hot-summer areas.

Helleborus niger **(Christmas rose),** ***Helleborus orientalis*** **(Lenten rose), and hybrids.** One of the joys of an effective North-by-South landscape is having something in bloom at all times of the year, including winter. In zone 6 and colder regions, attaining this is somewhat difficult without the numerous varieties of hellebores now on the market. In my opinion, these are essential perennials in any shade or partial shade landscape. Hellebores are small, evergreen, clumping plants that thrive in dry shade, even competing with established trees and shrubs. They establish slowly, but in a few years begin reproducing vegetatively via rhizomes, eventually forming large masses of plants. Hellebores flower in late autumn through winter and early spring, even in the North. In our area Christmas rose flowers from around late November through February and Lenten rose flowers from February through April. Flower color is highly variable, and hellebores readily hybridize, set seed, and generate new plants that can have wildly different colors from the parents.

Hibiscus moscheutos **(rose mallow) and hardy** ***Hibiscus*** **cultivars.** *Hibiscus* shrubs, with their enormous showy flowers and tropical aspect, are much prized in warm-climate areas. But one species, rose mallow, a common native wetland plant throughout zones 5–9, is also an excellent and readily available ornamental that will do well in dry as well as wet areas. It dies back in winter even in warm areas, and regrows the next season to perhaps 6 ft (1.8 m) with 1-ft (0.3-m) diameter flowers. Flower color is white to pink to red, depending on the cultivar. In recent years, nurseries have also developed, from tropical and subtropical evergreen parents, numerous strains of hardy *Hibiscus* hybrids that also grow as die-back perennials in colder areas (plate 6). These are now for sale at every home center. With proper mulching, these plants are root hardy through at least zone 5 and probably colder and look even more tropical than the rose mallow. *Hibiscus* hybrids are excellent when used with architecturally bold palms and other evergreens.

Hosta **species.** You simply cannot have a temperate garden without hostas to fill in borders, brighten up dark shady areas, and add color and interest throughout the landscape. But hostas are also premier companion plants for palms, bamboo, and other warm-climate specimen plants (see plate 3). Literally thousands of *Hosta* cultivars exist, and new ones are developed each year (see Arden 1990). Grow these for their foliage, which ranges from green to yellow and white to blue and all shades and patterns of variegation therein. The purple flowers in summer are an added benefit. Hostas are clumping plants that quickly fill in an area and function as a border or a ground cover. Clumps can easily be divided and transplanted. Although most cultivars prefer at least some shade, others grow well in full sun. About the only problem is that deer and rabbits love to munch hostas; I have found that combination taste-odor foliar sprays deter these herbivores.

Houttuynia cordata **(chameleon plant).** This is a wonderful, tropical-looking but completely winter-hardy ground cover for cold-winter areas. The leaves look somewhat like those of an English ivy, and its habit of spreading via rhizomes is similar. But chameleon plant has leaves that are a riotous variegation of red, green, white, pink, and yellow (plate 7). This plant requires no maintenance—just stand back and enjoy. Chameleon plant grows in dry areas, in very wet habitats, and even as an aquatic plant.

Pachysandra terminalis **(Japanese spurge).** This plant is probably familiar to most gardeners as one of the very best, trouble-free ground covers for deep-shade areas with intense root competition, especially naturalized woodlots. Japanese spurge is very effective with tropical-looking plants. Evergreen through at least zone 5, this species rapidly spreads via underground runners, forming a pleasing carpet perhaps 8–12 in (20–30 cm) tall with white flowers. Variegated forms exist to brighten those dark areas in your landscape. Browse damage by rabbits and deer is minimal.

Polystichum acrostichoides **(Christmas fern) and other ferns.** Ferns are wonderful companion plants in any landscape but especially those with warm-climate specimens. I favor the evergreen species such as Christmas fern that brighten the woodlot with deep green foliage even in the dead of winter. However, any temperate fern species is an excellent choice.

Annuals

Virtually any tropical species can be grown as an annual in a temperate climate. Likewise, virtually any tropical plant can be installed in the ground during the growing season and moved indoors during cold months. But there are a few species that stand out for ease of care, overall beauty, utility, and cost. In warmer temperate areas, some of these species can be overwintered in the ground.

Caladium bicolor (fancy-leafed caladium). Caladiums are native to tropical regions of the Americas. They are grown for their outstanding, almost translucent foliage marked with blotches of red, white, gold, silver, and green. Most varieties require shade and will not overwinter in zone 8 and colder areas, but you can dig the tubers in autumn and store them in a cool place over the winter.

Canna (canna lily). Cannas are a popular landscape staple in most areas of the United States. They require full sun, lots of heat, and heavy fertilizing. Gardeners are rewarded with wonderful tropical foliage with many patterns of variegation and stunning tropical flowers. Many newer hybrid varieties can be overwintered in the ground through zone 7 with mulching, and several of my neighbors have successfully overwintered these plants in our zone 6a climate (plate 8).

Colocasia esculenta (elephant's ear). The common name says it all. Elephant's ear, like canna lily, is a landscaping staple that is extremely effective with hardy warm-climate trees and shrubs. Tubers can be dug up and overwintered in a garage or other cool area, but some people report success in overwintering their plants in the ground with heavy mulching in zones 6 and 7 (figure 4).

Lantana montevidensis (shrub verbena). Lantana shrubs are a common sight in frost-free areas of the Deep South. Excellent growth form, drought resistance, and flowers that appear profusely throughout the warm months make this a great shrub for a sunny understory. Numerous cultivars exist that vary in size, flower color, and other characteristics. For several years now I have been seeing this species in northern gardening stores and nurseries and have had great success using it as an accent plant. It does not survive our winters, of course, but I feel that the modest

Figure 4 Elephant's ear (*Colocasia esculenta*), Colerain Township, Ohio (zone 6a)

investment for a 1-gallon plant that grows to 2 ft (0.6 m) high and 3 ft (0.9 m) wide and flowers from July through September is well worth it.

***Ricinus communis* (castor bean).** I almost hesitate to call this a companion plant. Castor bean is so large and striking that it merits specimen status, but it grows as an annual in zone 7 and colder, thus I describe it here. Castor bean is grown from seed in cold-winter areas, and with very fertile soil (composted manure is ideal) and plenty of water it can reach 15 ft (4.5 m) in height in a single growing season. Few plants are so tropical in appearance, with its massive showy leaves with purplish highlights. This species makes a superb companion to other plants with bold leaves, such as bananas (plate 9). I have one caution, however: This is probably not a good plant to grow if small children are around. The seeds, which are the source of castor oil, are attractive and quite poisonous if ingested, and the seeds and foliage can cause severe contact allergies in some people. You can eliminate seed formation in lower parts of the plant by pinching off the burrlike seed capsules when they are small.

Preparing Planting Beds for Specimen and Companion Plants

Once you have a plan, you can begin the work of implementing your planting bed design. This is the time that the shovel meets the soil and the real physical work begins. Of course, plants should be installed so that they have the best chance of successful establishment. Soil and bed preparation are especially critical when you are attempting to grow species that may be marginally adapted to your climate. Any good gardening reference will have information about the basics of soil preparation and plant installation. What I want to focus on here are those factors that are especially important when working with warm-climate plants in temperate areas. The specific details of installing a new bed or modifying an existing planting area depend on the kinds of plants that exist at the site, whether you want to move existing plants or work around them, and the types of soil and drainage conditions found in each site.

Soils and Soil Drainage

Regardless of whether you are installing a new bed or working in an existing one, soil and soil drainage are major considerations. As a group, warm-temperate and subtropical plants thrive in well-drained, organically rich soils. Many warm-climate plants will also do well in soils with a lot of clay, as long as drainage is decent and some organic matter is added to the soil. (Decent drainage simply means that standing water does not remain on the soil for more than a few minutes after a heavy rainstorm.) If your prospective soils do not drain well, consider tilling in some construction sand and coarse organic matter, such as peat. You can avoid the issue altogether by growing plants that thrive in wet, poorly drained soils—trees such as bald cypress, sweet bay magnolia, and several of the clumping palms actually prefer wetland-type conditions.

Gardeners in much of the United States have to deal with heavy clay subsoils. In other areas, especially along the coastline, soils are mostly sand. Clay soils are fine for retaining water and contain a ready source of mineral nutrients, but they are slow to drain and inhibit oxygen penetration to the root zone. Sandy soils drain too well, and because they are low in organic material, nutrients rapidly leach away from plant roots with every rainstorm. To make heavy clay or sandy soils fertile, they must be amended with lots of organic matter to provide soil nutrients, promote optimal water retention and drainage, and sustain the metabolism of essential soil organisms. Depending on the kind of lawn care and gardening program a home owner employs, soils can remain poor in organic

Man's *heart*
away from *nature*
becomes hard.

~ Standing Bear

lecades after construction, especially if the
s of lawn clippings and autumn leaf debris
gs and leaf debris back into the lawn can eas-
ic matter yearly to the turf-grass soil profile.
ethods for determining soil organic matter
eristics. Many gardening books recommend
ocal cooperative extension office where, for
omplete work-up done. There is nothing at
but I submit that these days it is relatively
cated gardeners to do their own soil testing

om your prospective garden plot. If the soil
obably have an adequate amount of organ-
f soil and fashion a ball. Ideal soil will form
ise the best soil, termed *loam,* is an ideal
particles from the largest (sand) through the
imal amount of organic matter for good
nd to stick together in a gooey mass, and
ot form a ball at all.
rganic material to form friable soil, I recom-
s and peat moss in about equal proportions
sand. Humus can be purchased at a garden
est sources is composted leaves from the pre-
pacted alkaline (pH above 7) clay soils of the
States and Canada, the physical texture and
iproved by adding powdered gypsum to the
United States and most of the Southeast,
predominate, lime may be used in place of
erally had to use an ax to cut through com
n the front yard of our present home, I can
tiveness of gypsum treatment. This kind of
lly produce a finished product that has a
-6.5), good water retention, good availability
of mineral nutrients, and good friability, which is fine for most of the
plants I discuss in this book. I will denote those species that prefer truly
acidic soil conditions (below pH 6) or other variations on the above

general formula so that you can adjust your soil pH with sulfur (to produce more acidic conditions) or acidic fertilizers and make other modifications accordingly. Should you need precise soil pH measurements, you can purchase easy-to-use and inexpensive pH test kits at your local garden store.

Soil Preparation and Plant Installation

There is no getting around it: Preparing soils for planting is difficult work, even with a mechanized tiller. The first step involves removing any existing sod. You can rent a sod removal tool from your local hardware store, but for modest-sized beds, a sharp, flat-edged spade and a lot of elbow grease will get the job done. After determining the shape of your planting bed and marking the outlines, cut the sod down through the root zone along the perimeter and scoop out a chunk toward the interior of the new bed. Do this along the entire perimeter. You now have an outline of the bed with the grass removed. Using the flat spade, cut chunks of sod out at the same depth, moving progressively inward to the center of the bed with each chunk, much like using a spatula to remove slices of cake from a pan. Remove as little dirt as you can, and shake attached soils from the sod clumps as you go—the top few inches of the root mass often contain the best soil, so don't waste it. Once the sod is removed, you can begin to dig and improve the soil that was below the turf.

Professional landscapers often apply a contact herbicide to turf grass about ten days before they remove it. This kills the roots as well as the aboveground portion of the turf, making removal easier and eliminating root resprouting. If you have large areas of turf to remove, this is an attractive alternative. However, there is also a less work-intensive alternative to actually removing the sod layer and all its organic matter. Cut the grass very short and then apply contact herbicide. After the grass plants are killed, till the entire area, working the dead grass and roots into the soil. Or simply dig the areas that will become actual planting holes and mulch right over the short, dead turf in the rest of the bed. Within a month or two the dead turf grass will decompose, enriching your planting bed with organic matter and nutrients, and you will never know it was there. If you do not like to use herbicides, you can kill the grass by covering the bed area for a few weeks with heavy plastic or several layers of newspaper. I have also used a very heavy layer of autumn leaves to kill unwanted turf grass over the winter months.

Once unwanted grass has been removed, it's time to dig and improve the soils in the new beds. Of course, the better the soil, the better plants grow, but there are practical considerations. How large will your anticipated new plants be? If you plan to install large trees with 3-ft (0.9-m) root balls, your planting hole will need to be more than 3 ft (0.9 m) deep and perhaps 4–6 ft (1.2–1.8 m) wide. Does that mean you need till the entire planting bed to that depth? In an ideal world, yes, but practically speaking most experts now advise filling that large planting hole with a mixture of the soil you scooped out and some soil amendments, thus forcing the tree to work its growing roots into the native soil. With that said, there is no question that palms and other warm-climate plants will establish themselves more quickly and show more vigor in deep loamy soils. A good compromise is to dig down a full spade depth, or about 1 ft (0.3 m), and turn over and amend soil in the whole bed to this depth. Then dig individual holes for individual plants based on the sizes of their root balls.

The above advice must be disregarded if you are unfortunate enough to have a soil formation called hardpan in your garden area. Hardpan is a very tight, compacted layer of soil caused by natural conditions (that is, the caliche hardpan common to the American Southwest) or the action of heavy equipment on clay subsoils. Hardpan will not allow water or gasses to pass through, and if you plant over it, the effect is much like planting in a pot with no drain holes. Rain and irrigation water accumulate, and the plant will quickly drown or at the very least be severely stressed. If the hardpan layer is thin, you can break it up and amend the soil as above. If the hardpan layer is thicker or deeper in the ground, you may need to literally drill planting holes through it so that roots can grow down below the hardpan and into porous soils. In especially severe cases, you may even need to install drainage tile to move pooling water off your planting beds.

I provide specific tips on how to install warm-climate plants as each species is discussed in part 2. One tip, however, is germane to include here. One of the problems with installing a larger tree or shrub with plenty of foliage is that the plant is especially sensitive to drought stress in its pre-establishment phase. Drought stress is literally deadly to an evergreen tree or shrub being grown at the limits of its hardiness range. When installing a tree with a massive root ball, it is very difficult to water it deeply enough to be effective, especially in heavy soils. Soaker hoses are effective, but two low-tech solutions can also be used. First, you can use 5-gallon plastic pails to slow-water your trees. Just poke a small hole or two in the bottom, place the pail on the ground above the root ball, and fill it with water. The water will slowly drip out the bottom and percolate deep into the soil. Commercially available tree watering bags perform the same function. If you do not like the look of pails or other aboveground watering devices, install a section or two of 4-in (10-cm) plastic drain tile right next to the root ball as you place the plant in the ground. The drain tile should extend down to the bottom of the planting hole and should be the kind of tile that has perforations all along its length. Allow enough length so that once mulch is installed, the top of the tile will be just a bit higher than the top of the mulch layer. When watering the tree or shrub, you can get water right down to the base of the root zone by filling and refilling the drain tile with water from a garden hose, saving water over-all and getting the water exactly where it is needed. An added advantage of this method is that you can use the drain tiles to water your warm-cli-mate plants during cold winter weather, when frozen soils make surface watering impossible or ineffective. Just fill a bucket with warm (not hot) water and pour the water right down into the tile.

Two cautions are needed, however: An open drain tile connects the root zone directly to the cold winter air aboveground during winter, and it can promote root zone water loss during hot summer months. Prevent winter cold damage and summer water loss by capping the tile when not in use. Alternately, stuff some easily removable insulation into the drain tile or simply fill the tile with several inches of mulch or coarse gravel. Some experts recommend that the tiles be removed or filled with soil once the tree is established, but I find them very useful for low-waste watering during periodic droughts.

Chapter 4

Four-Season Care
for Warm-Climate Plants

> If it grows, it grows. A palm does not cease to exist, or even
> thrive, just because the "experts" . . . tell you it can't be
> grown the way you grow it. The proof is in the pudding. If a
> needle palm grew outdoors in the Aleutian Islands, even 100
> "experts" telling you that this could not be would not alter
> the fact.
>
> —Tamar Myers

Designing and installing an effective and aesthetically pleasing landscape is only the first step. The next order of business is taking care of warm-climate plants throughout the year. In chapter 2, I noted that as long as a plant's needs are being met, it will grow and thrive, *regardless* of where it is growing. In this chapter I examine the year-round task of routine garden maintenance necessary to provide for these plants' needs. Too often, we think of gardening as something that is done only during the growing season, that is, from the last spring frost until the first killing frost in autumn. In this way of thinking, the question of what to do with your plants during the winter months becomes almost an afterthought. By extension, winter care and maintenance become winter protection—a form of cheating that a respectable gardener would not get involved in. In this chapter, I argue that the distinction between growing-season care (that is, gardening) and winter care is artificial and needlessly inhibits the successful adventurous gardener. Let's think, rather, about how best to care for each type of plant over a full annual cycle.

A temperate gardener is used to caring for plants that enter a dormancy period during the cold months, thus avoiding winter cold.

However, all plants are attuned to a full-year seasonal cycle and dormancy is a matter of degree. A deciduous maple tree avoids cold by dropping its leaves, but the trunk, branches, and roots remain metabolically active, if at a much reduced level. Woody warm-climate plant species, which are native to areas with cool to mild winters, do not enter as pronounced a dormancy period during the winter. They may retain their leaves, which remain photosynthetically active. The important thing is that for *both* temperate and warm-climate plants, care they receive during the summer affects their viability and vigor during the winter and care during the winter affects plant performance in the next growing season.

Care of Warm-Climate Plants during the Growing Season

If you are a seasoned temperate gardener, you already know most of what you need to keep palms and other warm-climate plants in top shape during the growing season. For the novice gardener, I suggest purchasing a good general gardening reference with a section on plant troubleshooting. Here are a few essentials common to warm-climate plant species and suggestions for the least labor- and time-intensive ways to care for your plants.

Heed the Three-Year Establishment Rule

For the adventurous gardener interested in growing plants near the extreme of their climatic range, perhaps no maxim is more important than the three-year establishment rule. Simply stated, in temperate climates, it takes *at least* three full growing seasons for a newly planted tree, shrub, or nonwoody perennial to become fully established. In heavy, compacted clay soils the establishment period may be even longer. Until that time, a plant is extremely sensitive to drought, cold, and any environmental stress. The hardiness, size, and growth rate characteristics quoted on an identification tag at the nursery or in a gardening book refer to *established* plants, not those in their first few years in the ground. This is especially true of broadleaved evergreens and other warm-climate species.

The relatively small root ball of a newly planted tree or shrub is hard pressed to provide for the water and nutrient uptake needs of shoots and leaves. Most plants experience a period of transplant shock during which they may lose leaves and in general look pretty stressed. During the first few growing seasons you will probably see minimal aboveground growth in a newly planted tree. That is because the plant preferentially shunts photosynthesis products to growth and development of its root system. It takes several growing seasons for the root mass to extend below the usual winter soil freeze depth and enable the plant to access deeper soil moisture. Thus, a first- or second-year southern magnolia or other broadleaved evergreen can experience severe winterburn and even defoliation at temperatures that will barely damage an established tree.

There is an important corollary here. The smaller a plant is, the more sensitive it is to environmental extremes. A seedling live oak or a small palm can easily be killed by conditions that barely damage a larger tree. We have used this rule to our advantage in the Miami University Hardy Palm Project. By planting small seedling palms and other warm-climate plants as well as larger specimens, we have been able to establish very conservative cold-hardiness benchmark temperatures, much more so than if we worked with larger plants alone. This is doubly important because many of the plants people are interested in experimenting with are primarily available via mail order as fairly small, immature specimens.

Mulch and Water Well

Most warm-climate plants are native to areas with abundant rainfall and are very prone to drought stress, especially before establishment. A banana tree, for example, is basically a column of water held upright by rigid cell wall structures. The general rules of thumb in gardening—provide the equivalent of 1 in (2.5 cm) of water per week and water deeply and infrequently rather than shallowly and often—hold true for most warm-climate plants, but there are a few caveats. During the establishment phase, you must keep the root ball moist, and during hot, dry weather that means frequent shallow watering as well as deep watering.

Newly planted palms are especially sensitive to drying out, as I learned the hard way during the hot, dry 1999 growing season in southwestern Ohio. We got essentially no rain from late May through early September, and even though I tried to water at least once per week, it was insufficient to keep the small, shallow palm root masses moist enough to counteract water loss through the leaves. As a result, several small palms defoliated by late summer, many others entered winter in poor condition, and in some cases the plants failed to recover during spring 2000 and died. Although we've had better than a 90-percent survival rate in three-year palm establishment overall in Miami University test plots, we have lost far more palms to summer drought stress than to winter cold damage.

You can kill a plant with too much water as well as too little. Measure incoming precipitation with a rain gauge or simply a straight-walled bucket or coffee can. Use those same devices to measure how much water you are adding with a sprinkler or sprayer. Again, aim for about 1 in (2.5 cm) per week during the growing season, but during extreme heat this may not suffice. So, how do you know when a plant needs water? Leaf wilting is usually a good indicator of water stress, but in full afternoon summer sun many plants wilt a little bit because they simply cannot move water fast enough from root to leaves to overcome transpiration. A better indicator is if the plant is wilting in the morning or evening. For a small price you can invest in a simple soil moisture probe, or you can just poke your finger into the soil a few inches. If the soil about 2 in (5 cm) down feels dry and powdery, it's time to water.

Over the past few years soaker hose design has improved, and I recommend them highly for relatively small garden plots, especially those areas where you are trying to establish new plantings. The disadvantage is that most designs allow you to run no more than about 100 ft (30 m) of hose per water outlet, enough for a relatively small bed, but not a full landscape. However, if you lay separate soaker hoses out in various parts of your garden and water each area on a rotating basis, they will provide excellent results with maximum water conservation. For a low-cost alternative, poke a couple of small holes in the bottom of a 5-gallon pail, place the pail on the ground near the plant, and fill it with water. The water will slowly drip out the bottom and percolate deep into the soil.

Whatever watering system you use, mulching with a 2- to 3-in (5.0- to 7.5-cm) layer of pine, cypress, or hardwood mulch or pine straw (that is, pine needle mulch) will not only inhibit soil moisture loss and weed growth, but will also cool and condition the soil. More mulch during the growing season really doesn't help much (but see later discussion of winter mulching) and may actually inhibit water penetration into the soil. Hardwood mulch or even stone mulches are fine, too, although the latter will not enrich your soil. I prefer pine or cypress mulches for warm-climate plant beds because as these products decay they add organic matter to the soil and acidify it, an added benefit for many key species of interest here. Another note on mulching: Try not to pile mulch up against the trunk of your trees. There is some controversy about this, but most horticulturists feel that this practice promotes bark rot and encourages insect damage.

Fertilize with a Slow-Release, Complete Fertilizer

Fertilizing is perhaps the most misunderstood of all gardening chores. Plants need adequate nitrogen, phosphorus, and potassium, as well as iron, magnesium, calcium, and other trace minerals to photosynthesize and convert photosynthetic products into more plant biomass. In keeping with the minimalist approach for plant care here, you can meet these nutrient needs in most situations simply by applying a balanced, complete, slow-release granular fertilizer to your plants in early to midspring. (Generic-brand fertilizers are fine.) Look for a fertilizer that has a relatively similar amount of all three major (macro-) nutrients, with perhaps a bit more nitrogen than phosphorus or potassium. The ratios are printed on the label: A 20–15–15 fertilizer is 20 percent nitrogen by weight, 15 percent phosphorus, and 15 percent potassium. For most plants, avoid using lawn fertilizer (usually about 27–2–2) because it may stimulate too much foliar growth versus root and/or flower development (bananas, discussed in chapter 8, are a notable exception). Also, make sure the fertilizer you choose is complete—that, is, contains micronutrients such as iron and magnesium. These two minerals, in particular, are often lacking in native soils and are critical for proper plant metabolism. Finally, if you plan to fertilize only once, make sure to choose a slow-release formulation, which gradually dissolves over a three- to eight-month period (depending on the brand).

If you live in USDA zone 6 and warmer, the length of your growing season may dictate a second application of slow-release fertilizer, depending on which formulation you choose. For example, I use a three- to four-month formulation and apply in mid-March to early April and again in early July. If you live in a region with cold winters, the key thing to remember is not to apply fertilizer to your warm-climate plants late in the growing season because the plants will continue growing into the early winter, rather than easing into dormancy, and in general will suffer much more cold damage. Some palm experts in zone 7b and warmer maintain that autumn fertilization benefits these species, but I have not seen enough data in cold-winter areas to be convinced as yet. Also, do not add more fertilizer than you need. The excess just runs off, contaminates surface and ground waters, and can even burn the plant.

The issue of natural versus synthetic fertilizers and liquid versus granular application is a difficult one, and much depends on individual preference. To me, it is very much like natural versus synthetic human vitamins. Vitamin C has a unique chemical composition that is identical whether synthetic or natural. Similarly, ammonium nitrogen, the preferred form of nitrogen for most plants, is the same compound regardless of its source. However, there is merit to using composted manure, fish emulsion, and other natural fertilizers in your garden. Manure adds organic matter as well as mineral nutrients, and any natural fertilizer is likely to have at least some trace minerals that even complete synthetic fertilizers lack. There is also the issue of helping to find a good use for the waste products of farm animals. I compromise and add a handful or two of composted manure to each of my palms and other plants each spring, while continuing to apply synthetic fertilizers. And don't forget those autumn leaves. Leaf litter is nature's way of recycling nutrients within forests. Whenever possible collect your autumn yard waste to mulch plants over the winter. Leaf litter decomposes over the winter and early spring, returning organic matter and mineral nutrients to your soil and priming the plants for a quick start in spring. To aid decomposition, you may want to use a portable yard vacuum to grind the leaf litter into smaller particles.

Two other soil fertility issues deserve mention. Many palm growers in the southeastern coastal plain fertilize palms with Epsom salts, which supplies magnesium, a nutrient often in short supply in sandy soils. A spring treatment with Epsom salts (perhaps ¼ cup [60 ml] for a 3- to 4-ft [0.9- to 1.2-m] palm) also greens up palms growing in clay soils. If you live in an area with soils poor in iron, add a trace mineral fertilizer high in chelated iron to planting beds each spring.

Control Weeds, Insects, Other Pests, and Plant Diseases

This subject is too vast for me to cover completely. Again, a good general-reference gardening book is a must. The key thing here is to seek control, not eradication. If you try to completely eradicate a pest, chances are you will have to put so much insecticide or herbicide on your property that you could be creating a health hazard for yourself, your family, and your neighbors. I know what the advertisements imply—just spray it on and the bugs are all gone. We've come a long way since DDT, but hardly a week passes without science revealing yet another environmental cancer trigger or mutational agent lurking within common household products. For this reason alone, I advise caution. We simply do not know enough about the long-term human health effects of many of the more modern pesticides and herbicides.

Mulching alone will control many weeds, and you can either pull the rest or control with a cultivating hoe. Pre-emergence herbicides work reasonably well (use gloves), and I occasionally use liquid herbicides for poison ivy and other really tough weeds such as Canadian thistle. As for insects and grazing pests such as rabbits and deer, I have had reasonable success with pepper sprays and bitter-tasting liquids that are broadcast sprayed on target plants. In my experience, the best formulations are those that deter both by taste and smell and contain an agent that reduces rainfall wash-off. (Mix these with an antidesiccant spray to further reduce washing off.) I resort to pyrethrin-based insecticides only for Japanese beetles and aphids, which seem particularly fond of my crape myrtles and red tip bushes, and for spider mites, which can be a real problem on palms. The same is true of fungicides. You'll occasionally need to use them to control leaf spot diseases and powdery mildew, although for many purposes old fashioned sulfur sprays work pretty well without the environmental hazards. Copper-based fungicide/bactericides are very effective, have low toxicity when used judiciously and cautiously, and control both groups of pathogens with a single spray. Fungicide/bactericides also play a crucial role in winter care, as we will see later. Some warm-climate plants are prone to scale diseases that can be controlled with dormant oil.

Winter Care Principles

I have grown palms and other warm-climate plants in my yard now for several years. As I write this chapter, our Miami University demonstration plots are entering their fifth year. Every year in about late summer, when the crape myrtles are in full bloom and the palms and other broadleaved evergreens are looking particularly lush and full, I can count on two responses from garden visitors who stop and chat. First, of course, people are shocked and thrilled to see such plants in what they view as a completely unexpected part of the United States. This is especially true of transplanted Southerners who are already familiar with this vegetation. Almost universally, however, the next response goes something like this: "Those things won't take the winter. What do you do, dig them up and bring them inside?" I try to explain gently that, no, the plants they see are there to stay and, with proper care, they can in fact survive winter weather. I find that most people do not accept this explanation at first. It took two years for my neighbors to come around—prior to that I was considered a typical eccentric professor. Well . . . maybe they still think of me that way, but not in regard to my garden.

So how *do* you overwinter warm-climate plants in temperate climates with cold winters? Although most tropical plants can grow anywhere if brought indoors during freezing weather, this book is about growing plants in the ground year-round. In this chapter, I focus on the basics of winter care and protection—from the simplest to most elaborate strategies. I also discuss winter care and protection strategies from a regional perspective. If you live in USDA zone 7 (Sunset zone 33), for example, where arctic blasts produce temperatures below 0°F (–18°C) only occasionally, your dwarf palmetto will need minimal care to get through a typical winter unscathed, but you still need to be ready to step in every few years when a major arctic blast comes through. Grow that same species in zone 6 (Sunset zone 35), where temperatures below 0°F (–18°C) are likely each year, and the need for year-to-year protection increases.

Winter Protection is Not Cheating

This is a common but false viewpoint that we outside-the-zone palm fanatics hear all the time. It is inconsistent with the goals of North-by-South landscaping. I rebut it this way: Plants thrive when their biological needs are met. Do you water your garden during the growing season? Do you install heat-sensitive plants out of the afternoon sun and mist or cover them with landscape fabric during heat waves? Do you use mulch and fertilizers? Do you amend your soil with organic matter or other soil additives? Do you control insects and disease pathogens? Of *course* you do—it would be difficult to maintain a typical temperate (or subtropical) garden throughout the growing season without intervention of some sort. And unless you consider normal summer gardening strategies—summer protection, in other words—to be cheating, you should not consider winter protection to be unnatural or a form of cheating.

Levels of Protection

Winter protection can range from very simple to very elaborate. How far you want to go in protecting plants is purely up to you. With the simplest measures and attention to microclimate and summer care, you can easily push a plant's hardiness-zone limit by one to one and a half USDA zones. With the more elaborate and sophisticated set-ups, it is possible to move two full zones or more depending on supplementary heating. Remember, too, my earlier discussion on the range of cold-damage symptoms, from minor leaf-tip burn to plant death. In temperate and subtropical plants that range involves a temperature spread of perhaps 20–30°F (12–18°C). With that in mind, consider the types of plants you want to experiment with in terms of the amount of damage you are willing to put up with and then employ winter protection accordingly.

For example, if you want to grow a windmill palm, which is normally considered hardy to zone 7b, in your zone 6b Nashville garden, you have several options. If you are willing to put up with some leaf damage each year and defoliation every few years, knowing that these palms recover fairly quickly in spring, you can take a very minimalist approach. If you are willing to put in more effort, you should be able to overwinter your windmill palm with relatively minor damage in most years. As I discuss individual plants in part 2, I will include any known information on cold-hardiness benchmarks to facilitate your planning.

There Are Few Absolutes

Plants are individuals, and thus even within the same species or variety there is some variation in cold tolerance. Summer care, plant age, and time of establishment also affect winter hardiness. So, predicting how a specific plant will respond to cold stress is far from an exact science. All we can do is provide guidelines based on present knowledge.

Each year we learn more about the biology of cold hardiness, and each year experimental gardeners come up with new information on winter protection.

Recognizing Cold-Weather Patterns

With modern advances in weather forecasting and a little knowledge about winter weather patterns, it is possible to anticipate weather conditions that are apt to cause warm-climate plants problems. This is true even in the rapidly fluctuating continental climates of Diane Heilenman's zombie zones (USDA zones 5 and 6). With a few clearly noted exceptions, the plants discussed in this book are not appreciably harmed by temperatures at or above about 10°F (–12°C). Thus, for those living in USDA zone 7 or warmer, normal winter weather is really not a concern, and you need only prepare for the occasional cold spell that drops temperatures to 10°F or lower. Even in USDA zone 6, gardeners are apt to experience only several days and nights that are problematic each year. A lot of grief and extra work can be saved simply by anticipating the normal sequence of events that leads to bone-chilling cold, especially in the eastern two-thirds of the continental United States.

East of the Rocky Mountains, arctic high pressure systems from late December until late February usually produce the coldest weather of the season. Almost always, these "Blue Northers" sweep down from Canada on the heels of a low-pressure winter storm system, which deposits snow and/or ice on the ground, insulating the relatively warm ground from the colder air, and usually produce extremely cold wind-chill temperatures during and after the storm event. Storm winds tend to come in from the north and west. When the arctic air mass moves over snow-and/or ice-covered ground (even 1–2 in, 2.5–5.0 cm), solar rays are reflected back to space through very cold, very dry, and usually cloudless skies, rather than heating the ground. After sundown, these same conditions promote rapid radiational cooling, and nighttime temperatures drop precipitously. Instead of a daytime high of, say, 34°F (1°C) and a nighttime low of 15°F (–9°C), snow-covered ground and a cloudless sky together mean that it might only reach 25°F (–4°C) during the day and drop to below 0°F (–18°C) at night. These patterns usually persist only for a few days and nights, until the arctic high moves eastward.

The further north you live, the more frequent, severe, and long-lasting these outbreaks become. A series of successive weather fronts and persistent snow cover can lead to a bout of record cold. In zone 6 Cincinnati, Louisville, St. Louis, Nashville, and similar areas, it gets down to −20°F (−29°C) every five to seven years or so and the all-time record lows are about −25°F (−32°C).

It is a myth that such extremely cold conditions occur only in the northern states. This myth, more than anything else, is responsible for perpetuating the erroneous notion that warm-climate species can only grow in the South. In truth, temperatures liable to damage warm-climate species are possible almost anywhere in the continental United States, including the Deep South. Yet, these tender plants do quite well there, with little or no extra winter protection.

Let's use Atlanta, Georgia, in USDA zone 7b as an example. The average minimum winter temperature (1960–1990 data) at the official Atlanta reporting station, Hartsfield International Airport, is about 8°F (−13°C). Hartsfield is located about 10 mi (16 km) south of downtown Atlanta. The northern Atlanta suburbs, away from the urban heat island and 30–40 mi (48–64 km) north of the airport, are several degrees colder on average. An unofficial zone map for Georgia published by the Southeastern Palm and Exotic Plant Society (2001), based on 1970–1999 data, rates Hartsfield as borderline zone 8a (10.1°F, −12.2°C). Whichever dataset you prefer, this climate is fairly moderate and supports a plethora of southern vegetation types, including cold-hardy palms. But even in Atlanta it can get downright cold. A Blue Norther may hit Atlanta only every several years, but when an arctic front does come through, nighttime temperatures can drop below 0°F (−18°C)—the official all-time record low at Hartsfield is −8°F (−22°C)—and the northern suburbs get much colder.

In fact, the all-time record lows for *every* state in the American South are well below 0°F (−18°C), including −16°F (−27°C) in zone 8a Minden, Louisiana; −27°F (−33°C) in zone 7a and 7b New Market, Alabama; and even −2°F (−19°C) in zone 8b Tallahassee, Florida (National Climatic Data Center 2001). By recognizing that extreme temperatures follow a pattern and are possible even in mild-climate areas and knowing what your local pattern tends to be, you can gear up to provide extra protection only when needed. I discuss these short-term solutions later in this chapter.

Minimalist Techniques for Winter Care and Protection

There are simple things gardeners should do for the entire winter season to protect warm-climate plants. The winter care season starts in late autumn or early winter after there have been a few hard freezes. It is important not to pamper your plants too soon—a little cold weather actually aids the onset of dormancy and makes plants more cold hardy. (I point out exceptions to this rule as I discuss specific plants in part 2.) The goal is to minimize damage to leaves and stems and, above all, to preserve the tender bud tissue that is necessary for recovery from catastrophic cold. Minimalist techniques can add about one-half to a full zone equivalent to your garden, irrespective of microclimatic variation.

Mulching

Mulching is an essential part of four-seasons plant care. Any kind of organic mulch will do, although I favor pine straw, oak or maple leaves, or coarse wood chips because they don't mat down over the winter but retain their loft. Some palm enthusiasts use wheat straw. To keep the mulch pile from blowing away and/or looking untidy, construct a wire netting enclosure around the plant with garden stakes and fill it with mulch to a level of your choosing. Try to extend the mulch layer at least 1–2 ft (0.3–0.6 m) away from the trunk or stem of a small plant and several feet away for a larger tree or shrub.

The only difference with winter mulching is that during this season you want to mulch plants more heavily than during the growing season. A mulch layer 4–12 in (10–30 cm) deep, depending on your climate and the target plant, prevents the ground underneath from freezing deeply, thus protecting the roots and lower trunks of cold-hardy, warm-climate plants. This is critical for two reasons. First, an unfrozen root zone allows plants a chance to access soil moisture to replace winter transpiration losses, preventing or at least minimizing leaf and stem desiccation and winterburn. Second, many of the plants described in this book have underground buds that enable them to recover from complete above-ground death. For example, well-mulched dwarf palmettos (*Sabal minor*) have been known to completely recover from air temperatures as low as –24°F (–31°C) in a Kansas garden. A combination of heavy mulch and winter snow cover enables a zone 3b Wisconsin gardener to overwinter clump palms, hardy bananas, and other regionally unlikely plants (M. Heim, personal communication).

Mulch also helps to keep temperatures around protected plants relatively constant, preventing damage caused by rapid temperature fluctuations. On a sunny calm winter day, unprotected foliage can warm to summerlike temperatures, often breaking dormancy. After sundown temperatures plummet, and plants can be damaged. Similarly, unmulched plants can be damaged by springlike weather in late winter. Regardless of how you apply mulch, leave it on until about the average date of last frost in your area, and then remove it over a period of several days. Removing it gradually rather than all at once is not critical but has the advantage of retaining some protection against a late frost while gradually exposing the ground and plant tissues to increasingly stronger sunlight. Day length, sun intensity, and ground temperature are all environmental cues that break dormancy, and a gradual approach is best. Of course, be ready to cover your plants again if a late frost threatens. New growth in spring is particularly sensitive to frost damage. In experiments at Miami University we have evaluated most, if not all, winter protection strategies. Heavy mulching, simple and low-tech as it is, has proven the most effective technique for minimizing foliar damage and maximizing plant survival.

Winter Watering and Antidesiccant Sprays

Mulching will help to keep the root zone and available soil moisture from deep freezes. However, research with overwintering crop plants, such as winter wheat, has shown that root water uptake is much reduced at soil temperatures below about 40°F (5°C; Al-Hamdani et al. 1995). To make matters worse, cold and dry winter winds and afternoon sun desiccate the evergreen leaves of palms, southern magnolias, and hollies, causing winterburn and defoliation. Do everything you can to maximize water availability to the leaves while minimizing water loss from green tissues.

To maximize water availability, ensure that plants enter the winter season well watered and the root zone is saturated with moisture throughout the winter. This is usually no problem if you live in a marine climate like the Pacific Northwest or the United Kingdom, with regular winter rains, or in the warmer parts of zone 7 south. But if you live in a dryer climate or in zones 6 and north, you may need to supplement winter precipitation. Melting snows can provide ample soil moisture, but in many parts of the central latitudes of the United States winter snowfall is unreliable. Also, it takes roughly 10 in (25 cm) of snow to equal 1 in (2.5 cm) of liquid precipitation—more if the snow is dry. Rather than risk ice damage to my hoses and exterior faucets, I haul a few buckets of lukewarm water from inside the house to perk up my magnolias, palms, and other evergreens a couple of times between late December and mid-February (see the tips on installing watering drain tiles in the soil preparation and plant installation section of chapter 3). Lukewarm (not hot) water has the added benefit of warming the ground somewhat, thus aiding in water uptake.

To reduce winter water loss from leaves, I recommend the application of antidesiccant sprays to leaf surfaces and stem tissues. Frankly, there is not a lot of hard *scientific* data supporting the effectiveness of antidesiccants in reducing winter injury, but the large body of available anecdotal evidence is convincing. Antidesiccant sprays, as the name implies, are water-soluble polymers that coat the surface of a leaf, preventing water loss much as a natural waxy cuticle layer does. They do not inhibit photosynthesis or harm the plant. I use antidesiccants for winter protection and whenever I want to transplant an evergreen or deciduous tree during the growing season, because the sprays do help reduce post-transplant shock and wilting. For cost-effectiveness, purchase concentrated solutions and dilute about 1:5 with water as per the directions and apply with an inexpensive hand sprayer. Spray all plant surfaces, top and bottom, until the solution runs off. Here in zone 6a, I usually make my first application in mid-December. Because antidesiccants gradually wash off in rain and snow, I reapply in mid-January or so. The only requirement is for air temperatures to be above 40°F (5°C) and no rain or snow for several hours after application. The effectiveness of fungicide/bactericide treatments can be prolonged by adding these agents to antidesiccant spray.

Antidesiccant sprays will not protect delicate plant tissues from freezing, although this claim has been made. I also cannot imagine how they could protect very tender plants from frost damage, although this claim is also made and research continues. I experimented with Japanese fiber bananas (*Musa basjoo*) and *Impatiens*, both species that are damaged by even a light frost, and could not detect a positive effect of antidesiccant spray on prolonging the growing season. A bed sheet or landscape fabric draped over the plant is still the best preventative measure to combat light frosts.

Snow Can Be a Good Thing

Snow cover is an excellent insulator full of air spaces. Leave it where it falls (plate 10). A few inches of snow can insulate the ground as well as a similar thickness of mulch. Air temperatures just a few inches down in a snow cover can be as much as 30°F (17°C) warmer than the air temperature.

Gardeners who live in areas that receives regular snowfall are actually in some ways better able to grow warm-climate plants that those in a slightly warmer zone where snow is sporadic and melts right away. In fact, gardeners in zone 6 and northward (myself included) have had good success with clump palms and other low-growing plants by banking the snow around the plant tissues if a real Blue Norther threatens. It is much better for a 3-ft (0.9-m) tall needle palm to be covered with snow than to have its leaves sticking out into air that is –10°F (–23°C) with –30°F (–34°C) wind chills.

Beware, however, that very heavy snows (either a lot of it or the wet variety) can stick to evergreen leaves and branches and break them. The same thing is true of ice and freezing rain, which cause more problems than snow in the Southeast, Mid-Atlantic, and lower Midwest. There is some controversy on whether to remove accumulated snow from the crowns of palms and the branches of other evergreen trees. You run a real risk of causing more breakage and damage to cold-stressed branches by going out with a broom and trying to knock snow off than by leaving them alone. In general, just let it be. In many parts of the United States, the snow will begin to melt and blow away fairly quickly, and most trees and shrubs will recover their normal shape. After all, a palm frond is very flexible and tough—so much so that it can endure hurricane-force winds. If you feel you must remove heavy snow, however, do so very cautiously. A heavy coating of ice is almost impossible to remove without damaging the plant.

Active Winter Protection Techniques

Most of you will probably want to experiment with at least some forms of active winter protection to reduce damage or to extend the zone even further that minimalist treatments permit. Let's look at these techniques, from the easiest and least intrusive to the most elaborate. Here I simply cover the basic principles involved, leaving specific details and tips to be covered as each plant group is discussed in part 2.

Simple Shelters

When a cold front looms on the horizon, one of the simplest and least intrusive ways to extend minimalist care is to cover marginally hardy plants with removable box structures. Cover the plant with an appropriate-sized cardboard box waterproofed with spray water repellant or other treatment and weighted down with a brick or stone. People also use bell-shaped jars and large plastic plant containers left over from planting season. If you use plastic containers or coverings, make sure that the plastic does not come in direct contact with plant leaves or severe leaf burn can occur. Mulch around the base of the box or container to seal out wind, and you have created a microhabitat that is 10°F (6°C) or more warmer than the external temperature and out of the wind. Alternately, you can simply drape a sheet or blanket over the plant, again weighted down or otherwise secured against the wind, and gain several degrees of warmth. Boxes and other temporary covers should be removed after a few days. It is also important to at least partially open a box cover on sunny days—even if the air temperature is well below freezing—because the air can easily heat up to damaging temperatures inside a completely closed box on a sunny winter day.

Wind Barriers and Enclosed Leaf Piles

In the section on minimalist techniques for winter care I discussed using wire mesh screen enclosures to contain loose mulch. For more active winter protection, replace the wire screen with burlap or synthetic landscape fabric (figure 5). This will not only hold in your loose mulch, but the burlap or landscape fabric will provide a barrier against cold winter winds. In wind-exposed sites, the windscreen along with a modest mulch layer will greatly reduce winterburn.

For the ultimate in low-tech winter protection, spray the plant stem and leaves with a broad-spectrum fungicide/bactericide and completely cover the entire enclosed plant with a *loose* pile of pine straw, whole deciduous tree leaves, or wheat straw. A loose pile will permit enough light penetration and air circulation around the leaves to prevent mortality, but will insulate the entire plant from frigid winds and extreme temperatures. Do not use fine-particle pine bark or hardwood bark mulches because they will compact down too much over the winter and can suffocate the plant. When using pine straw mulch with this method in zone 6 and colder, I strongly urge you to add in deciduous tree leaves at about a 50:50 mixture. If you have ever made a compost pile to recycle organic debris, you know that it gets really warm in the center of the pile, even on frigid winter days. This is because the decomposition process liberates considerable heat, which is retained in the pile by the insulating blanket

Figure 5
Needle palm
(*Rhapidophyllum
hystrix*) in a burlap
enclosure, Oxford,
Ohio (zone 6a)

of organic material. Decompositional heat is a major benefit of the leaf pile protection method, and pine straw decomposes too slowly to release much heat.

In my experience constructing enclosed leaf piles is *the* optimal method for overwintering small, marginally hardy palms and other warm-climate plants in zone 6 and colder. This method also has great utility in warmer climates for overwintering subtropical species. As part of our work at Miami University, we have overwintered small windmill palms in leaf piles through prolonged temperatures below 0°F (–18°C) with little or no foliar damage—no other method short of a mini-greenhouse produces comparable results.

If you don't like the look of a full windscreen enclosure in your yard, consider a variation of this method. I have overwintered clumps of Chinese fan palms, a true subtropical species, here in Oxford, Ohio, by allowing the leaves to senesce naturally (the leaves suffer complete winterburn below about 15°F, –9°C). I cut the dead petioles off several inches above ground level, then spray the crown with fungicide/bactericide before covering with a layer of landscape fabric or burlap topped with 10–12 in (25–30 cm) of pine straw and leaves. Temperature probes placed under the mulch layer revealed that the temperature never dropped below 15°F (–9°C), even when the outside temperature dropped to –12 and –10°F (–24 and –23°C) on successive nights. This temperature moderation and the small amount of light that passed through the mulch pile is enough to allow the basal portions of petioles to remain green and alive, facilitating rapid recovery and new growth in the spring. This technique is appropriate for any small mounding plant, whether foliage is cut back or not.

You might be thinking that under wet cold conditions, heavy mulching can promote the growth of fungi and bacteria that could attack the plant stem and, in completely covered plants, the leaves as well. This is why a fungicide/bactericide spray pretreatment is essential and why a leaf pile about 2 ft (0.6 m) thick is the upper limit—any deeper and you'll cause more harm than good to covered portions of plants. Some palm enthusiasts in zones 7 and 8 wrap the portion of the plant to be mulched in plastic to keep the moist mulch from direct contact with the plant. This technique is problematic in colder zones, however, because moisture will condense on the inside of the plastic wrap and be unable to evaporate away, thus promoting pathogen growth over the longer winter season. Wrap plants in synthetic landscape fabric or synthetic quilt batting instead. These materials breathe well and do not promote fungal or bacterial growth.

Preventing Crown Rot

In addition to spraying the foliage of heavily mulched plants with a fungicide/bactericide, you should also treat open-crowned plants, especially palms and yuccas. Because water collects in these open crowns, successive freezes and thaws can damage tissues and provide the ideal growing environment for fungi and bacteria. As noted earlier, much cold-damage and lethality in these plants is due to secondary infection and not the cold itself. I will discuss wrapping the crowns to keep water out, but whether you elect to wrap or not, it is advisable to spray a good shot of copper-based fungicide/bactericide into the crown of your palms and yuccas in very early winter and again in mid to late winter to prevent crown rot. As a safety precaution, always wear waterproof gloves when handling fungicides or other potentially toxic chemicals.

If palms are exposed to temperatures that kill the leaves, especially the emerging spear leaf, you must treat the plant as soon as possible to prevent possibly lethal bud rot. How can you tell if the spear leaf has been severely damaged? Just tug on it—within a day or two of lethal damage, you will be able to pull it clean out of the crown. A burned but not killed spear leaf may look bad but cannot be pulled easily from the crown. Sometimes lethal damage to the palm spear and bud tissue is delayed quite a bit and does not show up until early spring. I tend to be conservative and treat after a major cold event, regardless of whether the damage looks very bad.

As with many of my gardening lessons, this one came hard. In the late winter of 2000–2001, all four of the trunked windmill palms on campus looked reasonably good, despite the prolonged cold spell that winter. The leaves had lots of tip and margin burn, but the spears looked great. I tugged away, concluded that everything was fine, and congratulated myself on getting our prized trees through the winter. However, after a couple weeks of spring weather, I noted that the spear leaves and existing expanded leaves were not growing. I checked and, sure enough, the still-green spears pulled right out, along with all of the existing leaves. In fact, the crown rot disease had progressed enough that I had to cut the trunks back severely until I found green wood. I treated these stumps repeatedly over the next few weeks with a combined fungicide/bactericide. Slowly two of the four trees began to recover, poking up the first green tip of a new spear leaf in May and adding several more expanded leaves and a spear by summer's end. I probably could have avoided much of the major rot damage had I treated the crown right way rather than after the fact.

Trunk and Foliar Wrapping

Mulches and snow cover conserve soil heat and can protect the lower stem and foliar structures. For trees and shrubs with a central trunk and a crown of leaves, trunk and foliar wraps can be used to conserve heat and reduce wind-chill damage in aboveground plant parts. Again, how far you want to go with this technique is up to you. From our admittedly incomplete field experiments under zone 6a conditions (below 0°F, –18°C), I don't think wrapping is as effective as covering the entire plant with leaf mulch. But it can be the most effective way to protect a larger trunked tree.

A simple trunk wrap can be constructed using burlap, landscape fabric, or synthetic quilt batting. Many palm enthusiasts swear by plastic bubble wrap, but in cold-winter areas I worry about the condensation that can form inside the wrap, thus promoting disease. Before putting down a finishing layer of winter mulch, spray the area to be wrapped with fungicide/bactericide. Cut strips of wrapping material and wind them around the trunk, making sure that they overlap completely. Even a single layer of burlap is sufficient to add the equivalent of a few degrees of thermal protection. Multiple layers, especially with lofted materials such as synthetic quilt batting (not the water-absorbent cotton kind) or fiberglass insulation material, can retain enough heat and block wind chill to add about a full zone of protection. Some practitioners recommend placing sticks around the plant before wrapping so that the wrap does not directly contact the trunk. This method may minimize the chance for fungal and bacterial damage, and it creates a space of air, which in principle should increase the insulation value of the treatment. An added benefit of wrapping with synthetic quilt batting is that it does not trap moisture and thereby contribute to trunk rot.

It is difficult to wrap the foliage of most of the plants discussed in this book. For example, it's impractical at best to try to protect a large southern magnolia or live oak with foliar wraps, although you can wrap a small tree. For plants such as palms with leaves concentrated at the top of the plant, there is an easy technique that I and other enthusiasts have used. Wrap the lower trunk as you would any other plant. Then cover the spear leaf and the base of the crown (where the petioles intersect with the trunk) with synthetic quilt batting or landscape fabric. To create a somewhat waterproof but breathable layer over the crown and around the spear leaves, I spray the fabric wrap with silicone waterproofing spray— the same product used to waterproof a pair of shoes or a jacket. The waterproof layer is important because it keeps water from settling in the crown cavity, where it can cause freeze damage. Remember to spray fungicide/bactericide into the cavity before wrapping. Then simply extend your trunk wrap upward around the bases of the petioles. This treatment coupled with mulching protects the most vulnerable parts of the palm: its roots, lower stem, and bud tissue. Leave this wrap on until early spring.

As the trunk wrap is extended up around the lower petioles, you will note that the flexible leaves start to gather in a bunch. By continuing to wrap the petioles, in many palms you can draw this bunch of leaves fairly tightly together. The bunched leaves will not be damaged, and in this configuration it's fairly easy to drape a burlap or landscape fabric bonnet over the foliage during extreme weather events, removing the bonnet after the cold weather ends. For small palms, you can simply swaddle the entire leaf mass in wrapping and leave it that way for the entire winter— the so-called mummy wrap method. Experience shows that leaves treated with fungicide/bactericide suffer minimal damage. Overnight temperatures under the wrap remain about 6–8°F (4–5°C) warmer than outside the wrap, even under windy conditions with temperatures below 0°F (–18°C), adding another one half to two-thirds of a zone worth of protection above mulching and other minimalist techniques.

To take this technique a step further, consider creating a wrapped enclosure for your plant. Place stakes around the plant 1 ft (0.3 m) or more way from the trunk and cover the stakes with netting or mesh. Then fill the enclosure with dry leaves, straw, or pine needles, covering the entire plant. Finally, cover the whole enclosure with a waterproof covering of plastic or other material and secure to the ground with U-shaped landscape pins purchased from a hardware store or made from wire coat hangers. To make your enclosure more aesthetic, consider an outer wrap of burlap or pine boughs. When finished, the enclosure will keep the plant dry and warm through the winter, adding perhaps 15–20°F (9–12°C) of protection.

Temporary Greenhouses

As an alternative to wrapping, construct a miniature greenhouse or lean-to structure to retain heat and keep out wind and water. Simply cover a wood frame with a double layer of plastic sheeting (using staples or small nails), secure the frame and sheeting to the ground or house, and mulch up around the base. Make sure that your structure is larger than the plant to be protected, but recognize too that a smaller structure is easier to maintain, heat, and keep from being damaged by the elements. The specific frame design is up to you, but the roof should be strongly slanted to aid in rain and snow removal. Also, the framing and fastening must be strong enough to take whatever snow and wind is apt to come your way. Wet snow is very heavy, and I can tell you from experience that it is no fun at all trying to repair your lean-to at 7:00 A.M. in –20°F (–29°C) wind-chill temperatures. It's also necessary to incorporate a vent hole to prevent heat and condensation build up during the day. An easy way to do this is to leave part of the base of one side free and unsecured. Simply close the flap with duct tape or a strategically placed rock when cold temperatures hit. This sort of a structure can be left up all winter, and, with modest supplementary heat, can be used to overwinter small plants two full zones and even more beyond their normal limits. The sky is the limit with more extensive and elaborate greenhouse designs using Plexiglas sheeting, fiberglass framing, and the like. The Brooklyn Botanical Garden in New York City uses attractive metal-framed mini-greenhouses to enclose some rather sizable windmill palms each year.

A variation on the greenhouse theme that is useful in the milder parts of the temperate zone is the wall-of-water system, which is commercially available or can be homemade. This system uses water-filled baffles to enclose small plants. The warm water releases its heat slowly overnight, keeping the plant inside toasty warm. The downside is that these systems must be thawed after use (unless heated by the sun the next day) and are impractical for larger plants.

To Heat or Not to Heat

Perhaps nothing smacks more of cheating in the area of winter protection than the use of artificial heat sources. Again, in my view, there is no right and wrong here, just different approaches. Most of the new football stadiums constructed in the northern half of the United States (and even many of the baseball parks) incorporate some system of artificial turf heating to extend the growing season of the turf grass and melt off snow and ice. Thus, artificial heat sources are something to consider, especially as fail-safe measures to have on hand should a record cold spell threaten your plants. Depending on your climate and the plant you are trying to protect, some of these techniques work well and some do not.

The most common form of artificial heating is simply to string mini holiday lights (C9 lights) around the trunk and throughout the foliage of your plants, perhaps a bit denser than the normal holiday display. By turning these on during a cold night, several degrees of heat can be added to the air immediately around the plant, especially on calm nights. Research we conducted during the winter of 1999–2000 on red tip shrubs and palms (Francko and Wilhoite 2002) suggested that C9 lights add 2–3°F (1–2°C) to the ambient temperature (that is, not in immediate proximity to a bulb), provided that the winds were calm or nearly so. In windy weather the heat quickly dissipated. If a sheet of landscape fabric is thrown loosely over the lit shrubs, another 2–3°F (1–2°C) of heat can be added, and this will retain heat during windier weather. You can also use C9 lights under a wrap system, which easily adds 10–15°F (6–9°C) of warmth to a wrapped plant. Like all systems, this one is not foolproof. Sometimes the added heat simply dries the tender leaves more because they cannot access adequate liquid water from partially frozen root systems.

Holiday lights have proven to be very successful and popular among palm enthusiasts in the Deep South, especially to protect true subtropical and tropical palms from occasional frost and freeze events (Hilley 1999).

The next time you visit Disney World in Orlando, Florida, note the extensive use of arboreal lighting. It is a nice nighttime landscape touch, but it
also protects some of those true tropical plants on cold evenings. If you
live in an area without significant snowfall and simply need to add the
equivalent of a half zone to your plants now and then, this is an excellent away to do it, provided you don't mind having to explain to your
neighbors why your holiday lights are still on in February.

However, a caution is in order for those in zone 6 and northward who
might rely on snow cover as an insulator against extreme cold. At Miami
University we found that the C9 lights melted the snow cover around the
plants and left them fully exposed to ambient air temperatures and wind
chills. Thus, paradoxically, the plants that were heated by the lights actually received more foliar damage than plants covered with snow.

Another approach to supplementary heating is the use of low-wattage
heat cables. Available from hardware stores, heat cables are generally used
to wrap exposed water pipes to prevent freeze damage. They come in 3-
to 30-ft (0.9- to 9.0-m) lengths and can be used to wrap trunks and foliage
just like C9 lights. Newer versions of heat cables are extremely safe and
reliable, and most come equipped with a thermostat that activates the
cable when ambient temperatures reach about 38°F (3°C).

When needed, an incandescent bulb in a portable metal shop light or
heat cables can provide extra heating to a lean-to or temporary greenhouse. A 100-watt light bulb produces about the same amount of heat as
a 30-watt cable. Within a typical 4 ft × 4 ft (1.2 m × 1.2 m) lean-to or
greenhouse, each will add up to 10°F (6°C) of heat, more if you cover the
greenhouse with a blanket. Keep the bulb at least several inches away
from the plant tissue and any flammable materials—that bulb gets hot—
and always plug your shop light or heat cables into an external outlet
with a ground-fault circuit to prevent accidents due to shorts.

Another increasingly popular use for heating cables is to wrap them
around the root ball when installing a warm-climate plant and activate
them during prolonged cold spells to heat the root zone a bit, thus facilitating water availability. At present there are not a lot of hard data on the
effectiveness of this treatment for truly temperate conditions, but the reasoning is sound. A 30-watt heat cable should keep a well-mulched root

zone warm enough to prevent freezing, and anything that allows liquid water to move up into aboveground foliage will greatly aid in cold hardiness. Additionally, the relatively warmer water moving up though the root system should, in principle, provide some supplementary heating for aboveground plant tissues.

The search for the best winter protection strategy is akin to the search for the Holy Grail. There are many viable techniques that you can attempt, and I have tried to give you a flavor for those that might be the most successful. In our experience at Miami University, we got the best results with heavy mulching and antidesiccant foliar sprays. I emphasize, however, that experimental gardeners are still learning to fine-tune cold-protection systems, and you may devise a better mouse trap yourself. Also, plants are individuals and the variables are many. It is impossible to provide absolutes on how a plant can best be protected. Be innovative. Don't be afraid of setbacks. And, above all, have fun with the learning process.

Warm-Climate Plants for Temperate Landscapes

Chapter 5

Cold-Hardy Palms

> The righteous shall flourish like a palm tree.
>
> —Psalm 92:12

he palm family (Palmae) comprises more than 1500 broadleaved evergreen species, most of which grow in tropical or subtropical regions of the world. In the United States we are familiar with the palm-lined streets of southern California and Florida, and no group of plants better conjures up the image and flavor of the tropics in the public mind. In my view, no group of plants is a better keystone for designing and executing a North-by-South landscaping plan, even if you live well north of established palm country. Excellent tips on integrating palms into an existing temperate landscape may be found in *The Palm Reader* (Southeastern Palm and Exotic Plant Society 1994), Gibbons and Spanner (1999), McClendon (2000), Turner (2000a, 2000b), and Meiser (2001) as well as more general references listed in the bibliography.

Although most palms grow in warm climates, it is a myth that palms are *exclusively* tropical or subtropical species. Perhaps a hundred species (and probably more, as people experiment with newly available species and varieties) will easily take 20°F (–7°C) freezes, and a surprising number will survive at temperatures below 0°F (–18°C; Noblick 1998; Walters 1998; Francko and Wilson 2001). Thus, the terms *cold-hardy palm* or *temperate palm* are not oxymorons, but rather refer to members of the palm family that grow well in or at least tolerate temperate climates with cool to cold winters. Cold-hardy palms, like other cold-hardy broadleaved evergreens, have the genetic and physiological ability to survive extreme cold. I focus primarily on temperate palms in this chapter, but I will also introduce several subtropical palms that can be purchased from the tropical houseplant section of your local home center and grown successfully outdoors by an adventurous temperate gardener.

Palms can be found growing naturally in the high elevations of the Himalayas and Andes, where winter snows and frigid temperatures are common. They are cultivated outdoors as far north as coastal Scotland and Vancouver, British Columbia—in fact, some palms actually thrive in marine climates. Native stands of scrub or dwarf palmetto (*Sabal minor*) are found as far north as coastal Virginia and as far inland as southeastern Oklahoma. I participated in field trips when I was a botany professor at Oklahoma State University during the 1980s, and it always surprised me that most of our students (and many of the faculty) were unaware that dwarf palmettos are native to southeastern Oklahoma, extreme northeastern Texas, and southwestern Arkansas. Maybe I shouldn't have been surprised. After all, most people still think that palms won't grow outside the coastal Deep South, California, or Arizona. Fortunately, this mind set is changing rapidly. The next time you are working on the Internet, try doing a search using "hardy palms" as the key words. You will get dozens if not hundreds of hits; you'll find that people are experimenting with cold-hardy palms in virtually every state, in southern Canada, and throughout most of Europe. Especially illuminating are the web sites of various groups for hardy palm and subtropical enthusiasts (URLs are listed in the appendix).

Palms are angiosperms, although their flowers are generally not showy. In this regard a palm tree is like a maple tree or holly. But palms are unlike most deciduous and evergreen trees in that they are classified as monocots, meaning they grow from a single developing leaf and lack the secondary woody tissue of a typical woody shrub or tree. Monocots include grasses, lilies, cereal grains, and irises as well as the bananas and yuccas. All monocots grow new leaves from a single mass of bud tissue located near the top of the central stem. It's important to understand this botanical fact because it affects all aspects of palm cultivation. If cold, drought, or disease kills all of the bud tissue, the whole plant ultimately dies because a palm cannot grow new lateral branches and leaves the way a maple or an oak does.

Although the terms *tree* and *shrub* are somewhat subjective, they are useful when referring to the general growth habit of woody plants, including cold-hardy palms. Most palms are arborescent (tree-form) plants that feature a woody trunk. The coconut palm, date palm, and cabbage palm are common examples. But palm trunks are unlike regular tree trunks. The trunk and lateral branches of an oak tree grow thicker with age via secondary growth, as an annual growth ring of new wood is laid down each year just under the bark. New leaves and branches develop from apical (terminal) buds as well as lateral buds on existing branches. In contrast, a palm trunk is comprised of spongy water transport tissues and structural fibers, and it does not form annual secondary growth rings. No matter how tall a palm tree gets, with a few rare exceptions it still contains only a single growth bud near the top of the stem. This explains why palm trees have only a single whorl of leaves at the top—they all form through sequential growth and development of spear leaves that arise from the terminal growth bud.

As a group, arborescent palms are not as cold hardy as clump palms, which feature a shrublike growth habit with little or no aboveground trunk. Clump palms are not palm trees, but they are true palms. Many varieties are indeed beautiful and feature the characteristic palm stem and leaf architecture so effective in creating a tropical feel in a temperate garden. Clump palms tend to be more cold hardy than tree palms because, in many species, the growth bud is at or even under ground level and is thus insulated against the coldest temperatures. Also, as the name implies, most clump palms tend to sucker and form new lateral trunks, each with its own growth bud. Thus, part of the clump can be killed by cold, but the entire plant is not necessarily lost.

Both tree and clump palms have two basic leaf shapes and arrangements. Fan palms have palmate leaves, which are shaped like a human hand with its fingers outstretched. Most of the palms discussed in this book are fan palms. The leaves of fan palm differ across species mainly in terms of size (both the diameter of leaves and the length of the petiole) and degree of separation of leaf segments. As the name implies, feather palms have pinnate leaves that are shaped more like feathers. The common parlor palm (*Chamaedorea elegans*) familiar to houseplant enthusiasts is a typical feather palm. Finally, a few important palm species have costapalmate leaves, which look like a cross between a fan and a feather. Perhaps the archetypal palm tree, the cabbage palmetto (*Sabal palmetto*) of Florida and the coastal South, has costapalmate leaves.

I discuss cold-hardy palms roughly in order of descending cold hardiness. I say "roughly" because in many cases there are still too few hard data to differentiate one species or variety from another. Individual plants' characteristics vary somewhat, and how and where a palm is grown plays a huge role in how much cold weather it will tolerate.

Clump Palms for the Temperate Landscape

Rhapidophyllum hystrix, Needle Palm

The needle palm gets its name from the numerous needlelike spines that protect its crown. This species is native to the coastal plain of the southeastern United States, mainly as an understory plant in river flood plain forests. As rapid development destroys such habitat, the needle palm is rare and getting rarer in its native range.

In terms of foliar damage and survivorship, the needle palm wins the prize as the world's most cold-hardy palm, at least in climates with warm to hot summers. Mature specimens in good sites can easily tolerate −5°F (−21°C) with little or no damage to leaves, stems, or petioles and have been known to recover from −24°F (−31°C) in Knoxville, Tennessee, during the all-time record cold snap there in 1985 (Taylor 1999). This plant is being grown successfully in southern New England, northern Ohio, Michigan, and other places far north of its native range. However, because I have been quick to debunk myths about where palms will and will not grow, I am also obliged to debunk the new conventional wisdom that needle palms are bullet-proof in cold, wet winter conditions. Needle palms are indeed tough plants, but as more people grow them in marginal areas, it is becoming increasingly clear that they are not without hardiness problems.

Size and characteristics. Needle palms have beautiful deep green palmate leaves with silvery undersides. The petioles can grow as long as 3–4 ft (0.9–1.2 m), typically 1–2 ft (0.3–0.6 m), and the leaves range from 2 to 5 ft (0.6 to 1.5 m) in diameter, with fifteen to twenty deeply divided leaf segments. The aboveground trunk is typically short (less than 1 ft, 0.3 m tall), except in very old specimens, and is actually a leaf sheath comprised of fibrous material and black spines that enclose the petiole bases. The crown of each leaf sheath is comprised of ten to twenty leaves. Needle palms sucker profusely but grow very slowly. Fifty-year-old colonies in Florida have reached 10 ft (3 m) high and wide. The next time you visit Disney World in Orlando, note the very beautiful, perhaps 5-ft (1.5-m) tall needle palm clump near the Disney Marketplace bus stop.

Northern-grown needle palms can eventually attain 10 ft (3 m) as well, although few old specimens currently exist in zone 7a and colder. The largest specimens at Miami University are perhaps twelve to fifteen years old and 4–5 ft (1.2–1.5 m) tall and broad after three years in the ground, but there are some very large older specimens in the U.S. National Arboretum in Washington, D.C. (zone 7a). In summer 2001, my colleague Ken Wilson and I were privileged to visit the home garden of Charles and Diane Cole in rural east-central Tennessee (zone 6b). Among other amazing plants, we were in awe of their massive (perhaps 8 ft [2.4 m] tall and broad), unprotected forty-year-old needle palms (plate 11), which have attained their great size and vigor despite numerous winters at or below –10°F (–23°C) since the early 1960s and the –24°F (–31°C) spell in 1985. Most needle palms available to the home gardener are much smaller, three- to four-year-old plants that have perhaps 12–15 in (30.0–37.5 cm) of aboveground growth.

Cold hardiness. In zones 7 and warmer, a needle palms require little or no winter protection after the first year. Although Robert Riffle (1998, 301) rated this plant as fully hardy in zones 7b–10, he acknowledges that it is "being successfully grown by some adventurous gardeners in zone 6b with protection." My experiences and those of numerous other zone 5–7 gardeners and horticultural experts suggests that this estimate is overly conservative. I know of at least one gardener in zone 3b Wisconsin who has been successfully growing *Rhapidophyllum hystrix* for several years

(M. Heim, personal communication). An established needle palm (one that has been in the ground for at least three growing seasons) in a good site should be hardy in most years through at least zone 6a and hardy with leaf burn through zone 5b—about the same hardiness as the southern magnolia and many of the tree-form hollies already being grown in these areas.

In our experimental plots at Miami University (microclimates in zones 6b–7a) and my colder home landscape (zone 6a), first-year needle palms mulched with pine straw experienced tip and margin burn in exposed leaves beginning at about 0°F (–18°C), regardless of whether they were sprayed with antidesiccant (see winter protection section in chapter 4) *or* when exposed to wind chills below 0°F, regardless of air temperature. Tip and margin burn became progressively more pronounced with colder temperatures and with prolonged periods of cold weather, especially if the plant was not covered with an insulating layer of snow. Even so, the interior portions of the plant remained largely undamaged.

After a needle palm has been in the ground for at least three growing seasons, it will take about an additional 5°F (3°C) of cold exposure. There are numerous reports of needle palms surviving –20°F (–29°C) and lower temperatures, and I can personally vouch for –14°F (–26°C) survivability with perhaps one-third of the foliage damaged. Note, however, that like many palms the needle palm is markedly more cold hardy in climates that have long, hot summers. They are much more sensitive to cold in cool-summer regions such as the Pacific Northwest and the United Kingdom.

Needle palm foliage has proven to be exceedingly cold hardy, justifying the rave reviews about this species that appear in plant catalogs and the like. Although I do not recant my view that this is an excellent choice for zone 6 and even colder areas, foliar damage is only one component of cold hardiness. Experience in zone 5 and 6 (and even zone 7) suggests that, in about 10–20 percent of leaf bases the emerging spear leaves are killed by temperatures below 0°F (–18°C) and/or prolonged wind chills below 0°F, even if the established foliage is relatively undamaged. Surprisingly, spear leaf damage and loss can and does occur at even warmer temperatures (10°F, –12°C) if the palms are exposed to prolonged periods of wet, subfreezing weather. Following the winter season of 2000–2001, many of us palm enthusiasts in the eastern United States were dismayed to note spear loss in many larger, vigorous, and fairly well-established needle palms growing in excellent microclimatic sites, even though the foliage was in good condition. These palms were not subjected to temperatures below 0°F (–18°C), extreme wind chills, or strong afternoon sun. They were, however, exposed to record periods of wet subfreezing weather. I treated our campus palms with copper-based fungicide in mid-December, but, because the foliage looked so good and the temperatures never got horrendous, I did *not* treat them again in mid-January after the cold spell ended. And I paid the price.

Because the needle palm crown is open and can collect water and the bud tissue in the trunk is largely aboveground, these plants are especially prone to fungal and bacterial crown rot under prolonged wet, cold conditions, even if temperatures never approach 0°F (–18°C). This disease rapidly kills the tissue at the base of the developing spear leaves. Anecdotal evidence suggests that needle palms grown in very heavy clay soils may be more sensitive to cold and prone to lose spear leaves. However, I have noted spear damage and/or loss in plants grown in excellent, well-drained soils. One factor that may explain this tendency is that needle palms do not become completely dormant in normal winter weather, even in zone 6. The spears continue to elongate and expand, albeit at a slow rate, all winter, and this tissue is easily damaged when temperatures drop much below 10°F (–12°C).

If you grow this species in areas with cold, wet winters, be aware of this tendency toward spear damage and crown rot, and aggressively follow a fungicide/bactericide crown spray schedule. The other winter protection that helps tremendously is to mound leaf litter around the trunk, covering as much of the spear leaf as you can. In our experiments during the mild winter of 2001–2002, the spear leaves of mulched needle palms survived unscathed. In contrast, nearly one-half of unmulched needle palms suffered significant spear leaf burn and many lost their spears, even though temperatures never went below the typical zone 7b minimum (5 to 10°F, –15 to –12°C).

All is not lost if a leaf base loses its spear. If you treat the palm promptly with fungicide/bactericide spray, the surviving bud tissue often (but not always) will regenerate new spear leaves in the spring. Sometimes the crown recovers on its own, without treatment. In any case, a pup or two will usually emerge from the damaged leaf base via sucker growth. The clumping habit of the needle palm ensures that when damaged leaf tissue is pruned away in spring, new growth will restore the shape of the plant by midsummer. We have also noted that the spear leaf problem seems to be worse during the first winter, and palms suffer progressively less damage each winter as they become well rooted.

Culture, landscape use, and other notes. The needle palm may be used as a specimen plant or in groupings as an understory plant. The further north you go, the more a full-sun planting location is advantageous, but I have had success with plants in the dappled shade of a deciduous canopy. Needle palms are not picky when it comes to soil, but good drainage and abundant organic matter help. Mulch the base of plants with 2–3 in (5.0–7.5 cm) of organic mulch in summer and increase to 3–4 in (7.5–10.0 cm) in winter, with an additional thick layer of leaf mulch around the trunks and spear leaves. Fertilize annually in spring with a slow-release, complete, granular fertilizer. In zone 7 and warmer, needle palms do seem to benefit from a midautumn application of fertilizer; data from colder areas is inconclusive.

A word here about the so-called pot planting technique advocated for installing landscape palms in cold-winter areas (Tollefson 1999). This technique involves putting the plant in the ground container and all. In principle, this should keep the roots confined (palms, like other monocots, seem to like this) and force new root growth downward through the drain holes at the base of the pot or container, thereby facilitating a deeper root zone. The container is never removed; rather the growing root ball eventually bursts the container. We evaluated this technique using a number of palm species (Francko 2000; Francko and Wilhoite 2002), including needle palms, and the collective evidence did not support beneficial effects. In fact, in several species there was virtually no root growth into the surrounding soils during the first year after planting, thus delaying establishment and making the plants more sensitive to cold and drought.

Pay special attention to watering during the first few years—needle palms can withstand considerable drought when established but, like other palms, they are notoriously prone to summer drought stress during the first few years. Needle palms do not appear to be a preferred winter food for deer or rabbits, although these grazers do eat some other clump palms and will on occasion nip off a leaf or two from an accessible needle palm. Aside from easily controlled caterpillar damage in the summer, needle palms do not appear to be prone to mites or other common garden insect pests. Occasionally, these palms will develop scale diseases, especially if grown in the vicinity of magnolias trees infested with magnolia white scale. This should be treated immediately with dormant oil or an appropriate insecticide.

It pays to get the largest plants you can find. A larger plant is more cold hardy and *Rhapidophyllum hystrix* grows very slowly. It is possible to transplant suckers as they develop. Needle palms are easy (if slow) to grow from seed, but mature plants are dioecious, meaning that you will need a male and a female plant for successful pollination and seed production.

Winter protection. In zone 7a and warmer regions, heavy mulching and adequate watering prior to cold snaps are sufficient for all but the most extreme winter events (see chapter 4 for tips on short-term protection strategies). In zones 6b and north, spray foliage and crowns in mid-December and again in mid-January with an antidesiccant containing copper-based fungicide or other broad-spectrum fungicide/bactericide. A prolonged cold spell, even without extremely low temperatures, will freeze the root zone of recently planted needle palms and can cause major winterburn to unprotected leaves due to desiccation. Siting a needle palm in an exposed full-sun location will speed its growth rate; however, such a location will also produce more winter damage due to sun and wind exposure. In fact, wind appears to be much more injurious to needle palm foliage than any other physical factor, including cold and sun. If you grow needle palms in a windy location and want plants to come through winter in as pristine a condition as possible, I suggest erecting burlap windscreens around the plants during the winter months, perhaps adding a thick layer of leaf mulch as described in chapter 4, especially around the trunks and emerging spear leaves.

With regard to needle palms and other clump palms, snow is your friend. If there is some snow on the ground and an extreme cold spell threatens, carefully shovel or push snow up around the plant, covering as much of the foliage as you can. Experiments conducted by needle palm enthusiasts in Wisconsin and Michigan demonstrate that plant parts covered by even 1 in (2.5 cm) of snow will remain undamaged by air temperatures as low as –15°F (–26°C) and probably lower, even in windy conditions. This is a particularly useful technique for those who do not want the bother of erecting windscreens. In my experience, holiday lights are not very effective in protecting large needle palm clumps because it is difficult to string the lights densely enough and difficult, if not impossible, to tie and wrap the clumps without causing more damage to the plant than it's worth. When the snow melts away, spray the plants with a fungicide/bactericide to prevent crown rot. This is particularly important if the cold spell has been prolonged—there appears to be more threat of spear leaf rot in needle palms that are covered with wet snow for long periods of time.

Sabal minor, Dwarf Palmetto, Bluestem Palmetto

Sabal 'Louisiana', Louisiana Dwarf Palmetto

The common dwarf palmetto is native to the southeastern United States from eastern Texas north to southeastern Oklahoma and east to the extreme southeastern corner of Virginia. As such, *Sabal minor* is clearly the most cold-hardy member of the genus and rivals the needle palm in its ability to take cold, wet winters. *Sabal minor* resembles and is often confused with the saw palmetto, *Serenoa repens*. Unlike the saw palmetto, dwarf palmettos do not have spines on the sides of the petioles and do not form invasive colonies. Taxonomists disagree on whether *S. minor* var. *louisiana* is a true variety, a hybrid, or a separate species. To make matters worse, the names *S. minor* var. *louisiana* and *S.* 'Louisiana' are often used interchangeably. (I use the latter name hereafter.) The native range of the Louisiana dwarf palmetto is restricted to river floodplains in Louisiana and Texas, and it has several vegetative features (described below) that distinguish it from *S. minor*. Numerous local varieties (which may be ecotypes) of both the common dwarf palmetto and *S.* 'Louisiana' are readily available in the trade, and each performs similarly in the temperate garden.

Size and characteristics. *Sabal minor* features a clumping habit, but unlike the needle palm, each plant has only a single trunk. In the dwarf palmetto, the trunk is entirely or almost entirely underground, whereas older specimens of *S.* 'Louisiana' can have an aboveground trunk about 3 ft (0.9 m) high. The presence of an aboveground leaf base in *S.* 'Louisiana' is one vegetative characteristic useful in distinguishing it from *S. minor*. All *S. minor* plants grow very slowly, especially when young, and for perhaps the first three to four years after seed germination, the juvenile foliage consists of strap leaves. As the name implies, these straplike green leaves bear no resemblance to the mature palmate to somewhat costapalmate leaves. When mature, the leaves are medium to deep green in scrub dwarf palmetto and a striking bluish green hue in *S.* 'Louisiana'.

In all *Sabal minor* leaves there is a pronounced split ∨ in the middle of the leaf. Individual leaves are generally about 3 ft (0.9 m) in diameter and are borne on petioles that are about 3 ft (0.9 m) long. A variety new to cultivation, *S. minor* 'Tamaulipas', which is native to the northeastern Mexican state, is considerably larger than the type and may be equally cold hardy. Under zone 6 conditions, an individual dwarf palmetto typically has about six leaves and can reach 4–5 ft (1.2–1.5 m) in overall height and spread (figure 6; plate 12). A mature clump-form *S.* 'Louisiana' can be as large as 8–10 ft (2.4–3.0 m) in height and spread, even in zone 6 (plate 13). On Avery Island in southern Louisiana, specimens of old fully trunked *S.* 'Louisiana' are even larger and strongly resemble cabbage palmettos. An interesting question is whether specimens of this variety

Figure 6 Dwarf palmetto (*Sabal minor*), Oxford, Ohio (zone 6a)

growing in cold-winter locations will ultimately grow that large and form prominent trunks. I think this is entirely possible. The oldest specimens of *S.* 'Louisiana' that I am aware of in zones 7a and 6b Oklahoma and Tennessee are perhaps fifteen years old and are starting to form above-ground trunks.

Cold hardiness. Riffle (1998) listed *Sabal minor* as hardy throughout zone 7 and south and as marginal in zone 6b. The consensus among authorities (table 5.1) places this species just slightly less cold tolerant than the needle palm. I suspect that this species is hardy throughout zone 6 and will likely survive with defoliation even in zone 5 or colder if sited well. Heretical as it may sound, I am becoming increasingly convinced that *S. minor* varieties may ultimately prove superior to the needle palm in zone 6 and colder areas.

Established dwarf palmettos and *Sabal* 'Louisiana' specimens with mature foliage are largely undamaged by short exposure to 0°F (–18°C) temperatures and often a few degrees lower, especially in plants sited out of the wind and not exposed to full afternoon winter sun. Even in less sheltered sites, perhaps 30–50 percent of the foliar tissue will survive exposure to –5 to –10°F (–21 to –23°C) and prolonged periods of sub-freezing weather. In a sunny and windy site, there is often less damage to established dwarf palmetto foliage than there is to equally established needle palms. Juvenile strap leaves are somewhat more sensitive to cold, especially in windy sites. In any case, damaged growth is easily pruned off in spring and established plants recover quickly.

Because the growth bud generally remains under ground level, the species will recover from some intense cold. Until *Sabal minor* has been in the ground for several years, regrowth can be slow. However, even though this species may produce only two or three new leaves per growing season, the resultant plant is impressive, especially when several plants are grouped together. Raymond Sharon of Wichita, Kansas, has been cultivating a commercially available variety of dwarf palmetto called 'McCurtain County' (for the original population in southeastern Oklahoma) for more than twenty years in his zone 6a garden. His plants have recovered from exposure to air temperatures as low as –24°F (–31°C) and the extreme wind-chill values characteristic of the Great Plains. Many

Table 5.1

Estimated average minimum survival temperature (°F/°C) for established specimens of cold-hardy palms, without external shelters, supplemental heat, or extensive snow cover.

Taxa	Literature Source					
	Southeastern Palm and Exotic Plant Society (2002)	Noblick (1998)	Walters (1998)	McKiness (2000)	Avent (2001)	Francko (2000), Francko and Wilhoite (2002)
Clump Palms						
Rhapidophyllum hystrix	–20/–29	–5/–21	–20/–29	–10/–23	–20/–29	–14/–26
Sabal 'Louisiana'	–3/–19	—	—	–5/–21	—	–14/–26
Sabal minor	–11/–24	5/–15	–5/–21	–5/–21	–10/–23[a]	–14/–26
Serenoa repens	–11/–24	15/–9	–5/–21	0/–18	—	–12/–24
Aborescent Palms						
Livistona chinensis	15/–9	—	12/–11	15/–9	—	–12/–24[b]
Sabal palmetto	–5/–21	0/–18	7/–14	0/–18	0/–18	–11/–24
Sabal bermudana	—	—	—	15/–9	—	–3/–19
Trachycarpus fortunei	–11/–24	0/–18	0/–18	–10/–23	–10/–23	–12/–24
Trachycarpus takil	—	—	–5/–21	–10/–23	—	–12/–24

[a]According to Avent (2001), *Sabal minor* 'McCurtain County' is reputed to have survived –24/–31 in Kansas.
[b]Survival and recovery of a well-mulched specimen; defoliation occurs at temperatures similar to those given by other sources.

authorities suggest that *S.* 'Louisiana' is slightly less cold hardy than the common dwarf palmetto, but our experience at Miami University and that of many others in zones 6 and 7 suggests equivalent performance.

Culture, landscape use, and other notes. *Sabal minor* grows naturally as an understory plant in wet forested areas and in boggy habitats and often grows in standing water over the winter months. It is excellent as a specimen plant or in groupings. Dwarf palmetto thrives in full sun through partial shade. It prefers moist, well-drained, highly organic soils but will tolerate clay. It tolerates saline soils and marine salt spray, so it can be sited near walkways or driveways where de-icing salt is used. A grouping of dwarf palmettos creates a truly tropical look, especially when mixed with other broadleaved evergreens and suitable ground covers (plate 14).

Like the needle palm, the dwarf palmetto requires hot and humid summer weather and is considerably less cold hardy in cool-summer climates. This species also does not tolerate drought well during its first few years. Dwarf palmetto is easily cultured from seed, and individual plants can produce viable seed when sexually mature. Nonetheless, these plants grow slowly, and I advise obtaining the largest containerized plants available.

Winter protection. Follow the same protection strategy as outlined for the needle palm. It is fairly easy to wrap a clump of dwarf palmetto leaves should extremely cold weather threaten. Burlap windscreens are also useful if plants are sited in windy, sun-drenched locations. Because dwarf palmettos do not have open aboveground crowns, they are nearly immune to crown rot. Heavy mulching with leaf litter appears to add several degrees to foliar hardiness of exposed leaves. Do not completely cover foliage with a deep mulch layer, however. In experiments conducted during 2001–2002, we noted very poor survival of *S. minor* and *S.* 'Louisiana' leaves covered with a wet, heavy leaf layer all winter.

Serenoa repens, Saw Palmetto

Native to the Atlantic and Gulf coastal plains of South Carolina, Georgia, Alabama, and Mississippi and all of Florida, dense, weedy saw palmetto thickets often dominate the understory of piney woods and other dry forested areas. Saw palmetto thickets are easily visible from highways and thrive in areas that are frequently disturbed by fire, clear-cutting, or other major disruptions. The common name comes from the spiny projections that often exist along the petiole margins. Although clumps of saw palmetto superficially resemble those of dwarf palmetto, they are seldom found together in the same microhabitat. Saw palmetto fruits are the source of permixon, a pharmaceutical extract effective in the treatment of benign human prostate enlargement.

Size and characteristics. Saw palmettos sometimes have aboveground trunks, but usually the trunks creep along the ground surface or through the soil, rooting and branching as they spread. The aerial leaves form dense masses of stiff, palmately segmented blades that are about 3 ft (0.9 m) across and borne on petioles that are as long or longer than the blades. An established clump can easily be 15 ft (4.5 m) wide and 10 ft (3 m) tall. The leaves are either greenish yellow or blue to silvery blue, and clumps of saw palmetto can make an attractive and very tropical statement in the home garden (figure 7). Growth and establishment of clumps is very slow, even in Florida, and gardeners report considerable difficulty in transplanting and reestablishing wild plants (Putz and Pinard 1999).

Figure 7 Saw palmetto (*Serenoa repens*) growing with Sikkim banana (*Musa sikkimensis*), Miami University campus, Oxford, Ohio (zone 6a)

Cold hardiness. There is some evidence that the green form of *Serenoa repens* is more cold hardy than the silver form, but this remains to be proven definitively. Gerry McKiness, owner of Gerry's Jungle at the Neotropic Nursery, has recently brought into cultivation a silvery form of *S. repens* that was found growing wild in central Georgia, well north of the usual northern limit for this species. This ecotype may prove more cold hardy that the type. In any case, saw palmetto is generally considered fully hardy in the warmer parts of zone 7 and southward, although Riffle (1998) listed it as fully hardy throughout zone 7 and marginal in zone 6b (see table 5.1). In our admittedly limited experience with several small plants growing in zone 6a and 7a microclimates in southwestern Ohio (both green and silver forms), we have found that leaves are severely burned when the temperature drops below about 10°F (−12°C), and complete defoliation occurs around 3 to 5°F (−15 to −16°C). The leaves seem especially susceptible to wind chills below 0°F (−18°C), even when sprayed with antidesiccant. I have seen leaves severely burned by temperatures around 18°F (−8°C) if it is windy enough. Nonetheless, saw palmetto is worth growing in colder areas because, like other clump palms, the growing bud is underground and cold-defoliated plants quickly recover the following growing season.

Culture, landscape use, and other notes. These palms like full to partial sun and well-drained soils. Because saw palmettos are very salt tolerant, they can be grown near a seashore or next to a sidewalk or driveway that receives occasional winter salting. Saw palmettos don't do as well under the heavy shade and wet soil conditions favored by *Sabal minor,* although they will survive. They are very drought tolerant once established, but make sure specimens are well watered their first few years in the ground. Although wild plants survive without much care, saw palmetto looks much healthier with regular fertilization, irrigation, and an occasional dose of lime in very acidic soils.

If you are interested in cultivating this plant, purchase a specimen grown from seed by a nursery. It is tempting to dig wild saw palmetto clumps and transplant them; however, as the saying goes, "the only way to kill it is to try and transplant it." Putz and Pinard (1999) suggested that it may be possible to enhance transplanting success in Florida with very high watering regimes and a lot of patience, but gardeners outside the typical range of *Serenoa repens* are already operating with several strikes against them.

Deer and rabbits like to nip the leaves off near the petiole bases and then add insult to injury by refusing to eat what they browse. In thirty seconds, a single rabbit can nip off an entire season's growth in a young saw palmetto. The only way to prevent this is to enclose the young plant in a chicken-wire cage, although zealous use of taste/odor repellant sprays is also effective.

Winter protection. As with other clump palms, heavy mulching and anti-desiccant and fungicide/bactericide spray helps retain leaves, but don't expect *Serenoa repens* to keep its leaves in typical zone 7a and colder winters without additional protection. It's possible to wrap smaller specimens with fabric, synthetic quilt batting, or other materials to extend the zone a bit and even to wrap trunks and leaf bases with heat cables; however, because the leaves are very stiff it is almost impossible to fold and wrap them without extensive damage. I suggest constructing a leaf pile enclosed by a burlap windscreen to retain maximal foliage at temperatures below 0°F (–18°C).

Nannorhops ritchiana, Mazari Palm

Trithrinax campestris, Blue Needle Palm

Zamia pumila, Florida Coontie Palm

These clump palms are relatively scarce and new to the market but definitely worth a try if you can obtain them. The Mazari palm may be as cold hardy as (or even superior to) the needle palm, but specimens are difficult to locate, cultural conditions are not well worked out, and the species is extremely slow growing—even for a palm. In its native range in the cold deserts of the Middle East, Mazari palm is clearly exposed to and survives temperatures below 0°F (–18°C). However, it appears much less hardy when grown under the wet and cold typical of most areas of the temperate United States, Canada, and Europe. The green-leaved form from Afghanistan appears much more cold hardy than the blue-leaved form from Pakistan, especially in wet soils. If you want to try this palm and are willing to wait for several years to see significant growth, make sure to plant it in full sun in extremely well-drained soils (very sandy is best) amended with lime if acidic.

Another difficult-to-find but extremely desirable clumping palm, the blue needle palm, is native to dry areas in northern Argentina. In the wild, old specimens can reach 20 ft (6 m) in height and feature stiff leaves with bluish white upper surfaces and greenish lower surfaces. The cold hardiness of *Trithrinax campestris* is somewhat uncertain, but limited experimentation in the United States under excellent drainage conditions suggests it should at least be on par with *Serenoa repens* (McKiness 2000). Why not experiment with one? Who knows, this may in fact be one of the most cold-hardy palm species.

The Florida coontie palm is not a true palm but rather is the only cycad species (part of a larger taxonomic group that includes pines, spruces, and other cone-bearing trees) native to the subtropical southeastern United States. Coonties are extensively used in Deep South landscapes as a clumping understory specimen. I haven't tried coontie palms myself, but growers have been successful with this species in zone 7 regions of the southeastern Piedmont, suggesting it has temperature requirements similar to the more cold-hardy cultivars of saw palmetto. *Zamia pumila* has an underground caudex, or swollen stem, from which grow variably shaped and sized leaves that resemble those of ferns. Like all cycads, the cones are attractive and contain beautiful cherry red seeds when ripe.

Clump Palms as Die-Back Perennials

Several palm species that normally grow as trees or very large shrubs in their native range can be grown in colder areas as die-back perennial shrubs, greatly enhancing a North-by-South landscape. At first blush this sounds very strange. The average temperate gardener is used to growing butterfly bushes and other subtropical and tropical woody species as die-back perennials—but palms? Adventurous experimental gardeners have found that numerous palm tree species are killed to the ground each winter only to regrow when warm conditions return. A few obvious possibilities are listed below, but practically speaking almost every tree palm covered in the arborescent palm section can be grown as a die-back perennial shrub under climatic conditions that are two or more zones colder that conditions required to grow the same species as an outdoor tree.

Livistona chinensis, Chinese Fan Palm

This beautiful tropical to subtropical tree palm is commonly found in the tropical plant section of home centers. Chinese fan palm is cold hardy in the sense that it can take hard freezes, but its leaves are damaged by temperatures below 20 to 23 F (−7 to −3°C), and much below about 12°F (−11°C) it is defoliated. As such, *Livistona chinensis* can only be grown outdoors as a tree reliably in zone 9a and warmer and in very sheltered areas of zone 8b.

But this beautiful fan palm can also be grown as an understory or accent shrub in zone 6 and 7 and perhaps zone 5 as a die-back perennial (plate 15). When the leaves are finally killed back in early winter, simply cut off all the dead and damaged foliage to near ground level. Often, the bottom few inches of the emerging spear in each leaf base will remain green and alive well below the defoliation temperature. Give each leaf base a good spraying with an antidesiccant and fungicide/bactericide mix, allow the plant to dry, and cover it loosely with 15–20 in (38–50 cm) of organic mulch. I use pine straw mixed with deciduous leaves because this mixture retains its loft well throughout our wet, cold winters, but any mulch will do. As noted in chapter 4, you may want to cover the palm with landscape fabric or burlap before adding the top dressing of mulch, but either method works. To gradually reintroduce the plant to full sunlight, remove the mulch a little at a time in late winter and early spring, uncovering completely around the time of the last expected frost. Be prepared to cover the plants again if a major cold spell (below 20°F, −7°C) occurs. Leaves begin to poke up from leaf bases within a few weeks, and by summer you will be rewarded with a sizable palm with several beautiful fan leaves (plate 16).

Cycas revoluta, Sago Palm

Cycas taitungensis, Emperor Sago

Cycas panzhihuaensis, Chinese Cycad

Sago palm (*Cycas revoluta*) is another common denizen of the tropical plant section that can be grown successfully outdoors in zone 8 and warmer. This tough and very tropical-looking plant is not a palm at all but a cycad like the coontie palm. Leaves of sago palms and related

Figure 8 Emperor sago (*Cycas taitungensis*) near Oklahoma City, Oklahoma (zone 7a; photograph © Bryan Swinney)

species such as emperor sago (*Cycas taitungensis*) will easily take temperatures ranging from 20 to 25°F (–7 to –4°C). The latter species, although more difficult to find in the trade than sago palm, is more cold hardy and is being grown successfully outdoors as far north as Oklahoma City (figure 8). The Chinese cycad (*Cycas panzhihuaensis*) may prove to be superior to either sago palm or emperor sago in cold hardiness. Like the Chinese fan palm, a defoliated sago palm or related cycad (except for the truly tropical species) can be overwintered in the ground with reasonable success in zone 6 and warmer, provided the site is very well drained and the plant is heavily mulched.

Phoenix roebelinii, Pygmy Date Palm

Chamaedorea radicalis, Dwarf Bamboo Palm

Pygmy date palms are several degrees less cold tolerant than the cycads described above. I have not had success overwintering them in my zone 6a garden, but they should do well in zone 7 and warmer. *Chamaedorea radicalis* is a small trunkless shrub palm native to high elevations in northeastern Mexico, where it is regularly exposed to hard freezes and occasional snow. It has only recently become available as a garden plant and remains difficult to find, but I predict that this will change in coming years. Like its relative *Chamaedorea elegans* (parlor palm), *C. radicalis* is highly prized for its beautiful feather leaves, which are harvested by local peoples in Mexico and exported to florists for use in flower arrangements. Dwarf bamboo palms are leaf hardy down to about 15°F (–9°C) and perhaps lower, and there are reliable reports of the underground portions of the plant surviving 0°F (–18°C) temperatures with no extra mulching (McKiness 2000). We installed three specimens in our warmer campus microclimates in early 2001 (plate 17) and mulched them heavily in early winter. All three survived the winter with defoliation and began growing new leaves in April. *Chamaedorea microspandix* is another species to try in zone 7 and warmer, as it was proven to be leaf hardy through about 15°F (–9°C) in Georgia.

Arborescent Palms for the Temperate Landscape

When people talk about palms, they are usually referring to palm trees rather than shrub or clump-forming species. Many species of tree palms are surprisingly tolerant of extreme cold, especially when well established. A few species will even survive repeated exposure to temperatures below 0°F (–18°C) and frequent snow and ice. Let's look at candidates for temperate conditions, in rough order of decreasing cold hardiness.

Trachycarpus fortunei, Chinese Windmill Palm, Chusan Palm, Fortune's Palm

The genus *Trachycarpus* contains several closely related species with marked cold tolerance. If there's one genus of tree palms that can be unequivocally recommended to gardeners in temperate climates, it is this one. Windmill palms are native to northern parts of India, Myanmar (Burma), Thailand, Nepal, and southern China and are often found in mountainous terrain above 6650 ft (2000 m) in elevation. As such, they grow in habitats that regularly receive heavy snow and where temperatures drop well below freezing for extended periods of time. Whereas needle palms and dwarf palmettos require hot summers to do well through cold winters, windmill palms actually prefer cooler summer weather—making them ideal for the cool marine climate of the Pacific Northwest and the British Isles. All members of the genus have a slender solitary trunk and a compact crown of ten to twenty palmate leaves. The leaf bases on trunks form a fibrous network of material resembling burlap, which gives the trunks of these palms a characteristic and unique appearance.

The Chinese windmill palm was first identified in the wild on the island of Zhoushan in China and brought back to England in Victorian times by Robert Fortune, hence the species name and common name. When most people talk about windmill palms, this is the species they are referring to. Chinese windmill palms have been cultivated outdoors and without protection in the Pacific Northwest for decades. Thirty-foot (9-m) specimens abound in Vancouver, British Columbia; southwestern England; Scotland; and all around the Mediterranean. Containerized windmills have been easy to find in the southeastern United States for many years (also sold occasionally as *Chamaerops excelsa*), and now are widely planted throughout the coastal South. Clearly they are well suited to the Piedmont and Cumberland plateau of the southeastern United States as well.

Size and characteristics. Windmill palms, like other palms, tend to grow slowly when young—frustratingly so for the home gardener. Two- to three-year-old windmill palm seedlings, which are easy to obtain via mail order, are about 1 ft (0.3 m) tall with minimal trunks and are much more sensitive to cold than four- to five-year-old specimens with small but true trunks. Even in climates as cold as zone 6b, ten-year-old windmill palms may have 3–4 ft (0.9–1.2 m) of trunk and stand perhaps 7–8 ft (2.1–2.4 m) tall overall (figure 9), adding about 1–2 ft (0.3–0.6 m) of height each year.

Juvenile windmill palms have five or six deep green leaves that are about 1 ft (0.3 m) across. As the plant ages, the leaves become larger and more numerous. A 20-ft (6-m) specimen in the zone 7b or warmer can possess a crown with more than twenty, 3-ft (1-m) wide leaves. In some individuals, the leaves may droop at the ends, whereas in others the leaves are stiffly held. Because the crown of leaves is symmetrical and full, the overall appearance of this palm is very pleasing. However, windmill palms leaves can become ruffled and untidy looking if the plant is grown in a windy location.

The flower stalk or inflorescence is borne upright among the leaves. Windmill palms are generally dioecious—female (creamy white) or male

Figure 9 Mature trunked Chinese windmill palm (*Trachycarpus fortunei*), Quebeck, Tennessee (zone 6b; photograph © Kevin McCartney)

(yellow) flowers are found on different plants. Thus, for viable fruits to form one needs specimens of both sexes. The kidney bean–shaped fruits are bluish black and can be germinated easily to produce new plants. Again, seedling growth is extremely slow at first.

Cold hardiness. Because it has been grown for many years in many parts of the world, we know more about the cold-hardiness characteristics of the windmill palm than any other tree palm species. I go into a fair amount of detail here, because much of what can be said about the Chinese windmill palm will apply to most cold-hardy tree palms being grown in temperate climes.

Windmill palms are completely hardy throughout all of zone 8 and most of zone 7b without significant winter protection. They can be grown in zone 7a and sheltered zone 6 microhabitats (maybe even in warmer parts of zone 5), but can experience significant to complete defoliation during cold winters. With reasonable care, nearly all individuals can recover from even complete defoliation and loss of the spear leaf. In very marginal climates, think of these as deciduous palms in your landscape plan.

Several factors enter into the windmill palm cold-hardiness equation, making blanket generalizations and exact comparisons between sites difficult at best. First, there is a huge difference in hardiness between juvenile and mature windmill palms. As plants become established and develop extensive root systems and true trunks, they become *much* hardier. Experience shows that a fully trunked, well-established, and well-tended windmill palm is at least one USDA zone more cold tolerant than a juvenile plant or a large specimen in poor condition. In Bulgaria (Donov 2000) mature windmills have survived repeated exposure to –20°F (–29°C). Our plants in Oxford, Ohio, have survived –14°F (–26°C); similar results have been reported by other experimental gardeners in Tennessee, Kansas, and Colorado. Although individual plants vary, I would estimate that –10 to –20°F (–23 to –29°C) approximates the average lower survival threshold for an unprotected trunked specimen (table 5.1). Again, these are survival temperatures—foliar damage and loss occurs at much warmer temperatures. The very term *survival temperature* is somewhat subjective. Much depends on what happens to the palm after it is exposed to very low environmental temperatures. As I explored at length in chapter 4, windmill palms have been know to die from cold exposure even in zone 8 due to cold-induced crown rot that kills the bud tissue.

Windmill palm foliage appears especially prone to wind-chill damage. The degree of damage is directly related to the size of the palm and fortunately decreases as the plant grows larger. In small seedling windmills, the spear leaf can be lost at around 15°F (–9°C). Our experience in Ohio suggests that significant leaf burn starts to occur at about 8 to 10°F (–13 to –12°C) in calm weather and whenever wind-chill temperatures drop much below 0°F (–18°C), regardless of the air temperature. In calm air at just above 0°F, perhaps 75–90 percent of the leaf surface area in young windmill palms is killed, but some viable leaf tissue near the petiole (and the green petioles themselves) usually survives even down to about –10°F (–23°C).

Frankly, I don't believe that there is enough long-term data in zone 6 or the colder parts of zone 7 to provide accurate foliar damage benchmarks in *established, trunked* windmill palms. My best guess, however, based on experiences described in the literature and our experimental plots (including the particularly nasty winter season of 2000–2001 and the mild winter of 2001–2002) is that critical temperatures are perhaps 5–7°F (3–4°C) colder than those listed in the previous paragraph. Charles Cole's long-term experience with windmill palm cultivation in east-central Tennessee (zone 6b) seems to corroborate this estimate (see section on winter protection). A zone 7a gardener who plants a windmill palm in a wind-sheltered location can expect that the majority of its foliage will survive a normal winter once the plant is well-established, and even a zone 6 gardener can expect some leaf tissue to overwinter if the palm is sited in a favorable microclimate. Again, duration of the cold event, presence or absence of snow cover, exposure to wind, and variations between individual palms all factor into the equation. Even under more extreme winter conditions, a windmill palm will simply be defoliated. Tend the plant while it recovers and grows new leaves in spring and summer.

It takes a couple of years for a windmill palm to grow a full crown of twenty or so leaves. Thus, with annual winter foliar damage a windmill palm growing in zones 7a or 6b may never look as impressive as one in zone 8. But, in almost all years an established palm will retain at least some green tissue in existing leaves and grow five to seven new leaves per growing season. Trim off any dead tissue in early spring and take steps to preserve the spear. The windmill palm will start growing about the date of the average last frost (remember, they like cooler weather and often exhibit foliar growth during mild winters) and will look like a palm tree again by about the end of May. By the end of June you will forget the palm ever defoliated (figure 10), and you'll be able to enjoy those leaves well into the next winter at the very least. Keep in mind that during mild winters in zones 6–7, windmill palms may suffer little or no damage. In 2001–2002 we had a "zone 7b" winter; aside from minor tip burn, our windmill palms were undamaged.

To my way of thinking, having windmill palms with about eight months of nice foliage and four months of partially damaged foliage is a fair bargain and well worth the effort and angst. I admit that, after a hard winter, my first reaction upon looking at our windmill palms in early March is usually one of dismay. But then I realize how remarkable it is that

Figure 10 Winter damage in juvenile Chinese windmill palm (*Trachy-carpus fortunei*) after pruning away dead leaves in March (top) and in early July after recovery and regrowth (bottom), Oxford, Ohio (zone 6a)

the trees themselves, perhaps a quarter of their foliage, and the spear leaves are still very much *alive*. Buried not too deeply in my gardening psyche is a notion that I've heard other experimental gardeners profess: Plants are an affirmation of life and its ability to triumph in the face of extreme adversity. Not a bad reason in and of itself, I think, to grow palms in Ohio.

Culture, landscape use, and other notes. Windmill palms grow in any kind of soil, even heavy clay. In zone 7 and colder, grow them in full sun or light shade; in hotter climates, make sure they receive afternoon shade at least. *Trachycarpus* species are very prone to drought stress until established, so don't let the soil dry out, especially in summer heat. They thrive with ample soil fertility, so follow the fertilization schedule noted in chapter 4. Windmill palms seem to benefit from an application of Epsom salts (magnesium sulfate) in spring. In heavy clay soil poor in iron, spring application of a trace-mineral formulation high in chelated iron also aids in foliar greening and canopy development.

Windmill palms look great alone or in groups of differing heights, especially planted in front of a wall. They go well with virtually all companion plants and can anchor a planting bed, especially with flowering shrubs, hostas, and bananas.

There are numerous varieties of Chinese windmill palm available to the gardener, especially via mail order. Usually, these plants are named after the locale where the parent seed-bearing tree is located, for example, *Trachycarpus fortunei* 'Bulgaria', 'Charlotte', 'Taylor Form', 'Greensboro', and 'British Columbia'. It is possible that parental plants growing in more northerly and thus colder locales are more cold hardy that than normal, wild-type palms of that species and will produce more cold-hardy offspring. However, there are few hard data on the cold-tolerance characteristics of putative ecotypes of *Trachycarpus* (or for that matter other common palms). For now this remains a tantalizing but unconfirmed hypothesis. It does appear from our field trails in Oxford, Ohio (zone 6a), that 'Taylor Form' and 'Greensboro' may be a bit more cold hardy than normal varieties.

Winter protection. With regard to tree palms, our knowledge base on optimal winter protection techniques is far from complete, especially in climatic zones outside of traditional palm country. Heavy mulching and application of antidesiccant and fungicide/bactericide sprays are your best bets for minimalist protection, along with watering as needed during prolonged subfreezing weather.

But how do you optimize the chances for success with windmill palms and other true tree palms in areas that experience temperatures below 0°F (−18°C)? Despite uncertainties and gaps in our horticultural database, a few tips are especially important with *Trachycarpus fortunei*. The large, open crown cavity in windmill palms, from which the spear leaves grow,

tends to collect water. Repeated freezing and thawing of this water dam-
ages tender bud tissue. This damage manifests itself as a narrow, ringed
band of damaged tissue in spears and in fully opened leaves. Tissue damage also releases organic nutrients that favor the growth of bacteria and
fungi, which can cause crown rot, a disease that can kill the bud tissue
and thus the whole tree.

Most palm authorities recommend minimizing the amount of water
that gets into the crown cavity over the winter months. This is not easy
to do, however, because several spear leaves and numerous petioles of
expanded leaves poke out of the crown at different angles. Also, because
the palm will be transpiring water throughout the winter months, albeit
at a reduced rate, the covering cannot be completely waterproof or it will
trap internally produced liquid in the cavity. One trick that seems to work
is to stuff some insulating but porous material (synthetic quilt batting,
lightweight landscape fabric, or even heavy paper) into the crown cavity,
working it around the petioles and spears. The goal is to fill all of the obvious spaces with insulating material. Then treat this packing materials
with a silicone-based waterproofing spray—the kind you can purchase in
a sporting goods store to treat a coat or pair of boots. These sprays repel
liquid water by causing it to bead and run off, while allowing the crown
interior to breath. Some people have used plastic to cover the crown, but
this invites condensation to collect on the underside and also prevents
gas exchange.

Even with some form of crown covering, periodic treatment of the
crown cavity with fungicide/bactericide is a crucially important measure
to prevent crown rot and possible death of the palm. Treat once before
the onset of winter, once in midwinter, and once again in late winter or
early spring. The last treatment in the early spring is perhaps the most
important. Warmer temperatures mean more rapid grow of disease organisms, and sometimes spear loss does not occur until March or April. There
is no question that many of the windmill palms that succumb to cold are
actually the victims of infections caused by opportunistic pathogens that
destroy the bud tissue.

If in late winter or early spring your palm is defoliated and the spear
leaves are damaged enough to pull out, you must act quickly to save the
palm. Treat the cavity immediately with copper-based fungicide or other
broad-spectrum fungicide/bactericide. Wait a few weeks to see if the palm

will begin growing a new spear leaf without further intervention—a basically healthy tree will respond fairly quickly and begin growing new spear leaves from live bud tissue very early in spring. If by the end of April or very early May (a little earlier in zone 7, a little later if April was unusually cold) a new spear is not growing, it is likely that damage was fairly extensive and more drastic measures must be taken to save the tree. Cut off sections of the trunk with a saw until you encounter live, greenish yellow bud tissue. In extreme cases this means cutting the trunk to within about 1 ft (0.3 m) of the ground. Treat this tissue with fungicide every week or so. In almost all cases the palm will initiate a new spear and recover from there. Again, it's going to hurt you more than the palm to take such drastic action, but if you don't, the rot disease will rapidly destroy all the living bud tissue and the tree will die. I have one other tip: After cutting a trunk back, spray it with fungicide/bactericide during the entire growing season to prevent a relapse of disease, especially during wet years.

We spent several years dealing with windmill palm damage and trying lots of winter protection methods that were difficult to implement and/or ineffective. Our evidence suggests that it's hard to beat the leaf enclosure method for the best possible winter protection of windmill palms in cold-winter areas (Francko and Wilson 2001). Encircle trunked windmill palms with a wire or burlap enclosure, ensuring that the sides are at least 1 ft (0.3 m) away from the trunk (a bit more in zone 6) and that the enclosure is tall enough to protect the entire trunk, including the top of the crown cavity. Treat the entire palm with antidesiccant and fungicide/bactericide spray and fill the enclosure with dry leaves or pine straw mixed with leaves. This treatment will keep cold winds away from the palm and keep the trunk warm and at a relatively constant temperature; both processes minimize freeze-thaw cycles that lead to disease. If your palm is only about 3 ft (0.9 m) tall or surrounded by other plants, you can do without the enclosure and simply pile leaves around the trunk.

Veteran zone 6b windmill palm growers report that this treatment alone will allow the palm to survive temperatures below 0°F (−18°C), as well as preserve foliage well below normally lethal temperatures. These same people have reported that they do not attempt to cover the crowns or foliage, yet they rarely experience problems with trunk rot. During the winter of 2001–2002, however, we covered the leaf canopy with a 6-in (15-cm) layer of leaves—the concave slope of the leaf canopy makes this easy to do (figure 11). The leaves direct water away from the crown cavity, functioning like the thatched roof of a cottage. They also insulate the leaf tissue from cold, dry winds, adding several degrees of hardiness to the foliage. Palms protected in this way suffered no foliar damage or spear loss.

At Miami University we have been able to overwinter juvenile windmill palms with largely intact foliage at air temperatures as low as –12°F (–24°C) simply by covering the whole plant with a pile of leaves. Like the larger palms described above, this seems to keep the crown cavity dry and the leaves protected from chilling winds. Windmill palm enthusiasts in even colder climates with reliable snow cover report that covering small plants with snow during extreme cold works just as well. We have done fairly extensive experiments on trunk wrapping (see chapter 4) in windmill palms, but can report only modest success at temperatures below 0°F (–18°C). But for gardeners living in zone 7a and warmer, this is a viable strategy when a severe cold spell threatens.

Figure 11 Leave mulching, including the crown, protects a windmill palm (*Trachycarpus fortunei*), Miami University campus, Oxford, Ohio (zone 6a)

Other *Trachycarpus* Species

In recent years several closely related species of windmill palms have become available in the marketplace. Most of these species appear to have a cold-hardiness range similar to Chinese windmill palms, although there is considerable debate about this point. As the common name implies, *Trachycarpus wagnerianus* (miniature Chusan palm) is a dwarf version of windmill palm; it has stiffer and shorter leaves that are less sensitive to wind stress. *Trachycarpus martianus* (Nepal windmill palm) and *T. latisectus* (Sikkim windmill palm, Windemere palm) are both new to the marketplace, and, although apparently not as cold hardy as the Chinese windmill palm, they definitely deserve more attention. Both species are exceedingly beautiful in that mature specimens have a bare, ringed trunk, rather than the furry trunk of *T. fortunei*, and large elegant leaf crowns.

The discovery of *Trachycarpus takil* (Kumaon palm, Himalayan windmill palm) by noted palm hunters Toby Spanner and Martin Gibbons in the early 1990s was greeted with great enthusiasm by temperate palm enthusiasts. Here was a palm that grew unprotected in extreme elevations in the Himalayas, where temperatures regularly drop below 0°F (–18°C), winds are extreme, and snow cover is the norm. Early reports suggested that this species is considerably more cold hardy than the Chinese windmill palm, easily able to take –10°F (–23°C). Many cold-hardy palm enthusiasts believed this species to be their Holy Grail—a palm that would prove truly adaptable to zone 6 (and possible colder) conditions with minimal foliar damage. In addition, *T. takil* offers many benefits as a landscape subject aside from cold hardiness. It grows taller than *T. fortunei*, with a thicker, often bare trunk and a larger crown.

When containerized Kumaon palms began to appear on the market in the late 1990s they were snapped up, often for premium prices, and they continue to be an extremely sought-after species. With all that said, I wish I could confirm with hard data the promise this species may offer, but alas I cannot—at least not yet. Early reports from gardeners in zones 7 and 8 (as well as a few intrepid souls in zone 6) and two winters of experience with the dozen *Trachycarpus takil* specimens in our zones 6a–7a microclimatic plots in Oxford, Ohio, do not support the earlier rave reviews. The small plants available to date seem about as cold tolerant as regular windmill palms—but not more so—and there is some evidence that Kumaon palms are more sensitive to summer drought than Chinese windmill palms. To be fair, I am not aware of anyone in the United States who is experimenting with established, mature Himalayan windmill palms. It is entirely possible that larger plants have superior cold hardiness. Like so many aspects of hardy palm cultivation, time will tell.

Sabal palmetto, Cabbage Palm, Cabbage Palmetto, Sabal Palm

The cabbage palm is *the* archetypal palm tree for most Americans, who first encounter this common palm on a trip to Florida or the coastal Deep South. The genus *Sabal* contains sixteen species native to tropical and subtropical portions of the Americas, including the dwarf palmetto, *S. minor*, described earlier in this chapter. All members of the genus have palmate or costapalmate leaves, and most have prominent trunks. Cabbage palms and related species are surprisingly cold hardy, especially when large enough to form a true trunk.

Cabbage palms are so named because their terminal buds were often harvested and cooked like cabbage by wayfaring sailors. Native to extreme southern coastal North Carolina southward through Florida, the Caribbean, and the Gulf of Mexico coast, *Sabal palmetto* is widely grown throughout zone 8 and even in warmer parts of zone 7. This species is currently the official state tree of both South Carolina and Florida—and cabbage palm enthusiasts in Tennessee are touting their state, only partially in jest, as the new Palmetto State (Taylor 2000).

Size and characteristics. Cabbage palms grow slowly but ultimately reach 80–90 ft (24–27 m) in height, with a trunk diameter of greater than 1 ft (0.3 m). It takes many years for a seedling palmetto to develop a true trunk and then several more years for the trunk to attain significant height and thickness. Their trunks feature crisscrossed, wickerwork-like patterns of old leaf bases known as "boot jacks" or simply "boots." The dense and massive crown can contain up to forty large green to bluish green leaves held on 6 ft (1.8 m) petioles. A grouping of cabbage palms of varying heights uplit with landscape lighting is a truly beautiful sight and completely evocative of a tropical paradise.

Cold hardiness. Cabbage palms are fully adapted to zones 8 and 9, and there is ample evidence that this species can survive in much colder regions. A *Sabal palmetto* that is more than forty years old resides in Gainesville, Georgia, in the northwestern corner of the state at the interface of zones 7a and 7b. This tree has survived multiple bouts with temperatures below 0°F (–18°C), including a –5°F (–21°C) winter in the 1980s. Cabbage palm seedlings grown from seed collected from the northernmost native population at Bald Head Island, North Carolina, and from a mature tree in Mount Holly, North Carolina (zone 7a/7b), are widely available. These parent trees have clearly survived temperatures below 0°F (–18°C). Atlanta and other Piedmont cities have numerous cabbage palms, although many people living in these areas are unaware of this fact and still insist that this species is not hardy in the Piedmont. A large, booted specimen grew for many years in Fred Breeden's garden in Seymour, Tennessee, southeast of Knoxville (zone 6b; figure 12). Mr. Breeden moved to Brentwood, near Nashville, and transplanted his prized

Figure 12 Trunked cabbage palmetto (*Sabal palmetto*), Seymour, Tennessee (zone 6b; photograph © Fred S. Breeden)

tree to his new home. Unfortunately, it ultimately succumbed to transplant shock and was lost. Information from the Internet reveals lots of other untrunked cabbage palms that appear to be thriving in zone 6b and 7a sites in the middle to upper South.

Most authorities now agree that trunked, established cabbage palms will survive 0°F (–18°C) temperatures (slightly below with defoliation; see table 5.1) and likely colder. For the past four years we have been growing juvenile, untrunked cabbage palms in Oxford, Ohio. The leaves clearly begin to suffer minor damage below about 10°F (–12°C), and at around –5 to –8°F (–21 to –22°C) most of the leaf tissue is destroyed. Mummy wrapping helps (see the trunk and foliar wrapping section of chapter 4), but like the windmill palm, the best success in small cabbage palms is obtained with heavy leaf mulching.

The experiences of hardy-palm enthusiasts in zones 6b and 7a Tennessee and Oklahoma are instructive here. Several individuals have been growing cabbage palms successfully in these areas since the late 1980s and early 1990s (M. Prairie, D. Moorhead, and R. Ogletree, personal communications). They report that once a cabbage palm has been in the ground for a few years (remember the three-year establishment rule) the foliage becomes *much* more cold hardy, approaching and even exceeding the hardiness range of *Trachycarpus* species. With heavy mulching alone, major damage does not begin until about 0°F (–18°C), and most of the foliage remains alive through typical zone 6b winter conditions, with nothing more than a blanket for extra cover during extreme weather.

Although these cabbage palms are just beginning to grow trunks after a little more than a decade in the ground, the data suggest that large, untrunked cabbage palms represent an excellent choice for a prospective North-by-South landscape design (plate 18). Even without trunks, cabbage palms are large and full and make a tremendous architectural statement, especially when grown in groups. Also, until a true aboveground trunk forms, the bud tissue remains largely underground, thus protecting it from extreme cold much like *Sabal minor*. Our Ohio cabbage palms act much like die-back perennials if the foliage is not protected; by midsummer they regrow three or four leaves and stand perhaps 4–5 ft (1.2–1.5 m) tall. Plants surrounded by a burlap barrier and packed with leaves do considerably better through the winter. Experience suggests that these individual palms will eventually be marginally leaf hardy, at least, under our zone 6 conditions, without complete covering. A few years ago, I frankly did not believe people who said that cabbage palms were more cold hardy than windmill palms. After a few years of personal experience, however, I'm more and more convinced that the foliar hardiness of *S. palmetto* is at least equal to that of *Trachycarpus fortunei*

Culture, landscape use, and other notes. *Sabal palmetto* prefers loose sandy soil high in organic material, but this species will grow in clay. It does best in full sun and is tolerant of salt spray and salinized soils. For best growth and maximal crown development, provide regular watering and ample soil fertility. Cabbage palm transplants easily, provided that care is taken during the recovery period. Prune off most of the leaves so that remaining leaves can receive ample moisture from the smaller root mass. Some growers insist on giving transplanted cabbage palms a hurricane cut, meaning that all leaves except one or two are removed and these remaining leaves are trimmed severely. It takes such a plant approximately three or four years to produce sufficient leaves to recover from this treatment, even in zone 8 and warmer. It seems to me that a better approach in colder areas is a more moderate trimming. In any case, buttress or at the very least stake the trunk of a large, newly planted cabbage palm to prevent wind damage. For gardeners in zone 7a and colder, however, the chances of successfully transplanting a trunked cabbage palm and nursing it through its first few winters and growing seasons is remote. Perhaps the best approach is to purchase the largest, untrunked containerized specimen you can find. That way, the palm will have several years to establish itself and acclimate to cold winters without having aboveground bud tissue.

Cabbage palms look best when integrated into a planting bed that features palms of several heights and an understory of shrubs and other contrasting vegetation. In colder climates they work well when densely planted with clump-forming *Sabal* species to form a colony. They also pair well with windmill palms and feather-leaved palm species such as *Butia capitata*.

Winter protection. In addition to from heavy mulching and antidesiccant spraying, try trunk wrapping to conserve heat and preserve the bud tissue near the crown. Juvenile untrunked cabbage palms are easily mummy wrapped with good results. In zone 7 and warmer, try stringing holiday lights throughout the foliage for a 3–5°F (2–3°C) foliar heat boost when needed. Of course, the die-hard enthusiast will wrap the entire trunk with heat cables or lights, followed by an outer wrap of fabric or bubble wrap (but see chapter 4 on dealing with the condensation associated with bubble wrap). Data suggest that a simple trunk wrap, even without added heat, will add roughly one USDA zone of cold hardiness to the *canopy* of an established trunked cabbage palm, meaning that it may be possible to preserve viable leaf tissue down to 0°F (–18°C) or lower, at least in calm weather. Also, do not remove the trunk boots, even if you prefer the smooth trunk look found in Florida resort palms. The boots are full of hollow air spaces and provide excellent thermal insulation to the trunk. With untrunked juveniles, especially in zone 7a and colder, employ the wind-barrier leaf-pack method described in chapter 4. However, do not attempt to bury cabbage palm leaves in a deep layer of leaf litter—like *S. minor,* this will kill the leaves over the winter.

Other *Sabal* Species

Sabal mexicana (also known as *Sabal texana*), the Texas palmetto, is a native of extreme southern Texas and northern Mexico down through Central America. This species looks a lot like *Sabal palmetto,* except that the trunk tends to be more massive and the leaves somewhat larger and a bit more bluish. This palm appears to be as hardy as *S. palmetto* when established; a massive mature specimen in Dallas, Texas, has withstood 1°F (–17°C). Other anecdotal reports from northern Texas and Louisiana support survivorship at temperatures below 0°F (–18°C). McKiness (2000) listed *S. mexicana* as hardy to 5°F (–15°C) or lower, and Riffle (1998) rated it has hardy through zone 7b. We have had small untrunked specimens here in Oxford, Ohio, for a few years that are killed to the mulch line and regrow each spring.

Another palm that deserves more attention is *Sabal* ×*texensis,* the Brazoria palm, which is believed to be an interspecific hybrid between *S. minor* and *S. texana* that was first identified in Brazoria County in southern Texas in the early 1990s. As a hybrid, the Brazoria palm shares characteristics of both parent species. Individuals can reach more than 20 ft (6 m) in height and have massive trunks and large leaves that are palmate like *S. minor,* rather than costapalmate like *S. palmetto.* In terms of cold hardiness, this palm is also intermediate between dwarf palmetto and cabbage palmetto, probably around 0°F (–18°C) or a bit below for an established palm. But like so many species that are relatively new to cultivation, we really don't know the lower limit for individual Brazoria palms. Our plants in Oxford (small seedling stock) defoliate to the ground and regrow the following year during typical winters.

Sabal bermudana, Bermuda cabbage palm, was listed by McKiness (2000) as comparably hardy to *S. palmetto*. This species is more massive than a typical cabbage palm and very fast growing. At Miami University, our containerized, untrunked Bermuda cabbage palms are defoliated below about 8°F (–13°C) like other tree *Sabal* species, but when they regrow in spring and summer, their new leaves are more massive and fuller than cabbage palms and have a pleasing bluish green cast. Gardeners in zone 7a and colder regions could use this palm to excellent advantage as a die-back perennial in the understory of a planting bed, along with other shrubs and flowering plants.

Another palm deserves special attention, because it may ultimately prove to be the most sought-after tree palm for temperate conditions. *Sabal* 'Birmingham' is a putative trunked hybrid that has been grown successfully in zone 6b Tulsa, Oklahoma, since the early 1990s, where one massive specimen withstood –8°F (–22°C) with minimal foliar damage (plate 19). Seeds and seedlings from this exceptionally cold-hardy individual are now on the market. It will be very interesting to see how its offspring fare in other locations. This may ultimately prove to be the most cold-hardy arborescent palm available. In trials with juvenile, strap-leaved specimens derived from the Tulsa parent, this palm appears to be about as cold hardy as *S. minor* under our zone 6 conditions.

Butia capitata, Jelly Palm, Pindo Palm

The jelly palm is so named because the fruits can be used to make a tasty sweet jelly. *Butia capitata* is native to Brazil, Argentina, and Uruguay and is probably the most cold-hardy pinnate-leaved (feather shaped) palm available to the temperate gardener. Commonly planted in the coastal Deep South, it freely hybridizes with other members of the genus as well as palms from other genera. Some of these hybrids (for example, *Butia* × *Jubea*) are quite vigorous and are becoming more readily available. Although too new to wide-scale cultivation in the United States, *Butia yatay* (Yatay palm) is a larger member of the genus that may be even more robust and cold hardy than the jelly palm. Similarly, *B. eriospatha* (woolly butia) is another potentially very cold-hardy species to consider, if you can obtain one. Like so many new species and cultivars just appearing on the landscape market, more work is clearly needed to fully evaluate these palms under temperate conditions.

Size and characteristics. Jelly palms are medium-sized palms with stiff and gracefully arching, recurving fronds that are grayish green to bluish green and about 3 ft (0.9 m) long (figure 13). The short grayish trunks can be about 3 ft (0.9 m) at the base in old specimens and the overall height can exceed 20 ft (6 m). Petioles are long and feature wicked spines. Although the flower stalks are not particularly impressive, the clusters of mature fruits are, with their orange color and egg shapes nicely contrasting with the foliage.

Cold hardiness. *Butia capitata* palm has traditionally been grown only in the warmest parts of zone 8 and warmer—with good reason. In most individuals, even large established plants, leaf damage starts at about 15°F (−9°C) and generally at 10°F (−12°C) and lower the leaves are lost completely. Still, jelly palms have been reliably reported to survive 0°F (−18°C) cold spells in the middle South, provided they are well mulched, and they

Figure 13 Jelly palm (*Butia capitata*), Miami University campus, Oxford, Ohio (zone 6a)

recover rapidly in spring. Experimental gardeners in zones 7b and colder have been successful in mummy wrapping the trunk and lower leaves, thus preserving some green tissue and the spear leaf. In larger jelly palms, enthusiasts swear by the effectiveness of holiday lights in warding off the damaging effects of extreme temperatures.

This is an excellent species to protect within a leaf enclosure; for gardeners who attempt to grow this plant in zone 6b or colder, it may be the only way to go. In 2000 we obtained some 3- to 4-ft (0.9- to 1.2-m) specimens from a gardener in a rural area north of Charlotte, North Carolina. With minor trunk wrapping, the palms survived brief exposure to –10°F (–23°C) temperatures during the winter of 1999–2000 and recovered to grow several large leaves each by early June. However, we were only able to overwinter one trunk-wrapped jelly palm during 2000–2001, even in microclimates that did not go below 0°F (–18°C). Such treatments do not keep the root zone or trunk as warm as a leaf pile, especially during prolonged cold spells. I'm sure we will try again, with added winter protection this time. In my view, the extraordinary beauty and rapid growth of *Butia capitata* makes it a viable choice for the zone 7 North-by-South gardener (and zone 6 if planted in an excellent, sheltered site), even though leaf loss is virtually guaranteed each winter.

Culture, landscape use, and other notes. *Butia capitata* is an extraordinarily beautiful palm. In 2000 most visitors to our Miami University plots considered the jelly palms to be far and away the stars of the show. It is a wonderful specimen palm in warmer climates and can serve the same purpose in a colder garden, as long as the plant is heavily protected for winter. The form and leaf color of this species cannot be beat for creating a tropical look. For an aesthetically pleasing effect, trim off dead leaves so that the leaf bases are approximately the same length.

Jelly palms are tolerant of various soil types and are drought tolerant once established, but like all palms they do better with adequate water and fertile soil. Usually planted in full sun, they will tolerate some shade, but do not grow in dense shade.

Winter protection. Follow the directions for other trunked palms, making sure to treat the crown cavity with fungicide/bactericide. The leaves of jelly palms are relatively flexible and can be drawn up fairly easily to create an effective mummy wrap. I think it is futile to try and save all of the leaf tissue anywhere colder than the zone 8a, but if you are ambitious and want to try a full foliar wrap with supplemental heating, this could work, provided that the palm has access to soil moisture. That is, if you're going to heat up the aboveground portions of the plant, you must ensure that the root-zone soil is not frozen, either by mulching very heavily and/or installing an underground heat cable. Otherwise, the warm (and thus photosynthetically active) leaves and stems will rapidly dry out and die due to water stress. Again, in areas with winters that usually reach 0°F (−18°C) or colder, a heavy covering of leaves is probably the only viable option. In the spring simply cut off damaged foliage at the leaf bases and allow the plant to recover.

Washingtonia filifera, California Fan Palm
Washingtonia robusta, Mexican Fan Palm

The genus *Washingtonia* contains only two species, both of which are worth trying in warm-temperate gardens (zones 7 and 8 and perhaps zone 6). California and Mexican fan palms are native to desert and semi-arid areas of the southwestern United States and northwestern Mexico. As such, they tolerate considerable cold in dry-climate areas, but conventional wisdom has suggested that they are not as hardy under cold, wet winter conditions. However, Gerry McKiness reports good success in tests of young *W. filifera* in the wet-winter southeastern Piedmont, and established individuals have survived −11°F (−24°C) in the El Paso and St. George areas of western Texas and southwestern Utah, respectively. Decade-old specimens grow in zone 7a Oklahoma City and zone 6b Tulsa (plate 20), protected only with mulching and partial trunk wrapping during extreme weather. *Washingtonia filifera* gets much more cold tolerant as it becomes established. Paradoxically, *W. robusta* is nowhere near as robust as *W. filifera,* at least not with respect to winter cold, although Mexican fan palms can survive temperatures below 0°F (−18°C) if mummy wrapped and heavily mulched.

Both California and Mexican fan palms grow extremely rapidly and reach great heights in their native ranges: more than 50 and 80 ft tall (15 and 24 m), respectively. Mature California fan palms have wide, grayish green or yellowish green leaves with spiny petioles, a characteristic petticoat-like skirt of dead leaves below the crown, and massive trunks up to 3 ft (0.9 m) in diameter. Mexican fan palm trunks rarely exceed 1 ft (0.3 m) in diameter, and their leaves on spiny petioles are an exceedingly attractive rich green. Both species have cottony threadlike fibers associated with the leaves.

When grown outside their normal zone 8b and warmer range, California and Mexican fan palms should be planted in full sun and in very well drained soil. Use a full mummy wrap and, in zones 7a and colder, I would enclose the whole plant in a leaf cage during the winter until it is well established. Crown treatment with fungicide/bactericide is a must. Some people advocate supplemental heating of the roots and the bud tissue, but we have not been successful with this strategy in Oxford, Ohio.

In zone 7 and warmer parts of zone 6 it's relatively easy to cultivate these beautiful trees as so-called chainsaw palms—a colorful way of saying that they can be grown as deciduous palms under cold-winter conditions. Large 15- and 30-gallon specimens can be easily and inexpensively obtained from your local home center. Although completely defoliated below about 15°F (–9°C), *Washingtonia robusta* and *W. filifera* (the latter is perhaps 6–8°F [4–5°C] more cold tolerant) display a remarkable ability to recover rapidly in the next growing season, often adding eight to ten new leaves and 1 ft (0.3 m) or more of trunk. In my experience *Washingtonia* are *the* fastest growing palms available to the temperate gardener. A 5- to 6-ft (1.5- to 1.8-m) Mexican fan palm, with its stiff, large, rich green leaves and dark brown booted trunk is a truly striking specimen palm well within the reach of a zone 6 gardener (plate 21).

After the leaves have been killed in early winter, cut them off, treat the crown cavity with fungicide/bactericide, and wrap the trunk with synthetic quilt batting or heavy paper. Cover the batting or paper with a plastic bag or other plastic wrap to completely exclude liquid water from entering the crown cavity. Make sure the plastic wrap does not come all the way down to ground level, or it will wick soil moisture. Tie the bag or plastic wrap loosely at the bottom, so that some air is exchanged under the plastic wrap. Mulch the entire trunk with leaves or other loose material. After the worst winter weather passes, gradually uncover the trunk, but be ready to cover it again if a hard freeze is due. Once spring weather arrives, a healthy palm will rapidly grow its first new spear leaf. Sometimes you will need to cut off damaged sections of trunk bud tissue (see the earlier discussion in *Trachycarpus fortunei*) or treat the cavity with fungicide/bactericide spray. You can easily tell if a *Washingtonia* palm has been fatally damaged because the lower trunk will be distinctly mushy to the touch. If this happens, do not despair—just head down to the store and buy another inexpensive subtropical palm to replace it.

I have one additional note: *Washingtonia* species hybridize freely in nature, and a hybrid of *W. filifera* and *W. robusta* known as *Washingtonia* ×*filibusta* is becoming available on the market. Early trials suggest that this hybrid may be hardier than either of the parental species and well suited to conditions in the southeastern United States.

Chamaerops humilis, Mediterranean (European) Fan Palm

Native to northern Africa and the Mediterranean coast of Europe, this fan palm forms clusters of trunks that tend to lean outward from the center, creating a graceful and very tropical look. In the United States *Chamaerops humilis* is common in cultivation in regions with Mediterranean climates but is also grown extensively in the coastal South. Leaves, ranging from green to bluish green to silver, are relatively flat and stiff, and the petioles are spiny. This palm grows in virtually any kind of soil, although slowly, and can reach 20 ft (6 m) in height at maturity in the subtropics. One recently available variety, *C. humilis* var. *cerifera* (Moroccan silver palm), may prove to be more cold hardy that typical Mediterranean fan palms and is worth the effort if you can obtain one.

The Mediterranean fan palm is typically thought of as a true zone 8 and warmer species. It generally defoliates at about 15°F (−9°C) but has been reliably reported to survive temperatures of about 3°F (−16°F) without permanent damage. In 2000 we planted a single, relatively small specimen on the Miami University campus in a very sheltered microclimate, and protected it only with mulch during its first winter. It retained green foliage during nighttime temperatures around 8°F (−13°C), and although defoliated by spring, it recovered completely in 2001 and increased in overall size during the growing season. Performance was similar over the winter of 2001–2002, although by covering the entire palm with leaves we were able to overwinter a significant amount of green tissue after a winter low of 9°F (–13°C). Based on this positive result, we installed additional specimens, including several Moroccan silver palms. Due to its mounding habit the Mediterranean fan palm can be easily covered with landscape fabric during cold snaps, and its stiff leaves make it an excellent candidate for wrapping with holiday lights. This species also makes an excellent potted palm for use as a specimen plant on a patio or deck.

Brahea armata, Blue Hesper Palm

Trithrinax acanthocoma, Buriti Palm

Jubea chilensis, Chilean Wine Palm

Blue hesper palms are native to Baja California, whereas *Trithrinax* and *Jubea* species are found in dryer and colder climates of South America. Each holds great promise as a potential cold-hardy tree palm suitable for regions with cold, wet winters. Unfortunately, because these species are fairly new to cultivation in the United States, they are still expensive and difficult to obtain. Thus, there is just not enough information to provide precise and accurate cultural information for gardeners outside traditional palm country. Chilean wine palms, very beautiful tree palms that resemble huge jelly palms, are being grown with some success in zone 7 areas of the southeastern Piedmont, where they appear to rival windmill palms in hardiness. *Brahea armata,* with its striking bluish fan leaves, and *T. acanthocoma* may be better suited to zone 8 and warmer, but McKiness (2000) suggested that they may be hardy in zone 7. All of these species desire a lot of sun, and excellent drainage is a must in wetter climates. Once established, they are exceedingly drought tolerant. As noted earlier, these species are being hybridized with one another and with members of other compatible genera to produce hybrids with increased vigor and enhanced cold tolerance.

Chapter 6

Broadleaved Evergreen Trees and Shrubs

> Without some boldness the gardener will make no
> experiments, and his garden will be no more than a copy
> of his neighbour's.
>
> —Canon Ellacombe

> Nature never makes excellent things for mean or no uses.
>
> —John Locke

roadleaved evergreen trees and shrubs are the heart and soul of all warm-climate landscapes, providing the dominant architectural framework in a well-planned North-by-South landscape. They add interest and structure to the garden during the summer and break up the starkness of the landscape during the winter months when deciduous trees have lost their leaves.

Temperate gardeners outside the American South, Southwest, and Pacific Coast usually think of evergreens in terms of pines, spruces, yews, boxwoods, and arbor vitaes. There's nothing wrong with these plants, but there are so many other choices. As with the palms, the conventional wisdom about which broadleaved evergreens grow where is oversimplified at best or simply wrong. Thanks to advances in plant breeding and selection, the signature tree of the American South, the southern magnolia, can be grown in Cleveland, Ohio, as well as Cleveland, Tennessee—you just have to know which cultivar to select and how to site and care for it. Autumn- and spring-blooming camellias, traditionally the province of Deep South gardeners, can now be cultivated in more northerly climes. Again, the key is knowing *which* cultivars will do well in your area.

In this chapter I focus on those keystone landscape species and varieties that will provide the defining structure to your landscape—those essential woody plants that create a look and feel that set a warm-climate garden apart from the traditional temperate garden. What follows is not meant to be a completely inclusive list of possibilities. Rather, I start with two genera, *Magnolia* and *Ilex*, that have the largest number of candidate species and varieties. Then I survey, in alphabetical order, those genera that would probably be on any southern landscape architect's top 10 list for inclusion in a warm-climate garden, focusing on species and varieties that have proven hardy in cold-winter climates.

Evergreen Magnolias

Magnolia grandiflora, Southern Magnolia, Bull Bay Magnolia

This is my favorite tree species, hands down. To me there is no more stately or beautiful tree in the landscape than a southern magnolia. In her book *The World of Magnolias* (1994), Dorothy Calloway referred to this species as the aristocrat among landscape plants. As a specimen tree, the southern magnolia absolutely *defines* the southern landscape, even more so than palms (see chapter 5) and flowering crape myrtles (chapter 7). Michael Dirr put it succinctly in his landmark *Manual of Woody Landscape Plants* (1998): "Yankees would kill to be able to grow this species." By the mid to late 1990s, however, homicide was no longer a prerequisite for growing this species in areas colder than zone 7—sufficient experience on newer, more cold-tolerant southern magnolia cultivars had accumulated. In truth, massive old specimens can be found in home landscapes, arboreta, and public areas well into zone 6 (plate 22).

Size and characteristics. The genus *Magnolia* is one of the oldest among the flowering plants. Evergreen magnolias are native to the southeastern United States and many other mild-winter areas of the globe. There are more than a hundred cultivars of *M. grandiflora*, with more being developed all the time. Cultivars range in size at maturity from small trees of perhaps 20 ft (6 m) in height to massive specimens 100 ft (30 m) tall and perhaps half as broad. The large (5–10 in, 12.5–25.0 cm), glossy, deep green leaves range in shape from broadly elliptical to lance shaped. The undersides of leaves are lighter green and, depending on the cultivar, covered with varying densities of rusty brown, furlike material know as *tomentum,* which contrasts with the dark green upper surface and the grayish brown color of trunks and branches. Some people still insist that the more pubescent (furry) the leaf, the more cold hardy the cultivar, but there is little experimental evidence to support this view.

Magnolia flowers are among the most striking in the landscape. Creamy white and several inches to nearly 1 ft (0.3 m) across and extremely fragrant, the flowers are reason enough to grow these plants. The print medium is wholly inadequate to describe the lemony smell of magnolia flowers opening in late spring and early summer and sporadically throughout the rest of the growing season. Cut a few of them off, float them in a decorative bowl filled with water, and enjoy.

Cold hardiness. This trait varies greatly by cultivar. Nearly all cultivars are fully leaf hardy in zone 7 and warmer. I focus here on those cultivars that will do well in zone 6 and probably even colder, as well as being suitable for warmer areas.

It is worth repeating some information from chapter 4. Like all broadleaved evergreens, southern magnolias are prone to winterburn when low temperatures, strong winds, and bright winter sunshine dry the leaves and induce irreversible damage to photosynthetic pigments. You can reduce this damage greatly by proper siting, building windscreens, using antidesiccant sprays, and winter watering. But please remember that it takes several years for a newly planted magnolia to establish itself, especially in heavy soils. Until then, *expect* significant leaf burn damage from temperatures below 0°F (–18°C) or even prolonged periods of temperatures below freezing, especially on the side of the tree exposed to full winter sun and drying wind. In the winter of 1998–1999, I had the unfortunate experience of watching nearly every leaf on a first-year 'Bracken's Brown Beauty' turn purplish green and then brown after sequential nights of –14 and –12°F (–26 and –24°C) followed by bright, sunny days. In midspring all the brown leaves fell off, however, and the tree recovered fully from near complete defoliation. The next winter, after another growing season to extend its roots, it was only slightly damaged by essentially the same conditions. Understand that such behavior is a *normal* response to stress—by and large southern magnolias can and do recover from even complete defoliation. Once a tree is established, you can expect it to perform well under the conditions described below for each cultivar. Indeed, this same advice and caution applies to *all* evergreen trees and shrubs discussed in this chapter.

Culture, landscape use, and other notes. As a specimen, you can employ *Magnolia grandiflora* singly or in groups. Small varieties can be sited in tight places, but heed the information below on the ultimate size for each cultivar. Larger varieties require plenty of space, and southern magnolias are difficult to transplant without significant shock and loss of many leaves. Magnolias normally drop a fair number of leaves during autumn and spring anyway, and some gardeners like to clean them up because they decay very slowly and can be untidy.

Southern magnolias thrive in full sun but also do well in filtered sun or partial shade. They prefer well-drained soils high in organic matter but will tolerate wetter conditions and clay soils. In native habitats southern magnolias are found in moist woodlands, where they are often a dominant canopy species, with branches restricted to the crown. In landscape cultivation most individuals branch profusely from the ground up, and the tree takes on a pyramidal aspect. If you don't care for this shrubby look and prefer to expose the lower trunk—my preference because the sinuous trunk architecture is so pleasing—simply prune the lower branches to your taste.

Southern magnolias are available containerized or balled-and-burlapped. In marginal areas, larger specimens tend to establish faster than smaller (1- to 3-gallon) plants, and most cultivars do not flower until they are several years old, but I have had good success with 1-gallon 'Bracken's Brown Beauty'. I advise anyone growing *Magnolia grandiflora* for the first time to check out local nurseries and, if possible, purchase *locally available* cultivars. Nurseries lose money whenever someone returns a dead plant, so they tend to know which cultivars will do best in their climate. If you live well north of the Mason-Dixon line, your favorite local nursery may not carry this species yet, but they can order plants for you. There are also numerous mail-order firms that carry southern magnolia, but the plants sold are usually much smaller.

One additional tip from my personal school of hard knocks: Use extreme caution when purchasing and planting a southern magnolia early in the growing season. If you're like me, you cannot control the itch to get planting just as soon as the local nurseries open up for business. In our area, that's usually late February or early March. Although that is a good time to plant a still-dormant deciduous tree or shrub, a newly planted southern magnolia can be damaged severely by a late extreme cold spell or a heavy snow or ice storm. In addition, plants purchased early in the growing season are usually leftovers from the previous year, and for southern magnolias this can be a real problem. If the tree is not properly watered and cared for over the winter, the leaves and branches dry out and die, but the tree often remains green for weeks after death (one of the reasons why magnolia branches are often used in dried flower arrangements). Thus, the tried-and-true method of scratching the bark to search for green living tissue does not work well with *Magnolia grandiflora*. So, make sure you get a guarantee on any leftover evergreen magnolia, or you may wind up with a very expensive source of kindling for your fireplace.

Winter protection. Water and mulch well and spray with antidesiccant twice during the winter. Small specimens can be protected from wind and sun by burlap or fabric windscreens. In the spring following a difficult winter, I have noticed significant stem die-back in first-year trees that were drought stressed the previous growing season. Delayed drought stress is actually a common and underappreciated problem in all trees and shrubs but is especially problematic in broadleaved evergreens. Therefore, make sure to provide adequate water to pre-established magnolias during the growing season, or you may see problems the following year.

Magnolia grandiflora Cultivars

There is a vast and growing list of southern magnolia cultivars. A more complete treatment can be found in Dirr (1998, 2002) and Calloway (1994). Here are some of the more readily available cultivars in roughly descending order of proven cold hardiness.

'Edith Bogue'. This plant is readily available and is probably the most cold-hardy cultivar on the market, having withstood –24°F (–31°C) with defoliation. Once established, minor spotting and margin burn only occur down to –5 or –10°F (–21 or –23°C), depending on wind and sun exposure. With a vigorous pyramidal shape that withstands heavy snow and ice, this tree grows to about 30 ft (9 m) with a 15 ft (4.5 m) spread.

'Edith Bogue' bears large, dark green leaves with light tomentum on the underside. Originally a tree sent to Edith A. Bogue in Montclair, New Jersey (zone 6), established specimens are now found in many zone 5 areas of the United States. This cultivar is one of the best choices for zone 5 (and possibly colder) as well as zone 6.

'Bracken's Brown Beauty'. Introduced by Ray Bracken of Easley, South Carolina, in the late 1960s, this extremely popular and readily available cultivar has survived –20°F (–29°C) and colder temperatures in Ohio and elsewhere. 'Bracken's Brown Beauty' suffers minimal leaf burning above perhaps –5°F (–21°C), even in sunny sites. This tree is very dense and compact with narrow, medium-sized, glossy, dark green leaves that shed snow and ice well. The plant produces heavy dark brown tomentum on the undersides of leaves and forms multiple breaks (new shoots) from branch tips for added fullness. Flowers measure 5–6 in (12.5–15.0 cm) and are borne profusely at a young age. 'Bracken's Brown Beauty' transplants better than most selections, with less leaf shock and leaf drop; many specimens that exceed 30 ft (9 m) now exist (figure 14; plate 23).

Figure 14 *Magnolia grandiflora* 'Bracken's Brown Beauty', Miami University campus, Oxford, Ohio (zone 6a)

'**Victoria**'. A selection developed in Vancouver, British Columbia, this narrow-leaved, heavily pubescent cultivar is grown extensively in the Pacific Northwest and more recently has become available in other locales. 'Victoria' has taken −12°F (−24°C) with heavy snow loading and was rated as hardy in zone 6 and marginal in zone 5 by Calloway (1994).

'**Samuel Sommer**'. Introduced in 1961 by the Saratoga Horticultural Foundation (Florida), this cultivar is readily available. It was listed by Calloway (1994) as hardy in zone 6 and marginal in zone 5. 'Samuel Sommer' grows rapidly to 30–40 ft (9–12 m) and similar spread, with strong ascending habit, very large dark green leaves, and heavy rusty tomentum on the undersides. Flowers are exceptionally large (10–14 in, 25–35 cm).

'**D. D. Blanchard**'. The original tree of this cultivar grew in garden of D. D. Blanchard in Wallace, North Carolina, and was propagated and registered by Robbins Nursery in North Carolina in the 1960s. Its very broad, deep green leaves with heavy, coppery brown tomentum makes this an extremely attractive tree. 'D. D. Blanchard' has a compact, upright, pyramidal growth habit. It is perhaps a touch less cold hardy than the cultivars discussed above; in recent years, however, 'D. D. Blanchard' has become readily available in zone 6 Cincinnati, Ohio, and does well. In my experience, this cultivar suffers first-year damage comparable to 'Bracken's Brown Beauty'.

'**Little Gem**'. As the name implies, this is a dwarf cultivar. It was developed in the early 1950s by Steed's Nursery in North Carolina and tends to grow as a large dense shrub rather than a tree. 'Little Gem' is the one to try if space is an issue or if a magnolia screen or hedge is desired. It has become the small evergreen magnolia of choice in the southeastern United States. This magnolia grows slowly to perhaps 15 ft (4.5 m) and has small (4 in, 10 cm), narrow, dark green leaves with heavy pubescence underneath and small flowers. But it flowers at a very young age—it is not uncommon for seedling-sized trees to flower. Although 'Little Gem' has a reputation for being sensitive to cold, it is readily available in zone 6 locales in the eastern United States. In my limited experience, this cultivar appears about as cold hardy as those listed above, especially if sited out of the wind (figure 15; plate 24). A specimen planted in a fairly open site on the Miami University campus in the mid-1990s has survived many nights with temperatures below 0°F (18°C). However, it is not as full and healthy as trees planted in less windy sites.

'Claudia Wannamaker'. Widely planted in the Southeast for its vigorous, upright, and open growth habit, this early-flowering cultivar has somewhat small, dark green leaves with medium tomentum. I am not sure how cold hardy this cultivar will prove to be in zone 6 and colder areas. However, 'Claudia Wannamaker' has been locally available in the Greater Cincinnati area for the past few years and appears to do well in my zone 6a backyard. It suffers perhaps a bit more damage than the selections listed above but is worth a try.

Figure 15
Magnolia grandiflora 'Little Gem', Miami University campus, Oxford, Ohio (zone 6a)

Less Readily Available *Magnolia grandiflora* Cultivars

Numerous, extremely cold-hardy regional cultivars make excellent choices if you can find them locally. Some of these are now being offered in mail-order catalogs. What follows is far from an exhaustive list—check with a reputable nursery in your area, and you may uncover a local favorite.

'Poconos'. As the name implies, this is a cultivar from trees growing in the Pocono Mountains of eastern Pennsylvania. This magnolia is difficult to find but is now being sold via mail order. 'Poconos' is said to rival to hardiest known southern magnolias.

'24 Below'. This cultivar was selected from a tree that survived −24°F (−31°C) in Knoxville, Tennessee, in 1985.

'Tulsa' ('Winchester'). This magnolia was selected from a tree in the zone 6b Tulsa (Oklahoma) Rose Garden (figure 16). Specimens grow with only minor injury in Winchester, Massachusetts, just northwest of Boston (Dirr 1998).

Figure 16
Magnolia grandiflora 'Tulsa', Tulsa Rose Garden, Tulsa, Oklahoma (zone 6b; photograph © Bryan Swinney)

'Opal Haws'. This cultivar originates from parent tree in Boise, Idaho. It is hardy to –24°F (–31°C).

'Saint George'. Originated in Canterbury, England, this cultivar is hardy to at least –15°F (–26°C) with foliar burn.

Magnolia virginiana, Sweet Bay Magnolia

Native to swampy forested areas of the South and up the eastern seaboard as far north as Massachusetts, the sweet bay magnolia is already familiar to many gardeners in temperate areas. I include this species here because of its beauty and utility and because several cultivars are evergreen or nearly so. *Magnolia virginiana* is another essential tree or large shrub in any North-by-South landscape.

Size and characteristics. In the southern part of its range, the sweet bay magnolia is a large (up to 60 ft, 18 m) evergreen or semi-evergreen tree. In the North, it is used as a small, deciduous, multiple-stemmed landscape tree or large shrub (usually less than 15 ft, 4.5 m tall), although some individuals are semi-evergreen and grow quite large in zone 6 (figure 17).

Figure 17 Mature sweet bay magnolia (*Magnolia virginiana*), Miami University campus, Oxford, Ohio (zone 6a)

Leaves are elliptical to lance shaped, 3–5 in (7.5–12.5 cm) in length, and dark green above and distinctly silvery below. The creamy white flowers are borne in spring and early summer; they are smaller than southern magnolia flowers but with an exquisite lemony scent (plate 25).

Cold hardiness. *Magnolia virginiana* is clearly hardy in zones 5–9 and perhaps colder in good sites. There is some branch die-back in during extreme winters in northern part of its range. The hardiness specifics of cultivars are discussed below.

Culture, landscape use, and other notes. Sweet bay magnolias prefer rich, organic, and slightly acidic soils but will grow in heavy clay. Established plants will tolerate some drought but also do well in those wet and poorly drained areas of your landscape. Like other magnolias, *Magnolia virginiana* is pretty much left alone by deer and rabbits. This species can be grown in full sun to partial shade.

This is a graceful specimen tree or shrub, and even deciduous forms feature four-season interest due to an attractive branching structure and handsome bark. Walk by one of these trees when it's in flower and it will be difficult to turn away. *Magnolia virginiana* complements other magnolias, palms, and evergreen and deciduous shrubs; it is an excellent choice as a patio tree or grown in a natural woodlot.

Winter protection. Use the same strategy as outlined for southern magnolias above.

Magnolia virginiana Varieties and Cultivars

Most sweet bay magnolias are sold as unnamed containerized or balled-and-burlapped cultivars through the major plant suppliers. However, a few named cultivars are worth mentioning specifically.

var. *australis*. The taxonomy of this variety is uncertain, but many authors recognize Magnolia virginiana var. australis as a distinct southern form of the species. It is generally larger and more treelike than the species and evergreen. One commonly available cultivar is 'Henry Hicks' (figure 18), which is evergreen or nearly so as far north as zone 5 and fuller than the typical sweet bay magnolia. Another cultivar, 'Satellite', is a single-stemmed evergreen form that is often available via mail order.

Figure 18 *Magnolia virginiana* var. *australis* 'Henry Hicks', Spring Grove Cemetery, Cincinnati, Ohio (zone 6a/6b)

'Northern Lights'. This is a new, fully evergreen form of *Magnolia virginiana* available in southern Ohio and perhaps other locales. It is typical of recent efforts by several plant breeders to produce evergreen sweet bays. This cultivar appears to be about as leaf hardy as the hardiest southern magnolias in my garden. 'Northern Lights' is a promising plant, and I advise people to check with knowledgeable nurseries for locally available cultivars with similar characteristics.

***Magnolia grandiflora* × *M. virginiana* hybrids.** Cultivated hybrids of southern magnolia and sweet bay magnolia developed by Oliver Freeman at the U.S. National Arboretum in Washington, D.C., deserve special note here. The most commonly available Freeman hybrid, 'Maryland', is a very desirable small tree with foliage and flowers that resemble the southern magnolia parent. The leaves are olive green and slightly pubescent on the undersides, and the tree has an upright habit. 'Maryland' and Freeman hybrids 'Freeman' and 'Griffin' are more cold hardy than the typical southern magnolia—in my experience about on par with 'Edith Bogue'.

Evergreen Hollies

Hollies (genus *Ilex*) are critically important landscape plants. Along with the evergreen magnolias, they provide necessary structure and year-round interest to any warm-climate garden. Several species of deciduous hollies are commonly used in temperate landscapes, and northern gardeners are already familiar with the ubiquitous and evergreen Merserve hybrid hollies (*I.* ×*meserveae* 'Blue Boy', 'Blue Girl', 'Blue Prince', and 'Blue Princess') that are sold at nearly every garden center. These are beautiful, very cold-tolerant plants and well deserving of a place in the temperate landscape. But people living in the South or Pacific Northwest are aware of the many other choices of evergreen hollies available to the temperate gardener. What those of us living outside these areas have been slow to realize, however, is just how well most of these trees and shrubs will do in colder areas.

Evergreen hollies range in size from small shrubs to large trees. More than four hundred species and countless hybrids exist. All evergreen species feature glossy, dark green leaves, often (but not always) with spiny margins. Flowers are inconspicuous, but the fruits are very showy and often bright red. In most hollies, individuals are either male or female—so if you want lots of berries, make sure to plant both male and female specimens unless there are suitable males within about 0.25 mi (0.40 km; exceptions are noted in each species or cultivar description).

Hollies do best in slightly acidic, organic-rich soils that are well drained. They grow in full sun to partial shade. The plants prefer soils that are cool and moist, so a top dressing of mulch and adequate watering are important, especially in sunny locations. Most hollies are relatively disease-free, but leaf miners and mites can be problems.

Use tree hollies as specimens or in groupings with other deciduous and evergreen trees. Shrub forms can be used as understory plants or in foundation plantings. All are effective in front of a wall or contrasting structure and can be grown to form an impenetrable screen or hedge. See Bunting (2001) for a good overview of holly landscaping tips.

Unless otherwise noted below, all species and varieties below are fully hardy in zone 6 and most of zone 5, with some leaf burn in extreme winters. Watering, mulching, and antidesiccant sprays are effective winter-protection strategies. Small plants can be protected with windscreens.

Ilex ×*attenuata,* Foster's Hybrid Hollies

This group of evergreen tree hollies are hybrids between American holly (*Ilex opaca*; discussed below) and Dahoon holly (*I. cassine*), a species native to the Southeast.

'Foster's #2'. Foster holly is the most common selection of these hybrids in the trade and also the hardiest. This dense, slender tree grows to 20–30 ft (6–9 m) and is profusely covered with beautiful red berries in autumn and winter (plant a male 'Foster's #4' nearby for maximum pollination). Foster hollies are mainstays of the southern landscape trade—for good reason. They make exceptional specimen trees, especially in a formal area near a home or office, but are equally striking in a wooded area. The leaves are much more narrow (and usually more glossy and finer toothed) than those of an American holly, which to my way of thinking makes this a more elegant tree. Some authorities still list this plant as hardy only through zone 7, but that is *far* too conservative. Numerous mature specimens grow in southwestern Ohio (figure 19), and some large specimens can be found in zones 5b and 6a areas of northern Ohio as well (plate 26). In my experience 'Foster's #2' is at least as leaf hardy (easily –10°F, –23°C) as American holly and is much less subject to winter-burn in full-sun areas.

Figure 19 *Ilex* ×*attenuata* 'Foster's #2', Spring Grove Cemetery, Cincinnati, Ohio (zone 6a/6b)

'East Palatka'. Named after the town in Florida near where the first wild specimen was discovered, 'East Palatka' features entire to partially toothed leaves that are broader and somewhat larger than Foster hollies. It reaches about the same height as Foster holly with a bit more spread. 'East Palatka' is generally considered to be less cold hardy that Foster holly, but I have grown one from a seedling, and it has survived four winters (including –14°F, –26°C) with some defoliation and now is a 6-ft (1.8-m) sapling.

Ilex cornuta, Chinese Holly

Like Foster holly, Chinese hollies are grown extensively in the southeastern United States. Remarkably heat and drought tolerant, they make excellent foundation plants. Several cultivars can be trained to grow as large upright shrubs or small trees. Several selections of Chinese holly are hardy through zone 6 and warmer areas of zone 5 with winterburn and some defoliation in temperatures below 0°F (–18°C)—however, no more so than many of the hardy evergreen *Viburnum* species that are common in the North. In my experience, all *Ilex cornuta* cultivars recover from winterburn rapidly and completely the following growing season.

'Burfordii'. Commonly known as Burford holly, this is a shrub I'm very familiar with from our home in Stillwater, Oklahoma. It will easily take frequent bouts of temperatures below 0°F (–18°C) once established, as well as searing summer heat and drought. Lustrous, dark green leaves are armed with a single or double, very sharp terminal spine. Left on its own, this shrub can reach 10 ft (3 m) or more in height and nearly as much in spread (plate 27), but it can also be pruned upward as a dense tree. (I have seen particularly nice examples of this in the outdoor landscaping of a Lexington, Kentucky mall [zone 6b].) 'Burfordii' is one of the few hollies that will set fruit without a pollinator. 'Dwarf Burford' is a common cultivar with slightly smaller leaves that seldom grows more than 5–6 ft (1.5–1.8 m) tall (plate 28). The new growth of this cultivar is especially attractive—brilliantly shiny and lime green.

'Carissa'. This cultivar is a personal favorite of mine. The deep green, extremely glossy leaves are 2–3 in (5.0–7.5 cm) long and slightly cupped. This dwarf-form plant grows in a mounding habit, which makes it an excellent addition to a shrub border (plate 29), and unlike most hollies it grows fast, even in my zone 6a garden. Under zone 6 conditions, 'Carissa' does tend to winterburn more than some of the other hollies described here, especially in full sun, but recovers quickly in spring and continues to add new growth (which has a pleasing reddish tint) all through autumn and early winter. Of course, this new growth is the first to be killed when temperatures drop down around 3°F (−16°C), but that's what pruning shears are for.

'Needlepoint'. This holly is similar in habit and characteristics to 'Dwarf Burford', if a bit more sensitive to cold, but does well in zone 6. New spring growth is prolific and very attractive.

Ilex 'Nellie R. Stevens'

This cultivar is a putative hybrid between Chinese holly (*Ilex cornuta*) and English holly (*I. aquifolium*). Reputed to be one of the best hollies for the heat of the southern states, 'Nellie R. Stevens' is considered hardy in zones 6–9 (figure 20). This attractive, medium to large shrub (15–20 ft [4.5–6.0 m] in height at maturity) has the beauty of an English holly with

Figure 20 *Ilex* 'Nellie R. Stevens', Quebeck, Tennessee (zone 6b)

the toughness of a Chinese holly. It features extremely lustrous dark green leaves with prominent spines and a somewhat square outline. Its fruit set is outstanding, and the berries are very large and deep red. In recent years this cultivar has become readily available in many zone 6 areas outside the Southeast. 'Nellie R. Stevens' has a reputation for winterburn in full-sun sites, but its rapid recovery in spring and overall beauty are enough to overcome this liability. I've grown specimens for several years at our home, where they perform as well as American holly or Foster holly.

Ilex opaca, American Holly

American holly is native to the eastern United States. This species has long been recognized as hardy in zones 5–9, so one cannot really view *Ilex opaca* as a true warm-climate holly. But, like all evergreen hollies, it adds a distinct warm-climate look to a landscape. Surprisingly, this species remains underappreciated in the northern part of its range, and many people still don't realize just how tough this tree is. There are more than a thousand cultivars of American holly, and each region will have favorites that are readily available and well adapted to local conditions.

Ilex opaca can reach 40–50 ft (12–15 m) in height and about half that in spread, but most trees are about half that size. One disadvantage of this species is its extremely slow growth rate: 6 in (15 cm) per year is not uncommon. The leaves are about 1.5–3.0 in (3.8–7.5 cm) long and about half as broad, dull or only slightly glossy green, and generally with fully toothed margins. The trunks and branches are an attractive mottled gray. An American holly can take on a more unkempt appearance than a Foster holly, especially if neglected. This species is also more prone to damage from leaf miner and other insects. Still, it fruits heavily, can withstand severe cold perhaps better than any other tree holly, and with good care and soil fertility is quite handsome (plate 30).

The Secrest Arboretum in Wooster, Ohio (zone 5b), has nearly fifty cultivars of American holly in its collection, and most have grown into outstanding, beautiful, large trees with no special winter protection. American hollies really dislike cold winter winds, however, so site them well, especially in zones 5 and 6. If you do plant one in a sunny, wind-exposed area, make sure to water it well before and during the winter and do not skimp on the antidesiccant spray. If the tree is severely damaged by an exceptional cold spell, take heart—I have seen recently planted trees completely defoliated only to recover completely by mid-May.

Ilex vomitoria, Yaupon Holly

What an awful scientific name for such a nice plant! Native Americans used this species to prepare a purgative drink for medicinal use, hence the species name. Yaupon holly is an elegant, upright, irregularly branched shrub or small tree and is an exceptional landscape subject. The leaves tend to be smaller than the other holly species, and new growth has a pleasing yellowish green or reddish tint, depending on the variety. I have grown the dwarf cultivar 'Nana' successfully in a true zone 6a location of my garden. It resembles a rounded Japanese holly (*Ilex crenata*) or box-wood in aspect. 'Pride of Houston' is a common tree-form cultivar that I have not tried, but it is reputed to be hardy in warmer parts of zone 6.

Other Evergreen Trees and Shrubs

I covered the genera *Magnolia* and *Ilex* first because each contains numerous candidates for creating a tropical look in a temperate landscape. What follows are descriptions, in alphabetical order, of other woody plants worth trying. With the exception of the live oak, these plants tend to be shrubs, rather than trees, in climates with colder winters.

Aucuba japonica, Japanese Aucuba

It is difficult to envision a better plant to brighten up a temperate shade garden than *Aucuba japonica* 'Variegata', commonly known as the gold dust plant. The leaves are large and elliptical to ovate, with toothed margins; the glossy green color has yellowish gold variegation, which resembles the tropical crotons that many people prize as houseplants (plate 31). The growth habit is a dense shrub that can reach 10 ft (3 m) in height with similar spread in zone 7 and warmer, where this is a landscape staple. The overall net growth in height and spread in zone 6a appears to be a little less than 1 ft (0.3 m) per year.

In my zone 6a garden, temperatures below about –3°F (–19°C) begin burning exterior leaves, especially if exposed to winter sun and high winds. In protected spots, leaves will take temperatures that are several degrees lower, and we have not lost plants to –14°F (–26°C) weather. (I know of at least one adventurous soul experimenting with *Aucuba japonica* in zone 3b northern Wisconsin.) In early spring, simply prune off blackened leaves and cut off any dead shoot tips just above an undamaged node. New leaf growth commences almost immediately, and by midspring you will not be able to tell that the plant was damaged.

Easy to transplant from container stock into any decent soil, the gold dust plant is one of the few shrubs that grows well in the deep, dry shade of an established forest canopy. Deer and rabbits seem to leave it alone, although there is some nibbling during prolonged snow cover. *Aucuba japonica* also makes an excellent foundation plant or hedge on the shady side of a house. This species works well with hostas, rhododendrons, hollies, and other shade plants. Water well to establish, and use the winter protection strategies outlined earlier for magnolias and hollies. Another *A. japonica* cultivar to try is 'Rozannie', a nonvariegated, green-leaved form that appears equally hardy.

Camellia japonica, Japanese Camellia

Camellias are beautiful, evergreen shrubs or small trees with dramatic flowers—requisites in a Deep South landscape. Not too long ago, it would have been considered unthinkable to attempt to grow camellias in areas that regularly get down to 0°F (–18°C) or below during winter. Although most of the more than three thousand named camellias recognized by the American Camellia Society are best adapted to the milder parts of zone 7 and warmer, advances in breeding have yielded numerous hybrids and cultivars that are tolerant of zone 6 (and even zone 5) winters. Camellias are now being successfully grown in Ohio, throughout southern New England, the Mid-Atlantic, the Pacific Northwest, the lower Midwest, the United Kingdom, and even Ontario, Canada.

Here I cover a few of the more readily available and demonstrably cold-hardy cultivars in the trade. Without question, I'm leaving out some camellias that people are having great success with in northern areas. For the enthusiast, I suggest the more complete treatments by Michael Dirr (1998) and the *Sunset National Garden Book* (1997). Another excellent source of information (and plants, of course) is the extensive annual catalog put out by Camellia Forest Nursery in Chapel Hill, North Carolina (contact information is given in the appendix).

Camellias are not particularly difficult to grow, as long as you provide for a few requirements. They must be planted in extremely well-drained, highly organic, and slightly acidic soils, preferably out of the wind and in afternoon shade (although once established, most forms can take full sun). I use slightly raised beds in my garden and till in lots of peat and composted leaves. With anything other than excellent drainage, the roots will rot. Never plant a camellia so deeply that the trunk base is underground. Use an acidic fertilizer, but do not overfertilize. Water regularly, especially during the first few years and during summer droughts. And make sure to mulch plants heavily in late autumn and use antidesiccant sprays on the leaves. In fact, in zone 6 and colder, I would cover small specimens almost entirely with leaves in December.

Camellia japonica is the best known of the spring-blooming camellias. Unfortunately most cultivars are far too sensitive to cold for zone 6 conditions, and many are marginal even in zone 7a. However, several selections hardy in zone 6 are now available.

April Series, including 'April Dawn, 'April Blush', and others. This series includes a number of selections proven hardy in zone 6b. All have typical camellia foliage and habit; the flowers are white, pink, or red, depending on cultivar. The plants bloom in spring, with sporadic blooms in autumn, and reach heights of perhaps 5 ft (1.5 m). In my zone 6a garden, these cultivars have suffered little damage down to at least –5°F (–21°C).

'Berenice Boddie'. This camellia is an old standby with light pink semi-double flowers. It is a midspring bloomer that has performed reasonably well in my zone 6a garden. A few flowers open in autumn.

'Red Jade'. This 4- to 5-ft (1.2- to 1.5-m) shrub has survived –9°F (–23°C) conditions in North Carolina and has performed well on the Miami University campus for the past two years. The light red flowers tend to open early (late January through February in zone 7, March in zone 6), so they are sometimes damaged by frost.

Camellia oleifera, Tea-oil Camellia

This extremely hardy species is closely related to *Camellia japonica* and is rated to zone 6a and perhaps colder. A sturdy shrub with white flowers in early to midautumn, *C. oleifera* is primarily known as a parent of interspecific hybrids. Tea-oil camellia is not as well known in cultivation as other *Camellia* species, but it can survive temperatures below 0°F (–18°C) with only minor injury and reaches about 8 ft (2.4 m) in height in zone 6.

Camellia sasanqua × *C. oleifera* Hybrids

Crosses between *Camellia sasanqua* and *C. oleifera* have produced some of the most cold-hardy and easily cultivated of the autumn-blooming camellias. As a group, these hybrids represent the best chance of success for zone 6 or even zone 5 gardeners who want to experiment with camellias.

'Winter's Beauty', 'Winter's Charm', 'Winter's Star', and other Ackerman hybrids. Developed by William Ackerman at the U.S. National Arboretum in Washington, D.C., the so-called Ackerman hybrid selections (plate 32) probably represent the most cold hardy of the camellias available today. Several selections are rated to –15°F (–26°C) and have been cultivated successfully in zone 5 conditions. I obtained a few 1-gallon 'Winter's Charm' specimens from the Secrest Arboretum in northern Ohio (zone 5b) in spring 2000. The plants impressed me with their prolific flowering (pink, peony-like flowers) from early October through early December, even after hard freezes. 'Winter's Star' also does well in zone 6a without special siting or extensive winter protection. One-foot (0.3-m) seedlings planted two years ago are now 3-ft (0.9-m) specimens with dense, glossy foliage and excellent flowering from late October through early January.

'Survivor', 'Mason Farm', and other Camellia Forest hybrids. These autumn-blooming cultivars were developed by Camellia Forest breeders. They do well in zones 6a and 6b and may be as cold hardy as the Ackerman hybrids. 'Survivor', with showy white flowers, can grow to more than 20 ft (6 m) in height, and a specimen has successfully been grown in Ontario, Canada. A related selection rated to zone 6a, 'Carolina Moonmist', was developed at the Raulston Arboretum and performs well here in Oxford, Ohio.

Camellia sinensis var. *sinensis,* Small-Leaf Tea

Many varieties of *Camellia sinensis* are used to make green tea, popular for its antioxidant properties, but most people do not realize that this plant can easily be grown in the temperate United States. There is even a recipe for making your own tea leaves in the annual Camellia Forest Nursery catalog—amaze your friends. Small-leaf tea is hardy in zone 6 (probably colder with protection), and is adaptable to full-shade to full-sun locations. This excellent landscape shrub has small white flowers in autumn and grows to perhaps 6 ft (1.8 m) in height. Plants installed in 2000 on the Miami University campus and in our home garden are doing well after two winters; unfortunately, they are still not large enough for me to feel comfortable harvesting leaves to try the tea recipe.

Erica carnea, Mediterranean Heather

This member of the heath family (Ericaceae) is a mounding evergreen shrub with small green leaves and purplish pink or white flowers. Numerous varieties of Mediterranean heather are on the market. Heather requires organic, acidic soil, full sun, and excellent drainage. It does well with little or no fertilizer. One of the goals of a North-by-South landscape is to have something in flower virtually every month of the year—that is where Mediterranean heather comes in. Hardy through zone 5 and perhaps colder, in my zone 6a garden *Erica carnea* flowers from late November throughout the winter months and into early spring, adding a splash of color to the garden. It works well with other evergreens, and does not require special winter protection in zone 6 and warmer.

Eriobotrya japonica, Loquat

A small evergreen tree or large shrub, loquat has large (6–12 in, 15–30 cm), lustrous leaves with coarsely toothed margins. The undersides of leaves are covered with a grayish brown tomentum. *Eriobotrya japonica* is often used as a street tree or specimen in zone 8 and warmer, where its edible pear-shaped fruits have the chance to develop. Loquat is grown fairly extensively in warmer parts of zone 7 as a nonfruiting, autumn-flowering ornamental tree. Leaves are damaged by exposure to temperatures around 3°F (−16°F) and largely killed by temperatures below 0°F (−18°C), so this is probably not a plant that you can grow to tree size in cold-winter areas. But other experimental gardeners and I have had success growing this as a semi-evergreen shrub. In a sheltered zone 6 site some of the leaves and most of the stem tissues overwinter fairly well and recovery in spring is rapid. *Eriobotrya japonica* is very drought tolerant once established. Mulch heavily and use antidesiccant sprays.

Eucalyptus Species

Eucalyptus trees are native to Australia and, because of their beauty and drought tolerance, have long been a landscape staple in southern California and Arizona. Most species are tropical to subtropical in distribution and not particularly cold hardy. However, *Eucalyptus gunnii* (cider gum) is reported to be hardy down to about 5°F (–15°C) and has been grown with success in the Pacific Northwest. *Eucalyptus niphohila* (snow gum) may be even more hardy; the *Sunset National Garden Book* (1997) listed this species as hardy down to 0°F (–18°C). These trees are best grown in full sun, are remarkably drought tolerant when established, and will tolerate poor soils. There is very little solid cultural information on the success of these trees outside of traditional eucalyptus country, and plants are not readily available except along the West Coast and in the Southwest. I believe this will change in coming years, as more and more adventurous gardeners give these rapid-growing and picturesque trees a try.

In fall 2001, Plant Delights Nursery in North Carolina (contact information is given in the appendix) introduced a selection of *Eucalyptus neglecta* (omeo gum). Extensive trials showed the species performed well down to 0°F (–18°C) with tip burn, and they suggest that omeo gum may be root hardy to zone 5. This fast-growing tree may reach 30 ft (9 m); it has brown exfoliating bark and oval blue-green leaves. We installed specimens on the Miami University campus in spring 2002 and eagerly await the results.

Fatsia japonica, Japanese Fatsia

Japanese fatsia is a bold, very tropical-looking shrub with deeply lobed, palmate leaves. It prefers at least partial shade (although full shade is better) and acidic soils out of the wind. Most authorities list *Fatsia japonica* as reliable only through zone 8 or the warmest parts of zone 7 unless exceptionally well sited. However, gardeners are having success with Japanese fatsia in the cooler parts of the southeastern Piedmont. I am not aware of anyone attempting this species in zone 6 or colder, but I suspect it would have utility as an attractive die-back perennial. Japanese fatsia can be grown as an outstanding container plant as well.

Gardenia jasminoides, Cape Jasmine

Much as I like the smell of magnolia flowers, I do not think anything tops a jasmine in full bloom. The scent is simply sublime. Like so many of the plants discussed in this book, *Gardenia jasminoides* could not be readily grown in truly temperate climates until the introduction of a cultivar that was developed specifically for cold-winter areas, 'Kleim's Hardy' (plate 33). This dwarf shrub (2–3 ft, 0.6–0.9 m high) has typical glossy green gardenia foliage and fragrant white flowers in summer. It is reliably hardy to 0°F (–18°C) once established and will take considerably lower temperatures with leaf damage and branch tip die-back. I have seem small first-year plants killed nearly to the ground by –14°F (–26°C) and recover completely to flower the next summer. 'Chuck Hayes', a selection developed at Virginia Tech University, was listed by Dirr (1998) as possibly hardy in zone 6b. I have not grown this cultivar (it often sells out rapidly in mail-order catalogs), but reports on the Internet appear to confirm this. I have tried 'August Moon' in Oxford, Ohio; based on one winter's experience, this cultivar appears about as hardy as 'Kleim's Hardy'. Gardenias require extremely well-drained, highly organic soils. This species does best in partial shade and definitely out of the winter sun and wind. *Gardenia jasminoides* can be grown as a container plant but does not do well as a houseplant. Plant it near an entry way to your home or whatever part of your garden you happen to gravitate toward most.

Gelsemium sempervirens, Carolina Jessamine

Drive through the southeastern United States in early spring and you will see bright orange-yellow flowers scattered throughout the forest canopy, especially as the deciduous trees are just opening their new spring leaves. These are the flowers of Carolina jessamine, a woody vine that is hardy in zones 6–9, although in colder areas it may be killed to the ground in a harsh winter. After flowering, the vine's green leaves are lost in the surrounding tree foliage, but often turn purplish during the winter. *Gelsemium sempervirens* is a fine plant to naturalize in a woodlot or as a vining cover for a trellis, rock pile, or other structure. It prefers sun but will grow in dappled shade. However, be aware that this plant is highly toxic and may be fatal if eaten.

Gordonia lasianthus, Loblolly Bay

Related to the equally desirable and prized *Franklinia alatamaha* (Franklin tree), loblolly bay is native to swampy areas of the coastal southeastern United States. It is an erect and open tree with deep green leaves and showy white flowers that resemble those of a camellia, although it has a reputation for being difficult to cultivate. Nonetheless, *Gordonia lasianthus* should be used much more in the residential landscape because it really adds a tropical look and feel and complements other evergreens and flowering shrubs. Loblolly bay is listed by most authorities as hardy only through zone 7b. In my zone 6a garden I have managed to nurse a seedling through several winters, but it suffers extensive die-back at temperatures below 0°F (−18°C), and I suspect it will remain a small shrub at best. Plant loblolly bay in full sun to partial shade, in rich organic soils.

Illicium floridanum, Florida Anise Tree
Illicium lanceolatum, Lance-Leaf Anise Tree

Anise trees are underused but exceptional additions to the landscape. As the name implies, their evergreen foliage is scented of anise. The overall aspect reminds me of a large rhododendron, and anise trees grow in the same deep shade, wet woodland habitat as rhododendrons and azaleas. The most commonly available species, *Illicium floridanum,* grows as a large shrub or small tree with large, drooping leaves; red to maroon-purple flowers composed of twenty to thirty straplike petals are borne in spring. Dirr (1998) rated this species as hardy from zone 6 to 9 and reported that plants have survived −9°F (−23°C) under field conditions and even colder in laboratory hardiness tests. *Illicium lanceolatum* has smaller, narrower leaves and should prove similarly hardy.

Jasminum nudiflorum, Winter Jasmine

Seldom seem outside the South, winter jasmine is hardy at least through zone 5b and likely colder, although the flower buds that are not insulated by snow can freeze below about –5°F (–21°C). When our family lived in Oklahoma I always enjoyed the drifts of yellow-flowered winter jasmine that bloomed in late winter and brightened the landscape (plates 34, 35). Masses of spreading deep green branches arise from a center crown and spread laterally along the ground. The trailing branches of *Jasminum nudiflorum* develop adventitious roots and form new plants, quickly covering an area. The leaves are small and often lost during autumn, but the green stems are effective in the winter landscape. Winter jasmine is an excellent plant to use as a tall ground cover on a steep slope or trailing over a masonry wall. Control it by vigorous pruning and by digging out unwanted plants. This species prefers full sun and grows in virtually any kind of soil. A prolific performer in several years of growth in Oxford, Ohio, gardens (zone 6a), this species often begins blooming in late December and, during mild winters, flowers sporadically all winter. After a cold winter, winter jasmine still flowers a week or two earlier than the ubiquitous *Forsythia* bushes in our area.

Mahonia aquifolium, Oregon Grapeholly

Mahonia bealei, Leatherleaf Mahonia

Oregon grapeholly is a dense evergreen shrub that grows to 6 ft (1.8 m) in height. It has deep green, spiny leaves in summer that sometimes take on a reddish hue in winter. Leaf hardy to zone 5 and perhaps a bit colder with damage, *Mahonia aquifolium* is a fine addition to the shrub border or as a specimen, foundation plant, or hedge in partial to full shade (figure 21). It prefers acidic, organic soils and a wind-protected site. Bright yellow flowers appear in spring, and autumn fruits look like miniature purple grapes. Many cultivars exist that vary in form and leaf color.

Leatherleaf mahonia is one of those plants that you either love or hate. Hardy to zone 5b at least, it is a large shrub with thick, leathery leaves and prominent spiny margins. *Mahonia bealei* produces spiky clusters of flowers in early spring that give rise to showy powdery blue berries in autumn. This is an excellent specimen shrub for partial-shade conditions (plate 36).

Figure 21 Oregon grapeholly (*Mahonia aquifolium*), Miami University campus, Oxford, Ohio (zone 6a)

Nandina domestica, Heavenly Bamboo

This is another essential plant for your North-by-South landscape, with something to offer winter through summer. According to at least some references (thankfully not Dirr 1998), *Nandina domestica* will not grow in areas colder than zone 7. This is inaccurate. Heavenly bamboo is generally available in southern Ohio and other zone 6 areas, and I am aware of many zone 5 and even some zone 3 and 4 gardeners who have had success with this plant. Although defoliation and some shoot die-back can occur during prolonged temperatures below 0°F (–18°C), the plant recovers quickly in spring.

Heavenly bamboo gets its name from its resemblance to true bamboos, but it is actually in the barberry family (Berberidaceae). Its stems are canelike, and the foliage branches off from nodes like a bamboo (figure 22; plate 37). New foliage emerges an attractive pink or bronze red. In a shadier site the leaves turn a deep bluish green, but in full sun leaves become green with red highlights all through the growing

Figure 22 Heavenly bamboo (*Nandina domestica*) has an open habit in partial shade, Miami University campus, Oxford, Ohio (zone 6a)

season. In autumn, especially after a frost, the red color is excellent, and the leaves generally do not drop but persist throughout the winter. Even if the leaves are damaged by cold, the reddish brown color remains attractive. Another added benefit is the pinkish white to white flowers that are borne on clusters at branch ends. Successfully pollinated flowers develop into clusters of bright red berries that persist well into the late autumn and early winter. They are at least as showy as holly berries.

Nandina domestica grows in virtually any moist soils, although it performs better in rich organic soil and will tolerate some drought once established. Color is best in full sun, but I have grown heavenly bamboos in the deep shade of an established forest canopy as well. You can create a thicker, denser plant by thinning out old stems each year and/or cutting back old canes to near ground level in spring. An excellent shrub border selection, heavenly bamboo also works well in groups or as a specimen in a small area. This species is often used as a foundation plant in the South and can be massed to form a screen.

Numerous *Nandina domestica* varieties are available in an array of overall sizes and foliar characteristics. 'Harbour Dwarf' grows in a compact, spreading mound and makes a fine ground cover. 'Fire Power' and related cultivars are upright; some reach about 4–5 ft (1.2–1.5 m) in height and spread in zone 6, and the leaves are more persistently red throughout the season than most cultivars.

Nerium oleander, Oleander

While perusing my spring 2001 catalog from Plant Delights (Avent 2001) I was thrilled to note that the nursery is carrying cold-hardy varieties of oleander. This excellent, densely flowering evergreen shrub has generally been confined to zone 8 and warmer conditions in California and the southeastern and southwestern United States. When grown in zone 7, most of the more than four hundred *Nerium oleander* cultivars are killed back severely by normal winter weather. 'Hardy Double Yellow' and 'Hardy Pink' are rated only to zone 7b by Plant Delights, but the parent plants survived the –9°F (–23°C) deep freeze of 1984 in central North Carolina, and I suspect that this cultivar might perform well in good zone 6 sites. 'Hardy Double Yellow' reaches approximately 6 ft (1.8 m) in height and flowers profusely in late summer with masses of double yellow flowers. We installed several 1-ft (0.3-m) specimens in 2001, and by the end of the growing season they were 3 ft (0.9 m) tall (plate 38). Flowering was minimal in the summer of 2001. Most plants were killed nearly to the ground during that winter, but they have begun to regrow in spring 2002. A note of caution: all parts of oleander are poisonous if ingested.

Photinia ×*fraseri,* Fraser Photinia, Red Tip Photinia

Michael Dirr (1998) suggested that red tip photinia is so overused in the southern landscape that "the term *nauseous* is not sufficiently applicable"— the southern equivalent of a Japanese yew. I guess I would agree to some extent, but for gardeners outside the traditional South I feel this is an attractive option worthy of consideration. Red tip photinia gets its name from the distinct red of new leaves, which deepen into a dark green in a few weeks (plate 39). In zone 7 and warmer areas, *Photinia* ×*fraseri* can grow to a 15-ft (4.5-m) shrub (or small tree if limbed up), with perhaps half that much spread. It is often used as a foundation plant, screen, or hedge. The plant's white flowers are not spectacular but are an added benefit in spring.

Red tip grows in heavy clay soil as well as rich organic soil, and does best in full sun. Although listed by most authorities as hardy only through zone 7, I have noted in my recent travels that *Photinia* ×*fraseri* has become quite common in zone 6b areas of the upper South, from Oklahoma to the East Coast. In zone 6a Oxford, Ohio, late-autumn new growth is routinely killed back, and in exposed sites older leaves and branches experience significant winterkill below about –5°F (–21°C). Still, it is easy to prune off damaged growth in spring, and, because new growth is one of the most attractive features of this species, it's no great hardship. Established red tips in our area are often killed down to the bottom 2 ft (0.6 m) in cold winters and regrow to about 5–6 ft (1.5–1.8 m) in height through each growing season, making a splendid foundation plant or grouping. In more sheltered sites on the Miami University campus, with slightly warmer microclimates and less winter sun (and in less sheltered areas during mild winters), plants often come through winter with no damage, and I suspect these will grow much larger with time. After the mild winter of 2001–2002, some of the largest red tips on the Miami University campus should reach 8–10 ft (2.4–3.0 m) in height by the end of the growing season.

Photinia ×*fraseri* is adapted to high summer temperatures and periodic drought. The only major problem is that plants are periodically plagued by a fungal leaf spot disease that can completely defoliate a plant during humid summer weather. This disease produces rounded lesions in the leaves with distinctly purple halos. As the fungus spreads, the lesions coalesce and kill the leaf. The only treatment is a vigorous fungicide spray schedule, just as soon as the spotting is noticed. Copper-based fungicides work well here, although in some cases sulfur-based fungicides seem to work as well.

Pittosporum tobira, Japanese Tobira

Pittosporum undulatum, Australian Pittosporum

Pittosporums are excellent shrubs with dense whorls of leathery, deep green leaves that are suitable for full sun or partial shade. In the South, they are used as a foundation or accent plant or in a shrub border.

Japanese tobira is normally considered a zone 8 species (plate 40), but I have had a specimen growing near our house (zone 6a) for a few years that has done reasonably well. Despite considerable die-back, Japanese tobira regrows to an attractive 2-ft (0.6-m) mound each season. Variegated as well as fully green forms exist. Australian pittosporum is less commonly available, but is rated to zone 7. I've seen *Pittosporum undulatum* for sale in nurseries in the North Carolina mountains (zone 6b), supporting the view that it is more cold hardy than the Japanese species.

Poncirus and Other Hardy Citrus Varieties

Spend some time perusing the many web boards on the Internet devoted to experimental gardening and exotic plants and you will surely see reference to hardy citrus plants—and with good reason. The quest for an orange, lemon, or other citrus tree that can be grown outdoors and bear edible fruit in cold-winter climates is one of the Holy Grails of horticulture. Fortunately for breeders, members of the family Rutaceae (citrus and related species) are relatively easy to cross-breed under greenhouse and field conditions, and a large number of extremely cold-hardy selections have begun to reach the market in recent years. Because these plants are so new, their ultimate cold hardiness is still a matter of some debate, so what I present here is a best guess based on available information. I urge interested readers to keep current, because this is a rapidly evolving field.

As of 2002, I am not aware of a true orange, lemon, tangerine, or grapefruit variety that will withstand 0°F (–18°C) cold without being killed to the ground at best, although some satsuma mandarins, sour oranges, kumquats, and calamondin orange varieties can be grown in zone 8 with damage. There are a surprising number of citrus species and varieties, however, that can be grown in zone 7 and one that can even be grown in zone 5.

Even if you don't care to plant a hardy citrus, consider growing containerized citrus trees as patio or deck plants, moving them indoors over the winter. Numerous varieties of dwarf lemons and oranges do very well as container plants, and many are self-fertile—meaning that you can get crops of fruit even if you have a single plant. I have especially had success with dwarf lemon trees. The fruit is abundant and flavorful, and you cannot beat the fragrance of the blossoms.

Poncirus trifoliata **(trifoliate orange)**. Trifoliate orange is an extremely thorny shrub or small tree (figure 23) that is used as the grafting stock for many fruit-bearing citrus varieties. The leaves are comprised of three terminal leaflets, which are often lost in cold winter weather. Its spring flowers are typical of citrus in size and color and have some of the citrus fragrance. Fruits resemble small oranges but are inedible and are often retained well into the winter. This tough plant prefers full sun, grows in many soil types, and is clearly hardy through all of zone 5 and likely colder, although it can be killed to the ground by –20°F (–29°C). At Oklahoma State University (borderline zone 7a), trifoliate orange is used to create extremely dense and attractive hedges. The spines are exceptionally sharp, and care should be taken when planting this species in sites where people could be injured, especially small children. The most commonly available cultivar, 'Flying Dragon', is a dwarf form hardy to about –15°F (–26°C) with interesting contorted branches and thorns. This cultivar has performed well in our zone 6a trials through two winters; our 1-ft (0.3-m) seedlings are now about 3 ft (0.9 m) tall.

Citrus 'Yuza' **(*C. ichangensis* × *C. reticulata*)**. This Japanese commercial hybrid between Ichang lemon and mandarin orange features bright yellow fruits resembling lemons but with a sweet flavor. In Japan the plant

Figure 23 Foliage and fruits of trifoliate orange (*Poncirus trifoliata*), Quebeck, Tennessee (zone 6b)

often survives 10°F (–12°C) without damage, and limited experience by enthusiasts suggests that it may be hardy through zone 7. The *Sunset National Garden Book* (1997) listed this cross as hardy to about 0°F (–18°F). There is controversy over the hardiness of the Ichang lemon parent: The *Sunset National Garden Book* listed this species as hardy to temperatures below 0°F, but Riffle (1998) reported damage even under zone 8 conditions. Regardless of which temperature range is correct, *C.* 'Yuza' is a tough plant that I would like to see people experiment with in zone 6.

***Citrus* 'Thomasville' orangequat.** Developed by crosses involving trifoliate orange, sweet orange, and kumquat parents, this small tree produces a fruit with a limelike flavor that ripens in autumn. Established plants are hardy to about 0°F (–18°C).

***Citrus* 'Morton' and 'US-119' citrange.** These sweet orange × trifoliate orange hybrids produce fruits that ripen in autumn and taste much like a tart orange. They are reputed to be hardy to about 5°F (–15°C) or below. I know of one citrange tree that has been growing in Oklahoma City for fifteen years and has withstood several bouts of temperatures below 0°F (–18°C), although to date it has not fruited.

Prunus caroliniana, Carolina Cherrylaurel
Prunus laurocerasus, English Laurel

The genus *Prunus* includes many flowering and fruiting deciduous trees, for instance, cherry, peach, plum, and apricot, that are abundantly familiar to any gardener. However, this genus also contains some outstanding evergreen species that are often seen in the South, but seldom grown elsewhere.

The leaves of Carolina cherrylaurel are oblong, 3–4 in (7.5–10.0 cm) long, deep green, and somewhat glossy (figure 24). Limbed up, it makes an excellent multiple-stemmed small tree to perhaps 20 ft (6 m) or more in height. *Prunus caroliniana* can also be pruned into a dense hedge or left to its own design as a large and attractive shrub. The small flowers appear in very early spring and are somewhat lost in the foliage but are attractive nonetheless. Native to the southeastern United States, Carolina cherrylaurel grows very rapidly, will tolerate almost any kind of soil that is reasonably well drained, and can be grown in full sun to partial shade. The

Figure 24 Carolina cherrylaurel (*Prunus caroliniana*), Quebeck, Tennessee (zone 6b)

leaves contain hydrocyanic acid, which is toxic to animals, and deer and rabbits avoid the plant. Like nearly all members of this genus, seeds are abundantly produced, germinate easily, and can be a nuisance in a planting bed (but are also a source of more plants). Dirr (1998) and many other authorities have listed *P. caroliniana* as hardy though zone 7. I have seen numerous specimens in zone 6b landscapes, however, and a third-year shrub in my zone 6a garden does well with only minor winterburn. In full winter sun and wind, the exterior leaves do have a tendency to discolor, but the hardiness of this plant appears to be at least on par with an American holly or similar species.

Two varieties of English laurel are commonly available and both appear to be a notch hardier than Carolina cherrylaurel. They also tolerate partial to fairly deep shade, making them suitable for naturalizing in an established woodlot. Both varieties flower in summer. *Prunus laurocerasus* 'Otto Luyken' is a mounding form that grows to perhaps 3 ft (0.9 m) in height and twice as broad. 'Schipkaensis' (or Schipka laurel) is an upright, dense shrub that reaches 5–10 ft (1.5–3.0 m) in height. It has very attractive, glossy leaves that are toothed toward the apex; the foliage makes this a splendid screen or specimen plant. Once established, both of these varieties of English laurel should easily handle zone 6 winters with minimal if any damage and likely would do well in colder areas. In a shady part of your landscape, these plants provide structure, year-round green foliage, and a definite warm-climate look.

Quercus virginiana, Southern Live Oak

Another signature tree of the American South and the state tree of Georgia, southern live oak is generally considered in the literature as hardy only though the warmer parts of zone 7. Enough evidence has now accumulated from experimental gardeners across the temperate portions of the United States to revise this view considerably.

When we lived in Stillwater, Oklahoma (zone 7a/6b), I remember being told (incorrectly) by a number of experts that live oaks would only grow in the Gulf coastal plain area of extreme southeastern Oklahoma. I also recall, however, that our neighbors had several young live oaks in their yard, and I know that those trees survived the –14°F (–26°C) deep freeze of the late 1980s. In fact, although live oaks are still far from common in Oklahoma City and Tulsa, some fairly impressive specimens do exist there (figure 25) and across the rest of the middle and upper South.

Like many of the hardy palms, established live oak trees are quite cold hardy. Gardeners are now having success with this species in southern New England, the lower Midwest, and in other zone 6 climates. Clearly, this tree will survive 0°F (–18°C) with little difficulty, as long as it is well

Figure 25 Southern live oak (*Quercus virginiana*), Tulsa, Oklahoma (zone 6b; photograph © Bryan Swinney)

watered and mulched, especially during the first critical years after plant-ing. Gerry McKiness, owner of Gerry's Jungle at the Neotropic Nursery, lists *Quercus virginiana* as cold hardy to below 0°F (–18°C), a zone 6 hardi-ness rating. I tend to agree. I began experimenting with live oak seedlings a few years ago. I collected some roadside seedling recruits during a trip to Florida (Dad's infamous plant-collecting forays on family trips provide our teenage children with a wealth of anecdotes) and installed them in true zone 6a parts of my home garden and on the warmer Miami University campus. These seedling trees have all adapted and grown well through the equivalent of zone 5b winter minima. I installed a 6-ft (1.8-m) specimen in spring 2000 in an exposed area of our front lawn, and it has done well through two winters. In fact, it retained green leaves throughout the mild winter of 2001–2002.

Live oaks have elliptical to ovate, deep green leaves that are about 1–3 in (2.5–7.5 cm) long. They drop old leaves in spring, and the new leaves are an attractive olive green. In the colder parts of zone 7 and colder regions, live oaks tend to be semi-evergreen to almost deciduous and do not reach the massive size of Deep South specimens. In our zone 6a cli-mate, the leaves tend to remain green until the temperature drops to about 0°F (–18°C), when many (but not all) the leaves start to brown. I have noted at least some evergreen foliage down to about –3°F (–19°C).

Taxonomy of the *Quercus virginiana* is uncertain. Many geographic varieties exist, and some of these appear to be even more cold hardy than typical live oaks. One of these, *Q. virginiana* var. *fusiformis,* a native of Texas and Oklahoma, is now being grown widely as a landscape plant in areas as cold as zone 5b. Check with a local nursery and see if you can access a regional variety that is well adapted to your area. Also, if you are still not convinced that a live oak would be hardy in your area, consider a water oak (*Q. nigra,* see chapter 7), a deciduous to semi-evergreen species with leaves and habit that strongly resemble a live oak but with much greater cold tolerance.

It has become relatively easy lately to purchase live oak seedlings and small saplings via mail order. If you go this route, make sure to protect small plants well during the first few years, not only from the elements, but also from marauding grazers. Deer and rabbits especially like to munch on oak seedlings. I have found that deer-repellent sprays and similar products are fairly effective, but these need to be reapplied often. I also install a simple wire mesh cage around my small plants to discourage browsing. (Filling the cage with leaves during the winter enhances cold protection.) Finally, in cold-winter areas it is advisable to wrap the trunk of a live oak during the first few years to prevent scalding by the sun and bark splitting.

Rhaphiolepis indica, India Hawthorn

India hawthorn is a dense shrub much favored in zone 8 and warmer regions for its glossy leathery leaves, compact habit, tropical look, and white to red flowers that bloom profusely from late autumn through the next spring. The taxonomy of this species is confused, and Dirr (1998) believed that many cultivated varieties of India hawthorn available to the public may be hybrids of *Rhaphiolepis indica* and a closely related species. Maybe this explains why I have had marginal success with this supposed zone 8–9 plant, even in exposed zone 6a sites (plate 41). Although considerable leaf damage occurs below about 5°F (–15°C), the shrub generally recovers in spring and is easily pruned. Even a light snow cover seems to protect lower leaves and stems from all but minor damage during extreme cold. Again, this is a good plant to protect with a heavy leaf covering. India hawthorn makes a fine shrub border and companion to palms and other tropical-looking plants. Grow this species in full sun in virtually any kind of soil. *Rhaphiolepis indica* is now fairly common at plant outlets in the middle and upper South.

A Few More Species

Several other evergreen tree and shrub species are worth noting here, although my experience and that of other enthusiasts in zone 6 and colder regions is limited.

Araucaria araucana (= *Araucaria imbricata;* **monkey puzzle tree).** This is a very unusual looking and very tropical looking conifer that I thought could not be grown reliably in regions colder than zone 7, but I saw large and small specimens in east-central Tennessee (zone 6b) in 2001 (plate 42). Charles Cole reports that established 20-ft (6-m) trees were killed to the ground in the record winter of 1985 (–24°F, –31°C), but have been largely undamaged since, despite several winters at or slightly below –10°F (–23°C).

Cinnamomum checkiangensis **(hardy camphor tree).** This tree is a cold-hardy relative of *Cinnamomum camphora*, a species of the tropics and sub-tropics. But hardy camphor tree, a native of China, is rated as cold hardy through at least zone 7a in good sites. Shiny green leaves and coppery new growth hang loosely from branchlets and lend a tropical feel. *Cinnamomum checkiangensis* grows to about 20 ft (6 m) in height in zone 7.

Cornus angustata **(Chinese evergreen dogwood).** Dogwoods are a must for any warm-climate landscape, but the more familiar species are deciduous. The Chinese evergreen dogwood, formerly termed a variety of *Cornus kousa* (Kousa dogwood), is supposedly evergreen through zone 6 and has larger and more persistent white flowers that a typical *C. kousa*. It should also have the anthracnose disease resistance of *C. kousa*. Our specimens are too new to cultivation to be able to fully confirm the evergreen habit under zone 6 conditions, but it looks promising. A 3-ft (0.9-m) specimen on the Miami University campus was undamaged during the mild winter of 2001–2002.

Cyrtomium falcatum **(Japanese holly fern).** With lustrous, dark green, and serrated leaves, this plant is a true fern, as the expanding fiddleheads of new foliage in spring attest. Most holly ferns are intolerant of extreme cold, but *Cyrtomium falcatum* 'Fortune's Holly Fern' is sold locally in southwestern Ohio and is said to be leaf hardy in zone 6. Our plants tend to die back to the ground each winter, but regrow well in spring. Unfortunately, deer and rabbits love them. Still, holly ferns are such excellent plants for shade gardens with rich, acidic soil that they are worth the effort.

Daphniphyllum macropodum. I was not familiar with this genus until purchasing a few small specimens by mail order in 2000. Listed as hardy through zone 6, this dense shrub (in full sun) or small tree (in shade) has leaves that look like a cross between a rhododendron and a southern magnolia (plate 43). The petioles are an attractive red color. My plants have not suffered much herbivore damage.

Sciadopitys verticillata **(Japanese umbrella pine).** In truth, this is not a warm-climate tree, because it will clearly thrive in zone 5 and perhaps colder (plate 44). I list it here, however, because it *looks* very tropical indeed, much like a Japanese yew pine, which is most decidedly a sub-tropical species. Umbrella pines grow very slowly, about 6 in (15 cm) per year, and are thus expensive and difficult to find, but their foliage and habit are exceptionally beautiful. *Sciadopitys verticillata* is an outstanding complement to other plants or as a specimen. Old specimens in the Carolinas attain 40 ft (12 m) in height. Japanese umbrella pine does best with some shelter from full afternoon sun, and, other than typical mulching, it does not need extensive winter protection.

Skimmia japonica (Japanese skimmia). This very tropical-looking shrub with glossy green leaves is an excellent choice for shady foundation sites and in mixed evergreen borders in partial to full shade. The flower buds are red to maroon and open to white flowers. Japanese skimmia grows in many soil types but does better in slightly acidic loam. A lot of people grow this plant successfully in warmer zone 6 areas. I think it is an exceptionally beautiful shrub, and I would like to try it in southwestern Ohio.

Ternstroemia gymnanthera (Japanese ternstroemia). This plant grows in partial shade to full sun. The extremely glossy evergreen foliage starts out reddish green and retains attractive red highlights at maturity—one of the most attractive small shrubs I have seen. I installed small specimens in our landscape in 2001 (plate 45), and they are completely undamaged at 6°F (−14°C). Japanese ternstroemia is another landscape plant that used to be thought of as hardy only through zone 7b but that can now be found at many outlets in zone 6b areas of the South. This wonderful small shrub is often sold as Japanese cleyera, but that name applies to *Cleyera japonica,* a related but distinct plant.

Chapter 7

Crape Myrtles and Other Deciduous Trees and Shrubs

If at first the idea is not absurd, then there is no hope for it.

—Albert Einstein

nclude deciduous trees and shrubs in a tropical-look landscape? Absolutely. Even in truly subtropical and tropical regions, many of the best ornamental varieties are deciduous in leaf habit. The next time you make a winter visit to Disney World in Orlando, Florida, take note of how many deciduous trees and shrubs are used in their landscapes. In many cases, these species anchor a planting bed or other major landscape feature. You will note that even in their winter condition these plants offer considerable visual interest. The beautiful exfoliating bark and sinuous branching pattern of a crape myrtle, for instance, are reason enough to grow this plant. Add to this a blooming period that lasts summer through autumn, pleasing foliage, drought and heat tolerance, and excellent autumn color, and one readily sees a why a southern garden without crape myrtles is unthinkable. And, there are many other deciduous trees and shrubs that are essential for creating that gracious warm-climate feel and form in a North-by-South landscape. Think of a Louisiana bayou, and bald cypress trees immediately come to mind. A drive through the Carolinas in spring reveals masses of purple-flowering royal paulownia trees along the roadside. There are few trees more tropical in habit and flower than the mimosa or Chinese silk tree. In each case, these species can readily be grown in cold-winter regions. Best of all, because deciduous tree and shrubs lose their leaves over the winter, you don't have to worry about preserving tender foliage in the face of bitter winter winds. That makes winter protection much easier and, as a rule, the deciduous species covered here are a notch more cold hardy than most evergreens.

In this chapter, I focus on keystone species and varieties that create a tropical feel four seasons of the year and help define the landscape. I am probably going to offend some people by not discussing the many varieties of flowering dogwoods (*Cornus* spp.) and deciduous magnolias (*Magnolia* spp.) and architecturally elegant species such as the Japanese maple (*Acer palmatum*) that have long been mainstays in the northern landscape. Clearly, it is difficult to imagine an effective landscape plan in virtually any part of the temperate zone that does not incorporate such important deciduous plants. But my feeling is that most knowledgeable gardeners are already familiar with those long-standing landscape staples that are available each spring and summer in every home center's gardening section. Even if you are not familiar with them, every reputable gardening catalog, even those snapshot brochures available in the checkout lane of your local store, provide a perfectly adequate overview of common northern deciduous ornamental species.

My goal here is to compile a consensus list of exciting warm-climate candidates for cold-winter locations—those deciduous plant species that would be on any southern landscape architect's top 10 list for creating year-round drama and interest in the landscape. In some cases, these plants may be new to you. In others, you may be familiar with the species and have coveted examples you've seen in travels to the South and Southwest but were unaware you could grow it in your area or were unsuccessful in the past.

Crape Myrtles

Lagerstroemia indica, Crape Myrtle

Crape myrtles (also spelled "crepe") are ubiquitous in the South, Southwest, and California. Like the southern magnolia, the live oak, and some of the palms, crape myrtles are signature plants in a warm-climate landscape. Bar none, this is the *best* flowering shrub or small tree for hot-summer conditions. I cannot imagine landscaping without them and neither should you.

Northern gardeners have long coveted crape myrtles, of course. The conventional wisdom, however, has held that this is a zone 7–9 species—never mind that many areas of the South replete with crape myrtles actually lie in zone 6. Obviously, the plants appear to know something that the landscape manuals do not. And despite conscious-raising efforts by numerous zone 6 (and even zone 5) gardeners outside the traditional South who have had success with crape myrtles for decades and the many introductions of cold-hardy crape myrtle varieties in recent years, this view has been slow to change.

I'd like to dispel this myth once and for all. The fact is, there are *many* varieties of crape myrtle that are perfectly suitable for zones 6 and 5 and a few that will do reasonably well in even colder areas. Similarly, there is no reason to forgo crape myrtles in cool-summer, mild-winter climates like the Pacific Northwest and the United Kingdom, where conventional wisdom dictates that flowering performance will be poor.

It *is* difficult (but not impossible) to grow a large crape myrtle *tree* in areas that typically drop much below 0°F (–18°C) during the winter. It is also true that gardeners in Seattle or other areas of the Pacific Northwest need to site their crape myrtles well for optimal flowering. But these difficulties can be overcome with comparative ease. As is the case with palms, you need to know which varieties will do well in your area; how to site, plant, and care for them; and what to do during extreme weather.

Size and characteristics. Commonly available crape myrtles are either varieties of *Lagerstroemia indica* or hybrids of *L. indica* and the Japanese crape myrtle, *L. fauriei.* In recent years, cultivars of *L. fauriei* are becoming more readily available as well. There are many crape myrtle varieties discussed in the literature, and new varieties reach the marketplace almost every year. I refer the interested reader to Dirr (1998, 2002), Glasener (2000), and Sunset Books (1997) for a more complete listing.

Crape myrtle varieties and cultivars are typically grouped by height at maturity and by flower color. Dwarf crape myrtles are shrub forms below 3 ft (0.9 m) tall and as a group tend to be the most cold hardy. Semidwarfs are generally larger shrubs or small trees ranging from approximately 3 to

12 ft (0.9 to 3.6 m) in height, although some authors put the upper cut-off at about 6 ft (1.8 m). Tall forms are generally small to medium-sized trees that exceed 12 ft (3.6 m) in height at maturity. Habit ranges from broad and spreading to very upright and open. Flowers are six petaled, perhaps 1 in (2.5 cm) across, and borne in dense clusters called *panicles*, which are 6–8 in (15–20 cm) long and perhaps half as wide. Panicles form at the ends of stems and terminate each year's vegetative growth. Flower colors include white, pink, red, purple, and many gradations thereof.

Crape myrtles flower on new wood, so even if a plant is killed back severely by winter cold, it will regrow rapidly and flower the next summer. It is not uncommon for a single season's vegetative growth to exceed 6–8 ft (1.8–2.4 m) in taller varieties, so it's easy to grow flowering crape myrtles as large, die-back, flowering perennials even in hardiness zones that are too cold to ensure survival of the old wood.

Most crape myrtle varieties tend to grow multiple stems, although careful pruning can produce a single-leader plant. The trunks and branches have bark that is grayish to rusty brown, and as the trunk and branches grow larger in diameter, the outer bark exfoliates to reveal the characteristic glossy inner bark, which ranges from olive to tan to gray depending on variety or cultivar. This immensely attractive inner bark, coupled with the sinuous form of trunk and branches, is what makes large crape myrtle trees so striking even in winter.

Crape myrtles are among the last trees and shrubs to leaf out in spring. The leaves are opposite in the lower parts of the stem and sometimes alternate or in whorls on the upper branches. Leaf color is generally deep green, although new foliage is red-tinted and some cultivars retain at least some reddish highlights throughout the growing season. Most of the varieties described here have excellent autumn color, in many cases rivaling the maples and ashes. Some varieties drop their leaves in autumn; others retain old brown leaves throughout the winter.

Cold hardiness. This trait varies between cultivars and depends on age, growing-season care, exposure, and winter protection. In general, an established crape myrtle given no special winter protection is reliably wood hardy down to about 0°F (–18°C) and will take brief exposure to perhaps –5°F (–21°C) without serious die-back. At temperatures between about –5 and –10°F (–21 to –23°F) the old wood is killed, usually down to the snow or mulch line. First- and second-year specimens are only a couple of degrees less hardy than established plants because, as deciduous plants, crape myrtles enter a true winter dormancy period. As a group the National Arboretum hybrids are more cold hardy than the species—one of the reasons why they are such popular choices. The most cold-resistant National Arboretum hybrid, *Lagerstroemia* 'Hopi', is reliably wood hardy down to about –15°F (–26°C) once established. Again, duration of cold is as important as intensity, especially for recently planted crape myrtles. In the winter of 2001, for example, a small specimen of 'Hopi' I installed the previous summer was killed to the ground by –6°F (–21°C) winter minimum temperatures coupled with a record eighteen-day spell of below-freezing weather. My neighbor's established 10-ft (3-m) 'Hopi' tree was completely undamaged by the same conditions. Remember that even if the plant is killed to the ground, it will almost always regrow from undamaged buds at or below ground level. Winter protection strategies can add several degrees of cold hardiness to crape myrtles.

Culture, landscape use, and other notes. Crape myrtles are generally sold as container stock or balled-and-burlapped, and they readily transplant from the field. Like most deciduous trees and shrubs, it is best to transplant crape myrtles in the early spring before leaves have emerged but after all threat of extremely cold weather has passed. Crape myrtle leaves emerge in spring after the average last frost date. Unusually late frosts can damage new foliage, but plants quickly recover by producing new leaves. Small, 1-gallon crape myrtles are often available at home centers, even in many zone 6 areas. I would advise against purchasing such small plants if you live in zone 6 or colder—first-year survivorship, especially if the winter is unusually severe, is much reduced compared with larger plants. Try to find 3- to 5-gallon specimens (or larger) with robust trunks and a dense root ball. Not only do these plants perform better in their first year, but you have a better chance of nursing the old wood through the first winter in a larger specimen.

Crape myrtles are easily planted using the tips outlined in chapter 3. Although they grow in virtually any type of soil, including heavy clay, crape myrtles grow better and flower more profusely in fertile soil with plenty of organic material. Use a general-purpose, complete, balanced fertilizer, but do not overfertilize. Never use a high-nitrogen lawn fertilizer because this results in lots of vegetative growth but poorer flowering. For the same reason, if a large tree-form crape myrtle is killed to the ground by winter cold, you can improve flowering the following summer by using a fertilizer that is relatively low in nitrogen and high in potassium and phosphorus (for example a 12–12–12 blend). Also, in colder parts of zone 7 and colder zones, do not fertilize beyond midsummer. There is fairly convincing evidence that late-season fertilizing makes the plants less winter hardy. Once established, crape myrtles are very drought tolerant, but make sure the root ball does not dry out completely during the first year after planting and add a good top dressing of organic mulch. Most authorities also suggest that flowering performance is improved by regular, deep watering during periodic summer droughts.

An important consideration is that crape myrtles are sun-lovers and like summer heat. Unless a plant gets at least a few hours per day of direct sun, it will languish and flowering will be reduced. Winter hardiness is also reduced in shade-grown plants; less photosynthesis means less carbohydrate reserves in the root system to help with overwintering. In the Pacific Northwest, the United Kingdom, and other areas with marine climates, pay particular attention to proper siting in full-sun locations with warm microclimates. For example, site a crape myrtle in front of a south- or west-facing masonry wall that receives afternoon sun. Shade also increases the incidence and severity of diseases, especially powdery mildew and soot mold, two fungal diseases that are especially problematic with many crape myrtle cultivars. The National Arboretum hybrids and some nonhybrid selections of *Lagerstroemia indica* are resistant to these pathogens, another reason for their popularity. If fungal leaf diseases do crop up during the humid summer months, they can be controlled with fungicidal agents.

Perhaps no aspect of crape myrtle cultivation is more misunderstood than pruning. Anyone familiar with crape myrtles has seen the chopped and hacked stumps of poorly pruned specimens and knows exactly what I mean. Pollarding, as such pruning is called, can be effective if the object is to prune away dead wood or dramatically reduce the size of an overgrown specimen. You may want to create a low-growing and dense plant, in which case you do need to cut them back to 1 ft (0.3 m) or less above ground level each spring. Aside from these specific goals, however, there is no good reason to pollard a healthy crape myrtle. Severe pollarding does not induce greater flower formation (a common misconception).

Instead, let crape myrtles assume their naturally attractive shape and branch structure, and use pruning to enhance that structure. To develop a tree shape, cut off all the branches growing up from ground level except for three to five of the strongest and best-shaped leaders. Then judiciously prune away lateral branches perhaps one-third to one-half of the way up the stems as new growth commences in spring. Each year as the plant grows taller remove lateral branches higher up the stems. Crape myrtles tend to develop suckers, so cut these off at ground level as well. Thin out upper branches by removing dead twigs and cutting off other lateral branches that are smaller than pencil diameter. Ideally, major pruning should be done before foliage has completely developed, but minor pruning can be done anytime. Some authors suggest that the previous year's spent flower panicles should be cut off as well, but in my view this is not necessary.

If, like me, you are growing crape myrtles in zone 6 (or in a warmer zone that has experienced temperatures below 0°F [–18°C] over the preceding winter), you need to do annual pruning a bit differently. First, determine how far up from ground level live wood exists. The easiest and most foolproof way to do this is simply to wait until the plant starts to leaf out. Any part of the trunk or branches where new lateral leaf buds are emerging, by definition, is live wood. Simply make pruning cuts about 1 in (2.5 cm) above the last buds. I also use the scratch method on crape myrtles and many other trees and shrubs to find live wood. Simply scratch the bark gently with your fingernail. Live bark will scratch away easily to reveal green tissue—that part of the plant is alive. If your scratch uncovers brown or gray tissue, that part of the stem has died and should be removed.

I have two more tips for pruning crape myrtles in zone 6 and colder. First, resist the temptation to prune and shape crape myrtles after leaf drop in late autumn or early winter because this could stress the plant and result in poorer overwintering. Second, for the best chances of overwintering aboveground woody stems, it may be best to prune *very* judiciously, if at all, especially during the first few years after planting. I admit, however, that I don't have solid data on the latter point. But in researching this book I have observed numerous crape myrtle plantings in marginal areas and talked to the gardeners growing these plants, and we have done considerable experimentation with crape myrtle varieties in zone 6. Almost universally, gardeners who do little or no pruning (other than dead wood) have the most winter-hardy tree-form specimens. Maximizing the number of leaf-bearing branches does make botanical sense in marginal climates. On balance, this maximizes photosynthesis during the growing season, providing more energy for root growth and storage of carbohydrate reserves in the roots for winter metabolism and spring recovery. You can produce a nice, clean-looking crape myrtle simply by removing only the dead lateral branches and suckers, confining pruning of live wood only to those few branches that are problematic.

Winter protection. Crape myrtles require little, if any, winter protection in areas that do not experience temperatures below 0°F (–18°C), although a little mulch definitely helps. In colder parts of zone 7a and colder, a heavy layer of mulch is essential to preserve the trunk bases and root tissue during extreme cold. Use pine straw or other organic material that does not easily mat down and *loosely* cover the bottom 1 ft (0.3 m) of the trunk. The principle is the same as the maxim that keeping your feet warm helps your whole body stay warmer. This simple strategy will allow you to overwinter crape myrtles as die-back perennials well into zone 5—many people are reporting success in even colder climates. The following summer, the crape myrtle will be a full shrub with plenty of attractive blooms.

Of course, some of the real landscape benefits of *Lagerstroemia indica*— the attractive tree habit and exfoliating bark—are difficult to achieve unless the plant overwinters at least some woody tissue from year to year. First-year wood usually does not exfoliate. Happily, a few cultivars described below appear to be wood hardy in most zone 6 areas without extensive winter protection, and at least one is proving wood hardy under zone 5 conditions. There are several tricks of the trade that you can use to push the envelope.

I find that even though crape myrtles are deciduous, I can significantly increase wood hardiness by spraying trunks and branches with antidesiccant on the same schedule I use for broadleaved evergreens, namely an application in mid-December and another about four to six weeks later. This makes physiological sense, because crape myrtle bark is thin and exposed branches can easily desiccate and die if exposed to strong winter winds and sun. Second, heavy mounding of the trunk base with pine straw, leaves, or other noncompacting mulch (up to 2 ft, 0.6 m) usually prevents winterkill of the lower trunk tissue down to approximately −15°F (−26°C) or lower and appears to add 3–5°F (1.8–3.0°C) of wood hardiness to exposed wood. Finally, consider using trunk wraps. To retain heat and keep damaging winds away from trunk tissues, loosely wrap the lower part of the tree with burlap, synthetic quilt batting, or similar fabric material (never plastic). Even though the branches above the wrap are exposed, they seem to fair better as well. In a crape myrtle with multiple stems, it is easiest simply to wrap the entire stem bundle rather than to try to cover each stem individually. Leave the top of the wrap open a bit to ensure some air circulation, and mound mulch up around the base of the wrap (or, if you wrap a multiple-stemmed plant, fill in the center with mulch).

Trunk wrapping provides another key benefit for crape myrtles in exposed locations. Because the bark of these plants is both thin and light colored, crape myrtles are very prone to bark splitting and sun scald. Strong winter sun heats the trunk, causing the bark and trunk to expand. As the sun sets, temperatures drop and the bark and inner trunk contract. Rapid temperature swings cause the living bark tissue to split open and sometimes separate from the dead inner wood of the stem, ultimately killing the live bark and the whole stem. By wrapping the trunks, you prevent sun injury and the rapid temperature swings that cause mortality. In zone 6a and colder, for ultimate protection use wire mesh or burlap enclosures packed with leaves to entirely cover small crape myrtles or protect the lower 3 ft (0.9 m) of trunk on larger specimens.

Lagerstroemia indica Cultivars

I focus here on those crape myrtle cultivars that have proven successful under at least zone 6 conditions and are generally easy to find in the trade. The cultivars are discussed in alphabetical order. Unless otherwise indicated, flowering dates are given as average date of first flowering under zone 7 conditions. In general, once crape myrtles begin to flower they continue flowering throughout the growing season, with sporadic blooms all the way until the first hard freeze in autumn. In the colder parts of zone 6b and colder areas, when tall, tree-form varieties are killed to ground level by winter cold, they tend to invest most of their energy in vegetative growth the following growing season, producing a large, impressive shrub by season's end that may not flower very well. For good flowering and vigorous vegetative growth, it is doubly important during winter to protect as much of the woody tissue as you can.

'Carolina Beauty'. A common cultivar in the Southeast, this small, very upright tree form (to 20 ft, 6 m) has grayish tan exfoliating bark at a young age and brick red flowers. 'Carolina Beauty' has performed well on the Miami University campus (zone 6); first-year plants were wood hardy in sheltered microclimates down to –3°F (–19°C). Unfortunately, this cultivar is not very resistant to powdery mildew, but we've been able to control the disease with sulfur sprays. 'Carolina Beauty' has decent reddish orange autumn color. The flowers are borne relatively late (mid to late July) but are very effective if you desire a red crape myrtle (plate 46).

'Centennial' and 'Centennial Spirit'. These cultivars were developed in 1989 at Oklahoma State University to commemorate the centennial of the Oklahoma land rush. Both are wood hardy through zone 6b without extensive protection. 'Centennial' is a dwarf form that reaches about 3 ft (0.9 m) in height. Flowers are lavender and bloom in mid-June or later; its autumn color is orange. 'Centennial Spirit' is a large multiple-stemmed shrub or small tree that can grow to 20 ft (6 m). Specimens killed to the ground have been known to recover from –22°F (–30°C) and flower the next summer. The foliage has an attractive reddish green tint, and flower panicles are large and dark wine red, appearing in late June or early July. Stems are robust and keep the flower panicles from drooping, even after a hard rain. Autumn color of 'Centennial Spirit' is reddish orange. In exposed zone 6a sites, this cultivar performs well as a die-back perennial with no special treatment. Both cultivars have good resistance to powdery mildew.

'Dallas Red'. This is an older tree-form (to 20 ft, 6 m) cultivar that proved wood hardy through successive –9°F (–23°C) freezes in 1984 and 1985 in the Carolinas. I am aware of people growing 'Dallas Red' in zone 5b northern Ohio (plate 47) and other zone 5 and 6 locations. This cultivar is one of the few true red flowering forms. It has average mildew resistance and is fast growing. I have not tried this one in Oxford, Ohio, but I would like to.

'Glendora White'. This cultivar is often grown in the Mid-Atlantic region as a large shrub or small tree. It produces white flowers in midsummer and has red autumn color. My only experience is with 1-gallon plant that has done well as a die-back perennial.

'Peppermint Lace', 'Prairie Lace', and related forms. These semidwarf shrubs are also commonly grown in the Mid-Atlantic area. I have had success growing them as die-back perennials in exposed zone 6a sites. They have very small leaves and, beginning in mid to late June, bear interesting pink flowers with white banding on the outer margins of the petals. These cultivars have reddish orange autumn color and medium mildew resistance.

'Twilight'. A large, upright shrub or small tree with lavender to purple panicles, this cultivar is popular in the upper and middle South. It has grayish brown exfoliating bark and orange red autumn color. In my zone 6 garden it is often killed back to the bottom 1 ft (0.3 m) or so by temperatures around 0°F (−18°C), but 'Twilight' is a very fast grower and will reach 6–7 ft (1.8–2.1 m) in height the next summer before flowering. Again, under these conditions flowering is not spectacular, but it can be improved by a fertilizer low in nitrogen and high in potassium and phosphorus. Its upright habit makes 'Twilight' a good choice for an area of the landscape where space is a premium.

'Victor'. If you want an excellent true dwarf crape myrtle, this is it. 'Victor' grows to about 3 ft (0.9 m) in height. The flowers are dark red and begin blooming profusely in mid to late July in zone 6 (plate 48). This cultivar has good mildew resistance and decent yellowish red autumn color. Like 'Centennial Spirit', the summer foliage has an attractive reddish tint. Because 'Victor' is very cold resistant, this is probably the best dwarf selection for northern areas, but it is also spectacular in warmer climates.

National Arboretum Cultivars

The crape myrtle breeding program at the U.S. National Arboretum in Washington, D.C., has produced many outstanding cultivars through directed crosses between *Lagerstroemia indica* and *L. fauriei*. These hybrids offer excellent cold tolerance, exceptional resistance to powdery mildew and other common diseases, and vigorous growth and flowering. Make no mistake: Although these cultivars are especially good choices for gardeners outside traditional crape myrtle country, they are also some of the best choices for the South and Southwest. A full treatment of the twenty most popular National Arboretum cultivars is given in Dirr (1998). Here is an alphabetical listing of widely available cultivars that have proven hardy in zones 6 and 7 and, in many cases, colder climates as well.

'Acoma'. This cultivar is a broad, spreading semidwarf shrub that grows to perhaps 10 ft (3 m) tall and broad. 'Acoma' can also be limbed up to create a small tree to show off its excellent light grayish brown inner bark, which is revealed by exfoliation of outer bark at a young age (plate 49). As one of the most cold hardy of the National Arboretum cultivars, first-year plants easily remain wood hardy under typical zone 6b conditions, and third-year plants in exposed zone 6a locations in my home landscape retained a fair amount of live wood down to about –12°F (–24°C) with mulching alone. This is also one of the earliest crape myrtles to flower, beginning in late June in our area, and continuing on sporadically up to and sometimes even past the first killing frost in autumn. The flowers are white, and the dense panicles tend to bend downward, creating a pendulous effect. As with all of the National Arboretum cultivars, mildew is not a problem; I have never had to spray 'Acoma' for a fungal disease. Readily available even in nontraditional crape myrtle areas, this extremely tough and beautiful cultivar is perhaps the best overall white-flowering variety for zones 5 and 6.

'Hopi'. This is absolutely one of my favorite crape myrtle cultivars for a number of reasons. First, 'Hopi' is recognized as *the* most cold-hardy selection from the U.S. National Arboretum, although numerous earlier reports of this cultivar withstanding –20°F (–29°C) and colder without significant wood die-back appear to be incorrect. In Oxford, Ohio, old specimens were killed nearly to the ground by three consecutive nights of −24°F (−31°C) temperatures in 1994–1995 but were completely wood hardy through −14°F (−26°C) and −12°F (−24°C) in subsequent years with no winter protection. Clearly, this cultivar is one to try in zone 5 and colder areas, and I'm beginning to see it in the nursery trade in zone 5b areas. 'Hopi' has many other good qualities as well. It is a semidwarf shrub or small tree, generally with multiple stems, that can reach about 10 ft (3 m) in height and perhaps 7 ft (2.1 m) in spread, even in zone 6a (plate 50). Lower branches tend to die back naturally as the plant grows, so it is easy to limb up to create a tree-form habit without pruning much live tissue. The leaves are a slightly bronze-tinged dark green, and its orange red color is effective in autumn. 'Hopi' flowers profusely from late June through autumn, and its bloom period, lasting more than one hundred days, is among the longest of the crape myrtle varieties. The flower panicles are a medium pink. (I do not personally care for light pink flowers in a summer landscape, but this shade of pink is just right and complements a lot of other summer hues.) Like many of the other National Arboretum hybrids, exterior bark begins exfoliating even when the plant is young, revealing a light grayish brown inner bark (plate 51).

'**Muskogee**'. This is an upright large shrub or small tree that can reach 20 ft (6 m) at maturity. The exfoliated bark is shiny light gray, almost whitish from a distance. Leaves are glossy green in summer and rival the reds and oranges of a maple tree in autumn (plate 52). Flower panicles, which appear from July through September, are light lavender pink. 'Muskogee' is apparently a very cold-hardy selection and is being sold and grown in many zone 5 and 6 locations.

'**Natchez**'. People who have grown 'Natchez' for any length of time positively wax lyrical about this crape myrtle's numerous virtues. This cultivar, like 'Muskogee' and several others, is now becoming generally available in southwestern Ohio and other zone 6 areas. We installed out first specimens in several Oxford locations in 2000, and I am beginning to understand what all the fuss is about. If you want a large (potentially more than 20 ft, 6 m), tree-form, white-flowering crape myrtle, this cultivar is perhaps the best choice, whether you live in Georgia or Pennsylvania. The branching habit of this cultivar is sinuous and architecturally striking all seasons of the year (plate 53). The inner bark is a mottled cinnamon color that is attractive up close or at a distance. Most authorities rank 'Natchez' at the very top of the list for bark coloration. Reports in the literature and on various web boards suggest that 'Natchez' is reliably wood hardy in most of zone 6 with minimal winter care, and a fair number of people are having success with it in zone 5. Anywhere colder than the warmer parts of zone 6b, though, and I would use fairly extensive winter protection in the first few years. Like most tree-form crape myrtles, young, unestablished specimens of 'Natchez' can be winter-killed if temperatures approach 0°F (–18°C), and the next growing season you will get lots of vegetative growth and few flowers unless you switch to a low-nitrogen fertilizer in spring.

'Pecos'. This semidwarf shrub has medium pink panicles and a rounded, dense habit. Autumn color is maroon to purplish red. I have been growing this cultivar for a few years, and it does not perform as well in my garden (zone 6) as some of the other National Arboretum hybrids, although I have seen some nice specimens in other zone 6 and 7 locations. Like all of these hybrids, mildew is not a problem.

'Tonto'. A magenta-flowering semidwarf, 'Tonto' has been around for a long time. Many mature specimens can be found in zone 6 landscapes (plate 54). It can be trained as a multiple-stemmed and even a single-leader small tree—I saw a particularly nice example of the latter outside a motel in zone 6b Maryland—but usually people grow this selection as a dense shrub. The juvenile bark is a distinctive rusty brown, exfoliating to a beige tan color. 'Tonto' flowers prolifically, and the magenta panicles are exceedingly attractive. In my experience, this cultivar is a bit less cold hardy than 'Acoma' or 'Hopi'. I routinely lose a lot of the upper branches when it drops much below 0°F (–18°C), but mulched trunks do well at much colder temperatures. I suspect, however, that there is considerable variation among individuals. The owners of the zone 6a specimen in plate 54 told me that their twenty-year-old plant used to be a small tree, and they now cut it back each year by choice, preferring the denser shrub habit. This would mean that their 'Tonto' maintained a tree habit through at least one –20°F (–29°C) winter! In any case, 'Tonto' is a very fast grower; a plant cut back nearly to the ground will reach 5–7 ft (1.5–2.1 m) in height and perhaps 5 ft (1.5 m) in spread before flowering commences, and the spectacular blooms make it well worthwhile. Apparently, this cultivar blooms well regardless of whether it is killed back or the kind of fertilizer it receives

'Zuni'. This hybrid is another fine semidwarf shrub with rapid growth and medium lavender to almost purple panicles. Like several other cultivars, the leaves are dark glossy green with reddish highlights, and autumn color is orange red to red. As with 'Tonto', I have not had luck overwintering a lot of the upper woody tissue on this selection much below 0°F (–18°C), but again, regrowth is exceptionally rapid and the flowers are great. Although 'Zuni' is generally considered a globose or rounded shrub, I have found that specimens cut almost to the ground in spring tend to grow in a very upright, multiple-stemmed habit, making this a good choice for a confined area.

Proprietary Dwarf Cultivars

Do an Internet search for crape myrtles, and you will find a number of companies that produce patented dwarf and miniature crape myrtle cultivars for the retail trade. In recent years, many of the larger nursery companies (for example, Monrovia and Greenleaf) have also introduced proprietary cultivars. These cultivars are true dwarfs, some as small as 18 in (45 cm) tall at maturity. Many are extremely cold hardy, rivaling some of the best National Arboretum cultivars. As such, they are being extensively marketed to gardeners in zone 5 and even colder areas as die-back perennials and container plants. I do not have personal experience with these plants. In reviewing this group, Dirr (1998) suggested that they may be susceptible to mildew.

Some of the more generally available forms include the Dixie Series from Hines Nursery, the Chica and Petite Series from Monrovia Nursery, and the Pixie Series from Greenleaf Nursery. Numerous smaller companies produce their own proprietary miniatures, and weeping forms are available at retail outlets and via catalogs and the Internet. Check with your local nursery if these forms appeal to you.

Lagerstroemia fauriei Cultivars

One of the parents of the National Arboretum hybrids, the Japanese crape myrtle is a fine species in its own right. Unfortunately, this species has not been nearly as available as those discussed above, but that is changing. 'Fantasy' is an exceptionally promising white-flowered cultivar recently released to the trade by the North Carolina State University's J. C. Raulston Arboretum. Specimens in Raleigh have survived −10°F (−23°C) with little or no damage and reach heights of 25 ft (7.5 m) with a pleasing vase-shaped habit. The exfoliating bark, a dark reddish brown to cinnamon color, is thought by most to rival that of *Lagerstroemia* 'Natchez'. 'Kiowa', a lesser-known cultivar, also has cinnamon-colored inner bark that is uniform in color rather than patchy. The Raulston Arboretum has also introduced 'Townhouse', a small tree form with bark darker than 'Fantasy'. The flowering display of *L. fauriei* is not quite as spectacular or long-lived as *L. indica* but very effective nonetheless. These cultivars are very resistant to mildew and other foliar diseases.

It is still difficult to obtain specimens of *Lagerstroemia fauriei* outside the Southeast, but with its apparent zone 6 cold-tolerance range (possibly zone 5) and other exceptional characteristics, look for this species of crape myrtle to become a much more prominent part of the landscaping scene as it becomes more readily available. I was finally able to obtain a couple specimens of *L. fauriei* 'Townhouse' in 2002 from Yucca Do Nursery (contact information is given in the appendix), and I'm anxious to see how they perform.

Other Important Deciduous Trees and Shrubs

You could design a fairly effective North-by-South landscape using only broadleaved evergreens, crape myrtles, a few palms, and suitable companion plants. But to do so would mean neglecting some outstanding deciduous tree and shrub species that deserve a prominent place in your yard. Here is an alphabetical listing of some essential species and cultivars, each of which bring something special and unique to a landscape. Some of these trees and shrubs, although classified as deciduous, are semievergreen to evergreen in the warmer parts of their range. Let's focus on some species that most Northerners are unfamiliar with or think are ungrowable in their areas and revisit some old favorites that you may have had trouble growing in the past.

Albizia julibrissin, Mimosa Tree, Silk Tree

The mimosa or silk tree is a common sight in the Southeast and Southwest. It is so common, in fact, that some consider this almost a weed species, and seedling recruits do tend to colonize roadsides across its range. I frequently drive Interstate 75 from Ohio down to Florida; from Lexington, Kentucky, southward well into Georgia, summer-flowering mimosas with their characteristic pink, powder-puff flowers are literally everywhere. (I have noted that since the early 1990s, at least, the range has been extending northward by a few miles per year.)

A member of the legume family (Leguminosae), this small tree reaches 20–35 ft (6.0–10.5 m) in height with a similar spread. The mimosa tree has compound leaf foliage that somewhat resembles a locust tree, but much finer in texture. The overall habit of the tree is very tropical. The compound leaves fold up at dusk, adding another tropical touch. Like the crape myrtle, *Albizia julibrissin* leafs out very late in spring, and autumn color is nil.

Mimosas grow in any soil, and, when provided with adequate water and nutrients, they look elegant indeed. Growth is very fast—about 3 ft (0.9 m) per year is not uncommon. They prefer full sun but will tolerate some shade. In older texts mimosas were classified as zone 7–9 trees, and some authors still use this designation. Dirr (1998) listed it as zone 6–9, noting that some shoot die-back occurs below about –5°F (–21°C). Based on my travels and the trees in our area, I think that even Dirr is a bit too conservative.

Albizia julibrissin is another of the many species that I was told was rare in southwestern Ohio and not cold hardy here. But in actuality there are numerous older mimosa trees in the area that have survived the all-time record low of –24°F (31°C) in the late 1970s and again in the mid-1990s (plate 55). Respectably sized mimosas may be found in many zone 5 locales as well. I know of a person in zone 3b Wisconsin who has had success with this species, at least as a small tree.

In the southeastern United States mimosas have been plagued with an incurable vascular wilt disease that can kill a tree to the ground. The plant can regrow from suckers, and as Dirr (1998) noted, many of the I-75 roadside trees discussed above are resprouted sucker growth plants. I can only say that I have not noted a tendency for this disease to arise in more northern trees to date, perhaps because mimosa does not grow there at high population densities, and the disease has simply not had the opportunity to spread that far yet. Most people around here obtain their trees from local transplants rather than nursery container stock, so this explanation makes some sense. In any case, if you have access to small, transplantable trees grown from a disease-free parent tree, you are well advised to use this source. There are reportedly wilt-resistant cultivars appearing on the market; one of these, 'E. H. Wilson', is also supposed to be more cold hardy than the type species.

Cercidiphyllum japonicum, Katsuratree

Although known to be hardy in zones 4–8, katusuratree is an elegant, tropical-look tree that deserves to be used more in the colder parts of its hardiness range. Its leaves look much like those of an eastern redbud but are an extremely beautiful bluish green in summer (plate 56) and yellow to apricot in autumn. But this medium to large tree (20–60 ft, 6–18 m tall) has so much more going for it. Its aspect and form are exceptionally beautiful in all seasons of the year. Like a Japanese maple, its architecture and foliage complement warm-climate ornamentals such as bamboo, palms, and magnolias, especially in older specimens that develop a picturesque spreading habit in the canopy branches. Katusuratree does well in full sun but also takes a fair amount of shade, making it a good choice in a naturalized woodlot. It does require good, highly organic soil and prefers mildly acidic pH. Dirr (1998) noted that in its early establishment phase it is prone to drought stress, and I second this caution, especially if the plant is sited where it will encounter root competition from established trees and shrubs.

Ficus carica, Common Fig

Fig trees have large, lobed, tropical-looking leaves. Although most members of this genus are tropical and subtropical plants, the common edible fig is a widely planted ornamental in zones 8 and warmer. What is generally not known is that this tree can be planted and bears fruit in much colder areas as well. In zone 6 and colder, hard winters and exposed sites can kill a fig tree back most years, but many people are having success, especially if the tree is sited in a warm microclimate. If your tree is severely injured, just cut it back to live wood. I don't know that any particular cultivar of the more than seventy-five in the trade is markedly more cold hardy, but 'Celeste' is one that is often used. Many mail-order firms now carry small specimens of cold-hardy varieties, including 'Brown Turkey' and 'Desert King'. I obtained a 'Brown Turkey' fig sapling in 2001 from a Georgia nursery. It was killed to the mulch line by 6°F (−14°C) but has regrown vigorously during spring 2002. Although most people associate this tree with hot, dry climates, figs do especially well in the Pacific Northwest. Plant *Ficus carica* in virtually any soil; full sun produces the best fruit.

Franklinia alatamaha, Franklin Tree

Few trees have a more storied history than the Franklin tree, and few are more handsome in the landscape. The story goes that in 1770 John Bartram, the most famous of the early American botanists, discovered a single stand of this hitherto unknown species growing along the Alatamaha River in Georgia. Bartram was so taken by the wild trees that he collected some seeds and seedlings for propagation in his own garden, naming the species after Benjamin Franklin and the site of collection. This small endemic population had apparently disappeared by 1790, when another collecting trip was made, and it has not been seen in the wild since that time. Thus, it is thought that all specimens of Franklin tree alive today are derived from Bartram's original collection.

Franklin tree is in the same family as the evergreen loblolly bay (*Gordonia lasianthus*; Theaceae), and there is some resemblance, but the shiny leaves of *Franklinia* are deciduous and have a different pattern of venation. Few small (usually 10–20 ft, 3–6 m in height) deciduous trees have a more elegant combination of bark color, foliar form, branching habit, and flowering. The trunks and lower stem of mature trees have a fluted appearance and smooth gray bark broken up with vertical fissures—very nice even in winter. The flowers are white, very fragrant, about 3 in (7.5 cm) across, and borne from midsummer through early autumn. Autumn color is exceptional, with leaves turning color late and featuring orange, red, and purple hues. Franklin tree is considered by many a difficult tree to grow unless provided with excellent, rich, highly organic, and *very* well-drained soil—this species is plagued with a *Phytophthora* fungal wilt disease that often is present in container stock. This disease will rapidly kill a young tree planted in soil that remains wet for extended periods of time. *Franklinia alatamaha* is hardy at least through zone 5b.

Hydrangea macrophylla, Bigleaf Hydrangea
Hydrangea quercifolia, Oakleaf Hydrangea

Hydrangeas are an absolute must for any warm-climate garden, and they should find a prominent place in your North-by-South landscape plan. The large glossy leaves and showy flowers play well with all of the evergreen and deciduous plants discussed in this book.

Most temperate gardeners are familiar with bigleaf hydrangea, the common garden variety available in all zone 5–9 nurseries (plate 57). There are far too many cultivars to cover here, and I refer the interested reader to some of the references in the bibliography for a more complete treatment (for example, Lawson-Hall and Rothera 1995). All of these varieties, however, can be classed by their flowering habit into hortensias (also known as mopheads), with large spherical mass of sterile flowers, and the lacecaps, with fertile nonshowy flowers in the center surrounded by a ring of sterile showy flowers. Flower color ranges from white to pink to red to blue and gradations therein. Hydrangeas require acidic, organic, well-drained soil in full sun or partial shade.

Although bigleaf hydrangea is considered a zone 5 plant in terms of survival, people living north of zone 7 are often reluctant to grow this species because it does not flower for them. The reason is that, unlike crape myrtles, bigleaf hydrangeas flower on *old* wood. And, old wood exposed to the elements is seldom hardy in regions that experience 0°F (–18°C) cold. So, bigleaf hydrangea in colder regions get a large mound of beautiful leaves and foliage but no flowers.

There is a simple trick to prevent cold damage to tender old wood and next year's flower buds. In late autumn, after the hydrangea's leaves have dropped off and stems are exposed, simply mound hydrangeas with a pile of autumn leaves to a depth of 3 ft (0.9 m) or so, taking care to cover as much of the plant as possible. Even though this leaf pile will compress over the winter, the bottom 1–2 ft (0.3–0.6 m) or more or the stems will be protected from winter cold. The following spring, after the average date of last frost has passed, uncover the plants—the protected parts will be replete with green stems and viable buds. Those stems grow to full size and flower profusely in the summer. It isn't necessary to protect the whole stem—as long as *some* old wood overwinters, the plant will flower the next year. One added benefit of this simple method is that the decaying leaves naturally enrich the soil in which the hydrangeas are growing, and after a few years the plants will be huge and lush.

Oakleaf hydrangeas are less well known than bigleaf hydrangeas, and that is a shame. To flower, oakleaf hydrangeas require no special protection in all of zone 6 and most of zone 5, although newly planted specimens are a bit less hardy. These large woody shrubs have dark brown exfoliating bark and large white panicles of flowers in summer (figure 26). As the season progresses, flowers change to purplish pink and then to brown. While still pink, they can be cut off and used in dried flower arrangements. Oakleaf hydrangeas can get quite large and full, and make an excellent shrub border or specimen plant, especially in masses near a

Figure 26 Oakleaf hydrangea (*Hydrangea quercifolia*), Miami University campus, Oxford, Ohio (zone 6a)

foundation or in a natural woodlot. Cultural requirements are similar to the bigleaf hydrangea, except that *Hydrangea quercifolia* prefers a bit less sun and grows well in fairly deep shade. Most oakleaf hydrangeas are sold as unnamed cultivars, but 'Snow Queen' and 'Snowflake' are two widely available and excellent named cultivars.

Magnolia macrophylla, Bigleaf Magnolia

Deciduous magnolias are a must for any landscape, if only for their excellent and varied spring flowers and attractive habit, but one species deserves special note for its effectiveness in creating an exotic look during the growing season. Bigleaf magnolia is native to forests in the eastern United States from southern Ohio to Florida, mostly in upland terrain, and is hardy through zone 5 at least. Although a rather coarse, large tree, it lends a distinctly tropical look to a naturalized woodland landscape due to its enormous oblong-ovate leaves (about 12–30 in, 30–75 cm in length) and large (8–10 in, 20–25 cm) white flowers in late spring to early summer (plate 58). If you want to make a statement in your landscape with a really eye-stopping deciduous tree, this is a good choice, although the enormous leaves can make a mess in autumn. Therefore, *Magnolia macrophylla* is probably not a good choice for a lawn planting in a residential landscape.

Metasequoia glyptostroboides, Dawn Redwood

Like the bald cypress to which it bears a strong resemblance, the dawn redwood is a deciduous conifer. This tree is quite literally a living fossil, dating back some 100 million years in Earth's history. It was long thought to be extinct, until an extant population was discovered in China in 1941. Until its reintroduction into the United States in the 1940s as a horticultural species, dawn redwood had been extinct in North America for at least 15 million years.

Metasequoia glyptostroboides is a very tropical-looking large tree that is easy to plant into almost any kind of soil, although it prefers moist, deep, organic, and well-drained soils. It does best in full sun, but will do well in partial shade as well. Like the bald cypress, dawn redwood will also grow in boggy areas and has even been grown in standing water. Growth is very fast—2 ft (0.6 m) per year is about average—and the tree can reach 100 ft (30 m) or more in height at maturity. Dawn redwood has fine, alternate needle leaves. In autumn, the needles turn a nice orange brown before falling. The bark of young trees is a strongly reddish brown, a much deeper color than a bald cypress. At maturity, the trunk develops buttresses and a fluted form. You can differentiate a bald cypress from a dawn redwood by looking for the characteristic armpit-shaped depressions below branch attachment points in the latter species.

Dawn redwood makes an excellent specimen tree and complements magnolias, hollies, palms, and other key structural species in a warm-climate landscape. It also makes an effective screen. Many cultivars exist, but *Metasequoia glyptostroboides* is often available as an unnamed cultivar. Listed by most authorities as hardy through zone 5, it is also found in zone 4, with some stem tip die-back possible in northern regions.

Myrica pensylvanica, Northern Bayberry

Myrica cerifera, Southern Waxmyrtle

The waxy fruits of northern bayberry produce the scented wax for bayberry candles and soap, and you can smell this wonderful aroma in the cultivated plant. *Myrica pensylvanica* is a large (to perhaps 12 ft, 3.6 m), dense shrub which can be limbed up to create a picturesque small tree with nice white bark that is an excellent complement to palms and other warm-climate evergreen plants (figure 27). Leaves are about 3 in (8 cm)

Figure 27 Northern bayberry (*Myrica pensylvanica*), Old Woman Creek National Estuarine Research Reserve, Huron, Ohio (zone 5b/6a)

long, ovate to oblong in shape, and lustrous dark green. Hardy from zones 3 to 7, northern bayberry is evergreen to semi-evergreen in the southern part of its range, another plus. Although exceptionally cold hardy, bayberry deserves a prominent place in a North-by-South landscape and should be used much more as a specimen, screen, foundation plant, or addition to the shrub border. It grows rapidly in full sun to partial shade and will adapt to truly lousy soil, including heavy clay. Northern bayberry is one of my personal favorites for its adaptability and overall beauty.

The southern waxmyrtle (*Myrica cerifera*) is a southern evergreen relative of *M. pensylvanica* widely grown in the southeastern United States. Leaves are narrow, oblong to lance-shaped, glossy olive green, and toothed at the apex. Southern waxmyrtle grows to a large (to perhaps 20 ft, 6 m) shrub or small tree; limbing up produces a more treelike habit. Distinctly evergreen, it makes an excellent specimen or screen. Southern waxmyrtle is leaf hardy to about 0°F (–18°C) and stem hardy to much lower temperatures. Many cultivars are available that should prove adaptable to zone 6 and perhaps colder conditions. 'Hiwassee', developed at the University of Tennessee, has withstood –4°F (–20°C) with only minor leaf burn.

Passiflora caerulea, Common Passionflower, Blue Passionflower
Passiflora incarnata, Maypop

Passionflower vines produce perhaps the most distinctive and beautiful flowers of any tropical vine. The blooms are complex arrangements of ten sepals and petals that from a ring around the center of the flower, which is comprised of a series of twisting filaments and their very showy anthers and stigmas. Nothing else looks quite like a passionflower. Unfortunately, like the *Bougainvillea* and many other floral stunners, nearly all passionflower species and varieties are truly tropical or at best subtropical in their growth requirements and are killed by freezing temperatures. Temperate gardeners who have wanted to add a real tropical touch to the summer landscape have long grown these plants as annual vines. But like so many of the tropical genera discussed in this book, a few species of passionflowers are in fact adaptable to colder winter areas as die-back perennials.

Common passionflower is a prolific bloomer that produces 4-in (10-cm) flowers with greenish white petals and banded filaments adorned in lavender, pink, and purplish black. The lobed leaves of this vine are also a showy glossy green. The vine itself is hardy only through zone 9 or the warmest parts of zone 8, but a well-drained site and a heavy layer of mulch will allow the roots and rhizomes, at least, to be overwintered through zone 7 and likely in zone 6. Even as a die-back perennial, the vine can grow perhaps 20 ft (6 m) in a single growing season. Twine new growth onto a trellis, fence, or tree and enjoy the summer show. *Passiflora caerulea*, like all passionflowers, does best in full sun but will tolerate a bit of shade. It thrives on summer heat, so in areas with cooler summers make sure to plant it in a full-sun microclimate (a south-facing wall or similar site). Many cultivars, varying in flower color and form, are available.

Maypop, so called because of its propensity to jump out of the ground during its midspring growth spurt, is the only species of passionflower native to the United States and the only one that is wood hardy to 0°F (–18°C). But even in the warmer parts of the Southeast it is a deciduous vine that typically dies back to the ground each winter. *Passiflora incarnata* is fully root hardy through all of zone 7 and is adaptable throughout zone 6 (and maybe colder) with mulching and good siting. The flowers are a bit smaller than common passionflower, but spectacular nonetheless. The petals are lavender to greenish white, and the filaments are banded in purple, pink, and white. Several varieties are available in the trade.

Paulownia tomentosa, Royal Paulownia, Empress Tree

Considered almost a weed species in the southeastern United States, the empress tree is nonetheless an effective tree for creating a distinctly tropical look in a temperate landscape. The leaves are large (5–12 in, 12.5–30.0 cm long) and ovate to somewhat heart shaped. Autumn color is nil, and the enormous leaves can make a mess of a lawn when they drop in autumn. The empress tree grows amazingly fast, to 40 ft (12 m) in height, and its ability to grow in extremely poor soils makes it a popular choice for restoration of strip-mining spoil sites and other disturbed areas. In spring *Paulownia tomentosa* produces large panicles of purple flowers that are very handsome and dramatic (figure 28; plate 59). The fruit capsules are large and, like the fruits of a sweet gum, can be problematic in a lawn, as are the tree's surface roots and the deep shade produced under a mature canopy. Flower buds form during the preceding growing season and can be killed

Figure 28 Juvenile empress tree (*Paulownia tomentosa*) showing the species' typical massive leaves, Oxford, Ohio (zone 6a)

by temperatures below 0°F (−18°C), but established trees almost always flower in southern Ohio and Kentucky (zone 6).

Empress tree is fully hardy through zone 6, and can be grown through much colder areas (through zone 3) with stem die-back. This is not necessarily a bad thing. One of the most effective uses of *Paulownia tomentosa* in a tropical-look landscape design is as a cut-back perennial. By cutting the tree back to nearly ground level each spring, you produce a growth habit that features thick green stems up to 15 ft (4.5 m) tall with truly enormous leaves in a single growing season—very tropical indeed, even in zone 3 climates. Of course, this technique sacrifices the potential for flower production, but for many the trade-off is worth it.

Quercus hemisphaerica, Laurel Oak,

Quercus nigra, Water Oak

Quercus phellos, Willow Oak

I discuss these three deciduous to semi-evergreen oak species as a group because they share similar characteristics and utility in the North-by-

South landscape. Like the southern magnolia, I consider these oaks to be essential for creating a warm-climate look. All three species are very familiar to people in the Southeast as the predominant street trees in most southern cities. But laurel oaks, water oaks, and willow oaks deserve a much wider following. All three species used to be considered zone 7–9 choices, and the plant identification tags on nursery specimens often still carry this erroneous hardiness-zone designation. Dirr and most authorities rate laurel and water oaks as zone 6 species, and Dirr (1998) listed willow oak as hardy in zone 5. It's my guess that all three species are adaptable in zone 5, based on specimens I have seen in these areas, although experience with laurel oak remains limited beyond zone 6.

Laurel oak (sometimes listed as *Quercus laurifolia*) is an upright, pyramidal-shaped, medium-sized tree with narrow, glossy, lance-shaped leaves somewhat like those of a willow. Its relatively compact habit makes it an excellent choice for streetside or restricted residential sites. Many good specimens exist in Cincinnati, Ohio (zone 6b) that have endured −20°F (−29°C) and colder temperatures. Seedling-sized trees in my home landscape have survived similar conditions with some stem die-back. The fine texture of leaves, pleasing grayish brown bark, and attractive branching habit make this, in my mind, one of the most handsome oaks. In southwestern Ohio and similar areas, this species retains green leaves well into December, and in zone 7b and south it is nearly evergreen.

Water oak (also known as possum oak) is a large, bottomland species with lobed leaves that strongly resemble those of a live oak, so much so that the tree is often mistaken for a live oak. As I noted in chapter 6, this is the tree to grow if you are squeamish about trying a live oak in your area but desire a similar effect. A common residential tree favored in the Southeast for its adaptability to soil types, vigor, and beauty, water oak is almost certainly wood hardy into zone 5 and perhaps colder conditions. The Ohio Champion water oak in Spring Grove Cemetery in Cincinnati (at the interface of zones 6a and 6b) is more than one hundred years old; it has a trunk diameter of about 3 ft (0.9 m) and a height and spread of perhaps 80 ft (24 m). Young water oaks grow rapidly, 3 ft (0.9 m) per year in southwestern Ohio, and retain some green leaves well into December. When leaves do change color, they are an attractive yellowish brown and are largely retained through the winter, adding color to the winter landscape. Water oaks do have one drawback, however; the branches are sometimes weak and can break off in wind storms or when burdened by snow or ice.

Willow oaks are ubiquitous along southern avenues and streets; 50-ft (15-m) specimens can be seen growing out of grates set into sidewalks. As the name implies, the foliage of willow oak strongly resembles the leaves of willows, and the fine texture creates an elegant effect (figure 29; plate 60). Like the other *Quercus* species, green leaves are retained well into December. Autumn color in willow oaks is perhaps the best among oaks, a pleasing yellow with red, orange, and brown highlights that persists well into winter. *Quercus phellos* is an excellent specimen tree for full sun or partial shade and grows well in many soil types. Smaller trees need to be pruned to encourage a strong single leader. Several years ago I purchased small trees at a local garden center that carried a zone 7–9 hardiness designation on their identification tags, but this is grossly inaccurate.

Figure 29 Mature willow oak (*Quercus phellos*), Oxford, Ohio (zone 6a)

Mature willow oaks can be found in many zone 5 locales, and I would not be at all surprised if, like the bald cypress, it can be grown successfully in Minnesota and other northern locations.

Taxodium distichum Bald Cypress

Bald cypress is perhaps the best illustration of how inaccurate some of our notions can be about what plants will grow in which regions. After all, many people in the northern states still express shock when seeing a bald cypress at a local park or in a neighbor's yard. They believe that this species only grows in the Deep South and that bald cypress can only grow in swamps or wetlands. Both of these views are incorrect. Although far from common in most areas outside of the South, one can find mature bald cypress trees in upstate New York, the upper Midwest as far north as Minnesota, and in Canada. *Taxodium distichum* is a swamp species well adapted to growing in standing water; however, it will also grow to massive proportions in typical upland conditions (although trees rarely develop the characteristic knees associated with the aquatic habit).

There is some good-natured (usually) dispute over whether the Ohio Champion bald cypress resides in Spring Grove Cemetery in Cincinnati or on the Miami University campus, but there is no disputing that both of these century-old trees are impressive indeed. The former giant (its exact measurements are not available) is growing in an aquatic habitat, and the Miami University specimen, with its 7-ft (2.1 m) trunk diameter and 80-ft (24 m) plus canopy spread, is sited in an upland area in heavy clay soil. In a typical landscape setting, the bald cypress grows in a slender pyramidal shape, with attractive brownish red fibrous bark (plate 61).

Taxodium distichum prefers full sun but will grow in partial shade, although more slowly and with a more open canopy. Autumn color is much less effective than the dawn redwood, but pleasing. Beware that the dropped needles decay slowly and can be problematic in understory planting beds. This stately specimen tree adds a distinctly southern touch to a temperate landscape. In alkaline soils, leaves can become chlorotic due to iron deficiency and take on a sickly yellow cast. Cypress and pine straw mulches (as well as those dropped needle leaves) help to condition the soil over time. It is also a good idea to use acidic fertilizers with this species. Acute chlorosis can often be treated by applying ferric ammonium citrate or a fertilizer rich in ferrous citrate, forms of iron more readily assimilated by the tree under alkaline conditions.

A related species, *Taxodium ascendens* (pond bald cypress or pondcypress), is another good choice for the residential landscape, although less commonly available. Pondcypress resembles bald cypress, but the bark is lighter brown and deeply furrowed, even in young trees, and the habit is more columnar. Tree height at maturity is similar to bald cypress.

Chapter 8

Bamboos, Bananas, Yuccas, Cacti, and Other Exotic Temperate Plants

Possibly only pandas really appreciate bamboos; gardeners do not—if they did they would grow far more of these superb plants.

—John Kelly

Palms, broadleaved evergreens, crape myrtles, and other choice tropical-look deciduous species can be combined with companion plants to form an effective warm-climate landscape. But numerous other exciting plants do not fit into the above categories—plants that are so evocative of the tropics that they elicit an instantaneous reaction from passers-by when seen in temperate climes. A finished North-by-South landscape will feature many of these species and provide exceptional visual interest and texture throughout the year. Cacti and agaves are not just for semi-arid regions, and several banana species can be grown in-ground in zones 5 and 6. How about a bamboo thicket to screen your neighbor's garage?

Bamboos

Bamboo is woven into the very fabric of life for a large part of humanity. In the Far East and other tropical and subtropical areas it provides food, construction material, and the raw material for many of the arts and crafts. In China, bamboo is known as "friend of the people," and Colombians revere it as a "gift of the gods." A Japanese garden without bamboo is unthinkable, and, to my mind, a temperate garden without bamboo is equally unthinkable. Few plants are as elegant in form and few offer as many exciting possibilities for the temperate gardener seeking to create a tropical look. Many bamboos, represented by more than 70 species and 2400 species worldwide, are tropical and subtropical plants. But a surprising number of evergreen bamboos are true temperate species and will tolerate zone 5 and even zone 4 conditions (see Meredith 2001; Conner 2002). One species, canebrake bamboo (*Arundinaria gigantea*), is native to the United States.

One of the major problems with growing bamboo in past years was simply finding sources of plants. These days, there are several large mail-order firms that specialize in bamboo, and in most states local bamboo specialty nurseries have become fairly common. In Ohio, for example, which is hardly thought of as a bamboo Mecca, I am aware of at least three commercial bamboo specialty nurseries: Burton's Bamboo Garden in Morrow, southwestern Ohio (zone 6a); Plant Crafters Garden Center in Westlake, northeastern Ohio (zone 5b); and Buckeye Bamboo Company in Streetsboro, northeastern Ohio (zone 5b). Check your local nurseries.

I may be missing your favorite species or variety in the descriptions below. There are easily more than two hundred species and varieties of temperate bamboo in the trade, but many are rare and very expensive. I am also reticent to make a recommendation for species in which my own experience or that at least several acquaintances cannot solidly document shoot and leaf hardiness and overall vigor under zone 6 or colder conditions.

Size and characteristics. Bamboos range in size from small ground-cover species to giant timber bamboos that send up 75-ft-tall (23-m) canes that are several inches in diameter. All are members of the grass family (Gramineae) and share similar characteristics with other perennial grasses. Excellent, comprehensive treatments of temperate bamboos and their cultivation may be found in Adelman (1995), Reynolds (1997a), Bell (2000), and Meredith (2001).

Once a year, usually in spring, new growth arises as bamboo shoots (or culms) emerge from buds present on underground stems called *rhizomes*. The culm pokes out of the ground fully formed and at its mature diameter; over the next month or two the culm grows taller but not thicker. Some tropical timber species grow phenomenally—several feet per day is not uncommon—and even temperate culms can elongate several inches per day. As the culm grows, lateral buds present at the joints (nodes) produce lateral branches, and secondary buds on these lateral branches produce leaves. A culm lives for several years, becoming progressively more leafy but not taller. Dead culms persist for many years unless they are removed.

The key to successful bamboo cultivation under temperate conditions is understanding how and when different species of bamboo send up their new growth and what is needed to maximize growth but keep the plant within the boundaries set for it. Jerry Burton, owner of Burton's Bamboo Garden in Morrow, Ohio, and one of the best known hardy-bamboo pioneers, has summarized all you need to know about bamboo biology in one simple yet scientifically accurate phrase: "First they sleep, then they creep, then they leap." Patience is the name of the game when cultivating bamboo. When you plant a new clump of bamboo, whether a field-dug transplant or container stock, it will pretty much sleep and creep the first few growing seasons. A few new culms emerge the first year, a few more slightly thicker and taller culms the next year, and so on. And you may begin to wonder what you're doing wrong. Why doesn't *your* bamboo look thick, lush, and massive like the pictures in garden books? When do you get that bamboo grove that you desire?

Rest assured—you are probably not doing anything wrong. In its early establishment phase, the plant puts most of its energy into growing new underground rhizomes, from which new culms will appear in succeeding springs. Depending on the type of bamboo, these rhizomes can grow several feet per year. Because new culms emerge in spring, their initial growth and development is strictly dependent on photosynthetic energy reserves stored away in the root-rhizome system. As this system becomes more extensive and massive over the years, more energy from the previous growing season can be stored for growth the next spring. So, with each succeeding growing season after planting, new culms increase in diameter and mature height. An established bamboo plant has a dense and extensive underground rhizome system that permits it to "leap," sending up many vigorous, large culms each succeeding growing season. It takes several years, often five to ten, for a newly planted bamboo to establish a dense grove with culms of the characteristic thickness and height of the species or variety. But that should not keep you from getting a lot of enjoyment out of young bamboo plants. Just don't plan on harvesting those 3-in (7.5-cm) thick culms from newly installed timber bamboo in the first few years.

Two key, yet misunderstood, aspects of bamboo biology deserve special mention. First, many people hesitate to grow bamboo because it has a reputation for being extremely invasive. Second, everyone knows that when bamboo flowers it dies and you lose the whole grove. Let's examine the issue of invasiveness. There are two patterns of rhizome spread and culm growth in bamboo, creating two major functional groups into which all bamboo species can be placed. Running bamboo species spread by growing their underground rhizomes to varying distances from the parent plant before sending up culms. Unless constrained, such species can colonize large areas, forming a characteristic, single-species grove. Many of the large hardy temperate bamboos are runners, but, in contrast to conventional wisdom, such species need not be extremely invasive. A running bamboo can take over your yard, but only if you want it to. In the next section I will review several relatively easy strategies to use to constrain the spread of running bamboo. Clump bamboos, as the name implies, grow like the perennial bunch grasses most of us are familiar with. Underground rhizomes do not migrate far from the parent plant. Rather, the clump becomes denser and taller with each growing season, spreading modestly outward without becoming invasive. There are numerous species of clump bamboo available to the temperate gardener.

Another misunderstood aspect of bamboo cultivation is the tie between flowering and plant death. The key to sorting out confusion lies in understanding the reproductive biology of bamboo species—unfortunately, botanists still do not have all the answers. For those desiring a more complete overview of this topic, I refer you to excellent discussions in Jaquith and Haubrich (1996), Reynolds (1997a), Bell (2000), Jaquith (2001), and Shor (2001) as well as other references in the bibliography.

All clump or running bamboo species are flowering plants, although like most grasses the flowers are not showy. It takes a great deal of energy to produce flowers, the vehicles of sexual reproduction in flowering plants. Energy allocated to flower production and fruit set comes at the expense of growth and maintenance of the adult. Some of the smaller bamboo species flower nearly every year without affecting the vigor of the plant. Other species flower sporadically, and some have never been observed in flower. Many of the popular running and clump species flower on extremely long but fairly predictable time intervals of decades to more than one hundred years. And, unfortunately, for many popular bamboo species, flowering cycles remain poorly understood. The reason why flower cycles are so crucially important is that, unlike most flowering plants, bamboo species as a group tend to be hepaxanthic, reserving all of their sexual reproductive effort to a single event in their life cycle. This spasm of reproduction is so energetically taxing that it can result in mortality of the adult, a phenomenon perhaps better known in some animals. Salmon spawn a single time and then die. They put so much energy into the act of sexual reproduction that there is not enough left to sustain the adult.

To make matters worse, because it is easier to propagate bamboos vegetatively, commercially available bamboos of a single species or variety tend to be clones—genetically identical copies of a single parent. Many bamboos flower gregariously, meaning that all individual plants derived from a single clone tend to flower at approximately the same time—within a single grove but also in groves spread over great geographic distances.

Does this mean that parental death is inevitable when the plants flower? The best answer at present is "not necessarily." First, there is controversy over the dogma of gregarious flowering. Such flowering does occur and may involve many plants, but not necessarily all plants of that species or clone. And most of the common bamboo species available to the public represent many clones. Sometimes, even in a single clone, a flowering cycle appears to be sporadic rather than gregarious; a grove of the same clone down the street flowers, while yours does not. Remember than when you plant a single clump of running bamboo, new growth arises vegetatively via rhizome spread—all the culms in the resulting grove are, genetically speaking, a single individual. Even within a single-individual bamboo grove, botanists have observed that some culms flower, while others do not. When gregarious flowering does occur, it is true that the grove may die. Plantings of *Phyllostachys bambusoides* 'Castillon', a beautiful timber bamboo, were decimated almost completely in the United States and Europe during the 1970s and 1980s when that species flowered gregariously. Plants now available in commerce are derived from seeds of this reproductive event or a few clones that did not flower, and these plants should be fine for many years.

So, one way to minimize the threat of losing your bamboo plants through flowering is to purchase plants that are derived from clones that have recently flowered. Many companies and nurseries that sell bamboo now include this information in their plant descriptions. But predicting flowering cycles and the extent of flowering remains at best an inexact science, and there are few certainties or guarantees. If anything, the picture is less clear in 2001 than it was several years earlier (N. Jaquith and B. Shor, personal communications). Perhaps the best approach is to use some of the cultural techniques described later in this chapter to minimize the energy drain on parent plants when flowering does commence and to give the mature plants an extra dose of tender loving care to get them through the reproductive cycle without major mortality.

Cold hardiness. Most of the temperate bamboo species and varieties described here are leaf hardy through zone 5; several are adaptable to zone 4 and even a bit colder. If bamboo is grown near the limits of its cold-hardiness range, some of the foliage may turn beige, especially in a windy, full-sun site, but new leaves quickly replace damaged ones in spring. Under extreme winter conditions bamboo growing at the limits of (or slightly beyond) its zone rating can be killed to the ground, but the root-rhizome system will send up new culms in spring.

Culture, landscape use, and other notes. Bamboo is easy to grow as long as you follow a few guidelines. Most clump forms prefer some shade, especially from afternoon summer sun, and a few species do well in deep shade. Many running bamboos prefer full sun and will not migrate far into the dense shade of a woodland canopy. Small forms can be used as effective ground covers. First, decide where to site the plants, with an eye toward ultimate size, degree of spread, and the requirements of the species or variety for sun. In clump bamboos, degree of spread is not much or a problem, but in running forms you must decide on the ultimate size of the projected grove and plan accordingly.

Bamboos prefer well-drained, highly organic soils of roughly neutral pH. Well-composted manure makes an excellent soil amendment. You can obtain bamboo specimens as containerized or balled-and-burlapped stock. Many general-purpose nurseries are now beginning to carry bamboo, but the best sources continue to be mail-order companies or local bamboo-specialty nurseries that now are found in many parts of the United States, Canada, the United Kingdom, and many other countries worldwide.

If you purchase containerized stock, keep two things in mind. First, purchase the biggest plant you can afford. Small specimens take longer to establish and are more sensitive to adverse environmental conditions. Second, select the most root-bound specimens you can find. With bamboo, the more massive and crowded the root ball, the faster the plant will establish and grow. Containerized plants can be installed at any time of the year, but midspring is ideal.

One of the best bamboo sources are friends who have an existing bamboo grove or clump bamboo that they want to divide. The best time to transplant bamboo from the field is in spring just before new culms begin to appear. (In zone 6a southwestern Ohio, that is generally March to very early April.) You can transplant at other times of the year, but the risk of losing plants is greater during summer heat or winter cold. I have found it easiest to remove divisions with a sharp spade. Simply cut out a block of soil and root-rhizomes large enough to include two or three connected culms. Dig down 1 ft (0.3 m) at least, so as to remove a healthy mass of roots, and take care to keep the division and attached soil as intact as possible. A division of this size will contain sufficient roots to sustain the existing culm and will have enough rhizomes and underground buds to fill in rapidly.

Planting a containerized plant or a field division involves the same techniques. To maximize rhizome survival and establishment, dig the planting hole two times the diameter of the root mass and perhaps one and a half times the root ball or division height. Add several inches of composted manure and/or excellent organic soil to the hole, and place the plant so that the surface of the root ball is at the existing soil level. Backfill the hole with excellent soil amended with manure, and water deeply. Then, make sure to water regularly and deeply during the first growing season so that the root zone never dries out. Curled or rolled leaves indicate acute water stress.

To establish a bamboo grove using running forms, plant individual specimens with perhaps 5 ft (1.5 m) of space between them. Of course, a single plant will eventually send out rhizomes to fill any available space, but denser planting speeds the process by years. Similarly, a hedge or dense screen can be established using either running or clumping forms by setting the plants approximately the same distance apart as above.

Most bamboo authorities recommend that commercial inorganic fertilizers should not be used during the first year after planting. After the first year, fertilize as you would any other grass, in spring, midsummer, and early autumn, but use a more balanced N–P–K blend than you would use for turf grass. Purists insist that composted manure is always the preferable fertilizer for maximal bamboo growth. A layer of organic mulch is a must in the first year to conserve soil moisture, especially in sunny sites. I have found that leaf humus is especially effective, and it gives me an additional use for my autumn leaves. After bamboo plants have grown for a few years, they will develop their own mulch layer through natural leaf drop. To me that ground cover of bamboo leaves is one of the more aesthetically pleasing aspects of a mature bamboo grove, and you will find that such a layer is almost impervious to weeds.

When installing a running bamboo variety, you must consider the question of how to contain its spread. A healthy running bamboo does not respect property lines, and failure to plan ahead makes for unhappy neighbors. Even if you live on a rural property and bamboo trespass is not an issue, you will still want to consider containment options to maximize the beauty of the bamboo grove within the overall landscape. Fortunately, there are several relatively easy options. You need not fear bamboo taking over your life or ruining neighborhood relations.

In zone 7a and colder, most running bamboos are far less invasive that they can be in areas without cold winters. And even in warmer areas, if you plan a grove effectively, several natural controls will almost always keep running bamboo in check without the need for containment barriers. First, consider siting plants so that one side or more of the grove will be constrained by an existing physical barrier—a wall with a deep stone or concrete foundation or the side of a building is ideal. A very dense, well-established row of large shrubs can also be used, because the bamboo rhizomes have a difficult time penetrating through the intertwining shrub root masses. Bamboo will not extend its rhizomes into water, so a stream or pond constitutes an effective barrier. A running bamboo that thrives in full sun can be sited in the front of a deep woodlot, where it will migrate only partially into the canopy shade, forming a pleasing understory edge effect. A deciduous woodlot is much less effective in this regard, but even here root competition and shade prevent most bamboos from becoming very dense. Also, unwanted new culms can be easily and effectively removed. When bamboos send up new culms in spring, simply break them off at or near the soil line. In the same fashion, you can keep unwanted culms out of a lawn simply by regular mowing. A well-mowed swath of lawn approximately 25 ft (7.5 m) wide will prevent even the most invasive forms from crossing that area into new territory.

If you desire absolute containment, consider installing a bamboo containment barrier. Ready-made barriers can be purchased commercially, or you can construct one. This is not a small task, and considerable physical labor is required. Tips on constructing bamboo barriers are included with every bamboo supplier's catalog and on the Internet. A permanent barrier should be installed to a depth of 2–3 ft (0.6–0.9 m) to prevent rhizome spread; anything shallower is a waste of time. Excavate around the perimeter of the proposed grove and install either a poured-concrete barrier, strips of galvanized sheet metal, or heavy-gauge (30–40 mil) polyethylene sheeting. If you use metal or plastic materials, overlap cut edges by at least 1 ft (0.3 m) to prevent rhizomes from sneaking through seams. Backfill the hole and make sure that the barrier extends above the soil line by a few inches. Even with this technique, some surface rhizomes may grow over the barrier every summer and autumn; pinch these off right away.

I use a much less labor-intensive containment system to create small beds of running bamboo. A 30-gallon plastic container left over from the purchase or a large tree or shrub works well. Simply cut out the container bottom, dig an appropriate size hole to accommodate it, leaving a few inches of the rim aboveground, and plant running bamboo inside. A 55-gallon drum or deep trash bin will also work. In some of the larger running bamboos, you may need to thin the clump every few years, but this method works very well for small to medium running bamboo.

Should your bamboo begin to flower, there are several things that you can do to give the adult culms the best chance of survival. In a small grove of running or clump bamboo, you can cut off any flowering culms, chop them up, and bury them in the grove. (Nobody really understands why this technique helps grove survival, but it's thought that the decaying culms and/or flowers may produce a chemical that inhibits further flowering. The physical removal of the flower culms may also inhibit further flowering by interrupting the flow of phytohormones.) Then, fertilize the adult culms and water well. Sometimes this simple intervention prevents the plant from continuing the flowering cycle, and thus putting enormous amounts of energy into reproduction. Even if you are unsuccessful in staving off flowering, many bamboos will rejuvenate vegetatively if given a heavy dose of fertilizer and water. Although the flowering culms may die, the plant as a whole survives, gradually producing new culms from underground rhizomes.

Winter protection. In zone 6 and colder, make sure bamboo is well mulched and watered prior to winter. Leaves left over from autumn yard clean-up work well and condition the soil as they decompose, but any organic mulch will serve. Apply antidesiccant spray to bamboo foliage at the same time you treat other evergreens in your landscape.

Clumping Bamboos

Clumping bamboos make excellent specimen and screen plants, and most prefer or will at least tolerate considerable shade. These plants are ideal with other broadleaved evergreen trees and shrubs, flowering ornamentals, and palms. The hardiness temperatures quoted are for foliage; culms and underground rhizomes are considerable hardier. Plant heights and culm thicknesses listed are for mature plants grown under optimal conditions, and, where good information exists, I provide some background on flowering dynamics.

Bambusa multiplex, Hedge Bamboo

Most *Bambusa* species are tropical to subtropical, but hedge bamboo is leaf hardy to about 5°F (–15°C) and rated to zone 7a. I was not successful overwintering new plantings of this species in Oxford, Ohio, through the bitter winter of 2000–2001, but I think that established plantings could survive zone 6 winters in excellent sites. *Bambusa multiplex* is one of the few cold-hardy clumping species that prefers full sun, although it also tolerates partial sun. This species produces green culms that are densely branched from the ground up, with white sheaths at the branch and leaf nodes (see plate 3). It can reach 35 ft (10.5 m) in height with 1.5-in (3.8-cm) diameter culms, but in colder climates expect 8–10 ft (2.4–3.0 m) height. *Bambusa multiplex* has a very picturesque arching habit. The cultivar 'Alphonse Karr' has bright yellow canes with thin green stripes.

Drepanostachyum falcatum

This species is rare and therefore expensive—a bamboo connoisseur's delight. It features striking bluish green culms with dark green leaves. *Drepanostachyum falcatum* is hardy to 0°F (–18°C) and adaptable to sun or shade. It reaches 20 ft (6 m) with 0.75-in (2-cm) diameter culms.

Fargesia dracocephala, Hardy Dragon Bamboo

Far and away the most heat tolerant in the genus *Fargesia*, this species will thrive in the coastal Deep South as well as New England and in shady to sunny locations. It is hardy to –20°F (–29°C). *Fargesia dracocephala* has willowy leaves and a weeping habit and grows to approximately 15 ft (4.5 m) in height with 0.75-in (2-cm) diameter culms. Hardy dragon bamboo is a food source for giant pandas in its native range.

Fargesia murielae, Umbrella Bamboo

The genus *Fargesia* contains the most cold hardy of the clumping bamboos and also some of the most beautiful. Umbrella bamboo is cold hardy to –20°F (–29°C) and lower in a good site, and rhizomes have recovered from even lower temperatures. This species prefers shade. The culms, which measure 0.75 in (2 cm) in diameter, are bright green in the first year but mature to a powdery bluish green. The height is generally 6–8 ft (1.8–2.4 m), but can reach 15 ft (4.5 m) under ideal conditions. The attractive weeping habit of *F. murielae* is ideal near a pond, where it can reflect off the surface of the water. Some clones of umbrella bamboo began to flower gregariously in the early 1990s, and this is one genus that usually succumbs after massive flowering. Again, it is difficult if not impossible to say which clones will flower next or if any individual plant will flower and die. Fortunately, some bamboo suppliers have begun to propagate and clone individuals produced through recent flowering events. If you check before you purchase, you can acquire a plant that should be immune from flowering for many decades. The beauty and utility of this species makes it worth the chance in any case. The varieties 'Humbolt', 'Mary', 'Picturum', and 'Simba' differ from the species in overall size and foliar habit.

Fargesia nitida, Fountain Bamboo

There is some confusion in the literature concerning the cold hardiness of this *Fargesia* species, but most agree that the many available varieties of fountain bamboo are hardy to about –20°F (–29°C) once established. New culms are purplish green and mature to deep purple in the second year. As the common name implies, the foliage tends to weep or cascade down to ground level like water from a fountain. The overall effect is very graceful, even in young plants, although I have noted significant leaf loss in first-year plantings exposed to –6°F (–21°C). Mature height ranges from 6 to 8 ft (1.8 to 2.4 m) but can reach 12 ft (3.6 m) under ideal conditions, with an average culm diameter of approximately 0.75 in (2 cm). *Fargesia nitida* does best in shade to partial shade.

Many cultivars are available in the trade (the New England Bamboo Company lists ten) that differ from the species in height, foliar habit, and heat tolerance. 'Nymphenburg', or blue fountain bamboo, is very full from the ground up with especially attractive purple culms. 'Ems River' has slightly smaller leaves than the type and dark purplish culms year-round (plate 62). Some *Fargesia nitida* clones that last flowered in the 1880s are now coming into flower in Europe and are expected to flower in the United States over the next ten to twenty years. It is not clear whether flowering in these clones leads to mortality in the parent plants.

Running Bamboos

Running bamboos can be controlled or even grown in relatively small in-ground containers to mimic the habit of a clumping bamboo. But a running bamboo can also be used to create a magnificent grove. There are many species and varieties of runners available to the temperate gardener, and, in contrast to the clump bamboos, many running forms actually prefer full or partial sun and will tolerate summer heat well. As in clumping forms, I present information on plant size under different conditions and summarize current information on flowering dynamics.

Arundinaria gigantea, Canebrake Bamboo

Native to the southeastern United States, canebrake bamboo is absolutely one of my favorite bamboos. Some find its appearance a bit coarse, due to the persistent white culm sheaths, but to me its virtues far outweigh any liabilities. The overall habit of culms is very upright, with tight dense branching, making this an excellent choice for a confined area, especially in zones 5 and 6, where it is not very invasive. The deep green mature culms can reach 20 ft (6 m) with a diameter of about 1 in (2.5 cm), but generally 10–15 ft (3.0–4.5 m) in zone 6 and north. Leaves are likewise a deep green, even in winter, although the culms tend to turn purple after several hard freezes. Adaptable to sun or shade, canebrake bamboo is an excellent choice for naturalizing along a shrub or tree border or as a tall backdrop for lower-growing plants (plate 63). Some authors list this species as hardy to −10°F (−23°C), but the consensus is −20°F (−29°C). Based on experiences of numerous zone 5 and 6 gardeners, I suspect that the latter figure is more accurate.

There are reports of *Arundinaria gigantea* flowering somewhere in the United States almost yearly since record keeping began in 1872, but little is known about the flowering intervals of individual clones (Shor 2001). From these reports, however, it appears that this species either does not flower gregariously or that so many clones exist that wide-scale flowering is not observable.

Indocalamus tessellatus

This species has short (3–6 ft, 0.9–1.8 m), thin (2 in, 5 cm) culms and spectacular large leaves that remain fully evergreen through about −15°F (−26°C). Some plant manuals list *Indocalamus tessellatus* as hardy only to 0°F (−18°C), but I think this is far too conservative because it does well under zone 5 conditions (plate 64). Unlike many running bamboos, this species does best in shade or partial shade.

Phyllostachys aurea, Golden Bamboo, Fishpole Bamboo

The genus *Phyllostachys* contains a large number of popular and beautiful running bamboos that are exceptionally cold tolerant. Golden bamboo may be the most commonly cultivated bamboo in the United States through zone 7. Although sometimes killed to the ground at temperatures below 0°F (–18°C), it regrows vigorously from its root-rhizome system. *Phyllostachys aurea* is uncontrolled by barriers and tends to spread rapidly in warm-summer climates, making it an excellent choice for forming a dense hedge or screen that is especially effective with palms and other warm-climate species. Golden bamboo can reach 25 ft (7.5 m) in height under ideal conditions. As one common name implies, its strong golden yellow culms are fashioned into cane fishing poles. I made our son Tyler one such pole from a stand we had at our home in Stillwater, Oklahoma.

Phyllostachys aureosulcata, Yellow-Groove Bamboo

This species is one of the best choices for producing a dense, towering bamboo grove in zone 6b and colder (plate 65). Although plants grown in dense shade or with suboptimal water and soil fertility will only reach heights of approximately 15 ft (4.5 m) and culm diameters of perhaps 1.5 in (3.8 cm), well-nourished culms grown in even partial sun can reach 25–30 ft (7.5–9.0 m) or more with diameters of about 3 in (7.5 cm). *Phyllostachys aureosulcata* looks wonderful planted at the edge of a deciduous woodlot so that culms can grow into and among the canopy trees. Be careful, however; even in zone 6 this species can get out of hand quickly. The common name describes the green culms that possess yellow grooves on alternate sides between the nodes. Culms grow in an interesting upright but zigzag fashion near the base of the culm, and some winter foliage remains green down to –20°F (–29°C) and even lower if sheltered a bit from winter winds. Grow yellow-groove bamboo in sun to shade.

Extensive flowering records exist for this species. From these records, clones of *Phyllostachys aureosulcata* appear to flower sporadically, but again this does not mean gregarious flowering cannot occur in the future. Shor (2001) does not record extensive mortality in flowering parents of the species.

Several equally hardy subspecies and varieties of yellow-groove bamboo are available. *Phyllostachys aureosulcata* f. *aureocaulis* is about the same size and hardiness as the species, but has entirely yellow culms with green grooves. *Phyllostachys aureosulcata* f. *spectabilis* has bright to yellow culms with green grooves and occasional white stripes on the leaves.

Phyllostachys bambusoides, Giant Timber Bamboo, Japanese Timber Bamboo

There are several varieties of Japanese timber bamboo, the giants of the temperate world. Many of these clones were devastated by gregarious flowering in the 1970s and 1980s but have again emerged on the market from seeds produced during this period. 'Castillon' is the most popular variety and the most cold-hardy, to approximately –10°F (–23°C). It produces 40-ft (12-m) golden yellow culms with green stripes that are 3 in (7.5 cm) in diameter. Plant *Phyllostachys bambusoides* in sun or partial shade.

Phyllostachys bissettii, David Bisset Bamboo

One of the best performers in northern areas, this is a vigorous zone 5 or colder species (to –25°F, –32°C) with several available varieties. Culms (15–30 ft, 4.5–9.0 m, depending on variety) are very dark green with a pleasing branching habit. *Phyllostachys bissettii* is not very invasive in zone 6 and colder. Plant this species in sun or shade. Large specimens are growing at the Buckeye Bamboo Company in zone 5b northeastern Ohio.

Phyllostachys decora, Beautiful Bamboo

Approximately the size of smaller *Phyllostachys bissettii* varieties, beautiful bamboo is one of the most heat- and drought-tolerant species, even though it is cold hardy to about –15°F (–26°C) and will tolerate sun or shade. It grows well in sandy soil. This species has very straight upright culms and masses of drooping foliage. The culms turn yellow orange when exposed to the sun. Old culms of this Chinese native are extensively used to fashion arts and crafts.

Phyllostachys dulcis, Sweet Shoot Bamboo

Emerging culms of nearly all bamboo species can be eaten and are the staples of many Asian recipes. But sweet shoot bamboo is often grown specifically as a food source due to its excellent flavor, even though it is also a fine choice for a grove in the warmer parts of zone 5 and warmer. Culms grow to perhaps 30 ft (9 m) under ideal conditions, much shorter in shade. *Phyllostachys dulcis* is not very tolerant of summer drought. This species was thought to be ready to flower gregariously in the early 1990s, but to date it has not done so.

Phyllostachys nigra, Black Bamboo

This species is another one of my favorites. It is rated as hardy to about −10°F (−23°F), although the leaves are marginally evergreen under zone 6a conditions, especially if exposed to afternoon winter sun and high winds. In the Deep South black bamboo is capable of producing massive 45-ft (13.5 m) culms that are 3 in (7.5 cm) in diameter, but under temperate conditions it usually grows to perhaps 10–15 ft (3.0–4.5 m) tall with 1.5-in (3.8-cm) diameter culms at maturity. What is especially beautiful about *Phyllostachys nigra* is that the new culms are deep green in the first year and then turn black in the second year, even in young plants—the mixture of green and black culms is very striking (see plate 13). The black culms are often used in furniture-making and other crafts. Branches and leaves tend to be clustered near the top of the culm, giving the plant an attractive outline. Black bamboo is one of the best running bamboo choices for containers or planters and does well in small in-ground containers. This species is not very invasive in zone 6. It does best in light shade—the leaves tend to scorch a bit in the summer if in a full-sun location.

Several varieties are available that differ from the species in size and culm coloration. 'Henon', or blue bamboo, is a truly impressive giant, possibly 40 ft (12 m) at maturity even in zone 6, with 4-in (10-cm) diameter culms. The culms are a waxy pale blue at maturity. Sporadic reports of *Phyllostachys nigra* flowering have been recorded since the late 1980s, but no wide-scale events or mortality are known.

Phyllostachys nuda

This bamboo is another good choice for a zone 4–6 grove. *Phyllostachys nuda* grows to heights of about 30 ft (9.2 m) with 2-in (5-cm) culms under temperate conditions. Hardy to about –25°F (–32°C) once established, this species is considered one of the toughest running bamboos. Culms are olive green with powdery white rings beneath each node, and the habit is upright and full even in young stands (figure 30). This species does well in full sun and tolerates bitter winter wind, although the leaves tend to turn somewhat beige.

Phyllostachys rubromarginata

The species name refers to the red margins that appear on new shoots in spring. Mature culms and leaves are a rich green (plate 66). One of the tallest of the temperate running bamboos, *Phyllostachys rubromarginata* is reputed to reach more than 50 ft (15 m) in height under ideal conditions. This species is often used by artisans because, even in younger plants, the culms are very straight and the habit is upright. This bamboo is hardy to perhaps –25°F (–32°C) and is another good choice for culinary use.

Figure 30 *Phyllostachys nuda,* Miami University campus, Oxford, Ohio (zone 6a)

Pleioblastus variegatus, Dwarf Variegated Bamboo

The genus *Pleioblastus* contains numerous species and varieties of short running bamboos that are used for accents, shrub borders, or ground covers. Dwarf variegated bamboo is one of the most commonly available and most beautiful. A tall ground-cover species that seldom grows more than about 3 ft (0.9 m) tall, with pencil-thin canes, it is favored for the striking white and green variegation of its dense leaves. In full sun the white color tends a bit toward yellow, but in my mind that makes the plant even more attractive (plate 67). Dwarf variegated bamboo is hardy to about –10°F (–23°C). I note a lot of winter leaf damage in my zone 6a home landscape. Leaves protected by snow cover during extreme weather are fine, and in any case recovery is quick in spring. Be careful: This species is quite invasive, even in zone 6.

Sasa senanensis

I have not grown this species, but I would like to. *Sasa senanensis* is an attractive bamboo with large, leathery leaves. This species is reportedly difficult to grow in containers. Truly leaf hardy down to –25°F (–32°C), this excellent shrub bamboo (to perhaps 10 ft, 3 m) can be planted in deep shade to partial sun, making it ideal for naturalizing in a woodlot. This is perhaps the best bamboo choice for this application in zones 4 and 5, and likely even warmer parts of zone 3.

Semiarundinaria fastuosa, Japanese Palm Tree Bamboo, Narihira Bamboo

This bamboo species should be used more—it is one of the most upright, strong, and picturesque of the running bamboos. Like *Arundinaria gigantea*, it makes an excellent specimen or hedge to 10–25 ft tall (3.0–7.5 m), especially in tight spaces. Narihira bamboo is not very invasive and is easy to control. It has persistent culm sheaths like *A. gigantea* and dark green leaves. Some authors list this species as hardy only through zone 6b, but other list it as hardy to –20°F (–29°C); I suspect the latter is more accurate because good specimens can be found in zone 5.

Semiarundinaria okuboi

Although capable of reaching 20 ft (6 m) in height in warm climates, this species is excellent as a shorter shrub in cold-winter areas. The leaves are an interesting twisted shape and a shiny, light yellowish green. They retain their attractive color and glossiness through the heat of summer (plate 68). Although often listed as hardy only through zone 6, *Semiarundinaria okuboi* appears to do well in colder locations as well.

Temperate Bananas

If palms are the princes of the tropical plant kingdom, then surely the bananas are somewhere in the royal court. Of all the warm-climate plants installed in our home landscape and on the Miami University campus, the palms and bananas draw the most attention from passers-by. Our bananas generate the most oohs and aahs each time I give a slide presentation to a public audience. Yet, when confronted with a 10-ft (3-m) tall Japanese fiber banana tree in all its summer glory, even knowledgeable biologists are incredulous when told that such a plant is an in-the-ground perennial in our zone 6a climate.

Bananas positively exude a tropical aura in the landscape, and the majority of the world's more than forty banana species are tropical in distribution, including the two species that produce the bulk of edible commercial crops. The dozen or so banana species most grown in temperate regions will rarely if ever develop edible fruit due to cold winter temperatures and comparatively short growing seasons. But the real glory of temperate bananas is in their incredible vegetative growth habit and foliage, and, in *Musella lasiocarpa,* its unusual and decorative flowers. Along with palms and bamboos, bananas are one of the most important framework species of a North-by-South landscape.

Although popular for thousands of years in the Far East, cold-hardy bananas first came into vogue in the West in Victorian England, both as die-back perennials and as plants that were dug up and moved to greenhouses for overwintering. In the ensuing years they remained a popular choice for a small but devoted cadre of loyal subtropical-look gardeners in Europe and the Americas. Then, beginning in the mid-1990s, large numbers of gardeners began to rediscover hardy bananas as the plants became generally available through mail-order catalogs and the Internet. Almost every year a new species or variety appears, and these days it is not uncommon for some of the larger general nurseries and smaller specialty nurseries in zones 7, 6, and even 5 to sell containerized temperate bananas.

Size and characteristics. Bananas are large, clumping, herbaceous plants that take on a habit resembling a palm tree as they grow. Despite their treelike appearance, however, the massive central trunk of a banana plant is termed a *pseudostem* because it is comprised not of woody tissue but is rather a column of old leaf bases. Think of a banana as a column of water being held upright by a minimal amount of structural tissue, and you can readily see why they are so sensitive to freezing weather. Near the top of the pseudostem the plant bears giant oblong leaves, and unfolding new leaves are developed in the central axis of the plant. As new leaves unfold and elongate, the older leaves below senesce and eventually drop off, leaving only their bases.

Bananas, including temperate species, are among the fastest growing plants in the world, matched only by some of the tropical timber bamboos. In my garden, a Japanese fiber banana that had been killed to the ground can grow to 10 ft (3 m) in height between April and August; 1 ft (0.3 m) per week in summer is not uncommon. Better still, bananas do not need a long establishment phase to reach maximal growth potential. A 1-gallon plant obtained via mail order or transplanted from a friend's garden can reach this impressive size in its first growing season.

Bananas have shallow root systems and spread vegetatively by suckering. Each year, new pups arise from the underground root-rhizome system, gradually extending the size of the clump in a ringlike fashion. Young pseudostems can be dug up and transplanted with ease. Gradually, the center of a banana clump dies off, and it is sometimes necessary to transplant some young pseudostems back into the center of the clump. Most banana pseudostems have an eighteen-month flowering cycle, which explains why they cannot flower and bear fruit in cold-winter areas without extensive winter protection. The inflorescences are huge, pendulous, and often showy, and are borne as a terminal spike, signaling the end of vegetative growth and ultimate demise of the pseudostem (the reason why these stems are cut down after fruit production).

The huge leaves of bananas are glossy and beautiful, but because they are soft and easily torn by winds, a plant growing in a windy site can often take on a tattered look. Young pseudostems begin producing leaves immediately, giving a banana clump its lush, tropical look even during spring months. I have one caution: Although the sap of banana leaves and stems is fragrant (not surprisingly, it smells just like the fruit), it stains any fabric it comes into contact with.

Cold hardiness. All banana leaves, even those of temperate species, are damaged by frost and killed outright by a hard freeze. Some of the species I describe here can take a few hours of 30°F (–1°C) and even a degree or two colder with minor foliar burn, thus extending the growing season by a few weeks. And if plants are covered with landscape fabric or a bed sheet, it's possible to add a degree or two to these figures. The pseudostem will take temperatures several degrees lower, and the whole plant can recover from short-duration, one-time freeze events to produce new foliage.

Nonetheless, in zone 8 and colder, winter weather eventually kills the aboveground parts of unprotected bananas. What most people do not realize, however, is that the banana root-rhizome system is vastly more cold hardy. If properly mulched and sited in well-drained soils, most plants will survive typical zone 6 and even colder conditions, regrowing the following spring.

Culture, landscape use, and other notes. Bananas are best as specimen plants, where their dramatic look can be fully appreciated. There is no way to grow an inconspicuous banana tree in a temperate landscape, so make sure to site the plant in a location that the eye is naturally drawn to. The angle formed at the intersection of two exterior walls is an excellent place—a banana filling the corner and arching outward is particularly dramatic. Another excellent choice is near an ornamental yard lamp, where nighttime illumination will be reflected off the banana's shiny, cascading leaves. Remove yellowed or brown leaves as they develop, but watch out for the sap. I usually cut up the spent leaves and use them to augment the mulch layer and recycle nutrients.

Bananas are very easy to grow. Plant small pseudostems or transplanted clumps in any good, well-drained garden soil; even clay soils are fine as long as you till in a lot of organic material. Drainage is important because sometimes bananas will rot in the ground during wet, cold winter weather in poorly drained soils. Make the planting hole wide but not deep; bananas have extensive surface roots and rhizomes but no tap root. Cover the planting bed with several inches of organic mulch. For maximal growth, a site in full sun is best, but bananas will also do well in partial sun. As noted earlier, shelter from the wind is desirable to keep the leaves from becoming tattered.

It is almost impossible to overwater or overfertilize a banana clump—the old adage of providing 1 in (2.5 cm) of water per week does not apply here. Remember that bananas are essentially columns of water topped with huge leaves that transpire at a tremendous rate. In the summer, especially, it may be necessary to water deeply and heavily every few days. Bananas are also heavy feeders. They need monthly applications of balanced inorganic or organic fertilizers that have plenty of nitrogen. If you use a slow-release granular fertilizer, apply it heavier than suggested on the product label. I have found that an occasional dose of high-nitrogen turf grass fertilizer (usually a 27–2–2 blend or similar) is useful during midsummer, and bananas will also benefit from foliar spray applications of soluble fertilizer.

Winter protection. When it comes to winter protection of bananas, a lot depends on where you live and what your overwintering goal is. For those fortunate enough to live in the milder parts of zone 8 and warmer, it is possible with relatively minimal effort to keep a banana tree in the ground well enough so that it regrows the following spring from over-wintered pseudostems, thus completing the normal eighteen-month flowering and fruiting cycle. This is difficult, but not impossible, in zones 7 and 6—it is simply a matter of how extensive you want to be with winter protection.

The easiest strategy is just to let nature take its course and allow the pseudostems and leaves to be killed by a hard freeze. Then simply cut the plant down to ground level and use the plant remains plus a lot of extra mulch to cover the entire clump with a minimum of 8–10 in (20–25 cm) of mulch. Make sure to extend the mulch layer well beyond the edge of the clump. Some authors recommend covering the mulch layer with a tarp or other protective covering to keep moisture out, but I have never done this and have not lost plants, even in our relatively wet winters.

Around the average date of last frost for your region, remove mulch and any dead, rotted banana tissue so that sunlight can strike the top of the senesced pseudostem, thus initiating new growth.

The so-called zombie zones (zones 5 and 6) as well as the colder parts of zone 7 tend to have a long winter-to-spring transition with lots of springlike weather in February and early March. In our area the average last frost date is around April 12–15, depending on microclimate, and like many people, my gardening urge becomes almost uncontrollable by mid-March. I often uncover my bananas very early, perhaps two to three weeks before average last frost date, and have found that the plants begin growing almost immediately. I'm always ready, however, to jump in and cover those young plants should frost threaten. Please remember that the average last frost date is just that—an average—and for nearly all areas the frost-free period begins about a month after the average date of last frost. By taking such a chance in spring and covering bananas during light autumn frosts, it's possible to gain several extra weeks in the growing season, thus producing a much larger plant. And, in the case of one short-flowering-cycle banana species that is now appearing on the market (*Musa acuminata* 'Rajapuri'), it may be possible to produce fruiting bananas within a single growing season even in truly temperate areas.

But inevitably that autumn hard freeze will come, and your poor banana will be killed back. Is there any way to prevent this? Certainly, there are reasons for wanting to try. The disadvantage of allowing bananas to be killed to the ground is that they will never get as large as they might if allowed to complete their full life cycle, and unless you are growing a short-season species, you'll never get flowers or fruit. With some effort, it is possible to protect a major portion of the pseudostems through the winter even if only 1 ft (30 cm) or so survives.

After the first killing frost in autumn, but before even colder weather has a chance to freeze the pseudostem, cut off all the dead leaves about 1 in (2.5 cm) from the stem. Then carefully tie the stems together with straps or other wide banding material so as not to cut into them. Drive a few posts into the ground in a perimeter about 1 ft (0.3 m) away from the outside edge of the clump and string chicken wire or other material around the posts a little higher than the top of the plant. Fill the entire cage with leaves, straw, or other dry mulching material to cover the entire plant. Some sources recommend covering the entire cage with a tarpaulin or other protective cover to keep the pile dry. Stake or weight the edges down to keep it from blowing away, leaving a crack somewhere in the cover to allow moisture to escape. In the spring, uncover the plant. Although the pseudostems will be covered with a slimy mess of decomposed material, this will wash off in the first few rains, and in a very short time new leaves will begin growing from the overwintered pseudostems.

In the milder parts of zone 7 and warmer, with this strategy you should be able to overwinter enough of the first-year growth to allow the banana to complete its life cycle and flower later in the second year. Of course, the idea of having a giant tarpaulin-covered construct in your yard all winter may be off-putting—but think of the fun you can have in the second year with those impressive flowers and fruit.

I can only offer limited insights on the efficacy of this method in zone 6 and colder. By using leaf enclosures and 2-ft (0.6-m) leaf piles, we were able to overwinter the majority of pseudostems from the hardiest temperate species (*Musa basjoo*) but had very limited success with other species, even though the minimum temperature in campus plots dropped to only 9°F (–13°C)—in effect, zone 7b conditions (Nagy and Francko 2002). Our experimental procedure, however, used open leaf enclosures that did become saturated with moisture, and it's entirely possible that better success could have been achieved if we had excluded rain and snow.

Musa acuminata 'Rajapuri'

This exciting cultivar was new to the market in 2001, and our specimens have gone through only one annual cycle at this writing, so I can offer only personal insights. Rated as fully hardy in zones 8–10 and through zone 7 with protection, only about one-third of our specimens made it through our mild 2001–2002 winter. Those data notwithstanding, all the preliminary data suggest that this banana appears to offer significant opportunities for temperate gardeners. Unlike other temperate bananas, *Musa acuminata* 'Rajapuri' is capable of flowering and producing edible fruit in a single nine-month growing season. That timeframe is still a reach for anyone living in areas colder than zone 8, but as I indicated earlier, it is relatively easy to extend the banana growing season both early and late. For example, although the nominal frost-free period in rural areas of southwestern Ohio is about 185 days, simply taking advantage of warmer microclimates near our home adds perhaps 20 days to that total. On the warmer Miami University campus, the nominal frost-free period in especially favorable sites approaches 240 days. By allowing bananas to begin seasonal growth well before the average last frost date in spring and covering them during autumn frosts, another 30–40 days can be added. In 2001, campus plots did not experience a killing frost until 24 December. Thus, it may be possible to coax this hybrid banana through a full flowering and fruiting cycle in especially favorable zone 6 sites, and the likelihood of success increases greatly for zone 7 regions. We're running these experiments in 2002 on the Miami University campus using 'Rajapuri' specimens that survived the winter and began growing back in March.

Musa acuminata 'Rajapuri' is relatively small (reputedly no more than 8 ft, 2.4 m), but all our first-year specimens reached that height and featured massive pseudostems (plate 69) even though they were not planted until May. Leaves are very large, and a mature clump can be twice as wide as it is tall, intensifying the overall tropical impact in the landscape. Unfortunately, the leaves of this cultivar are not quite as frost-tolerant as others described here and, based on our experience, excellent winter drainage is an absolute must. All of the successfully overwintered 'Rajapuri' were planted in very well-drained, loose soils in sites sheltered from a lot of direct precipitation, so that the insulating leaf piles stayed relatively dry all winter.

Musa basjoo, Japanese Fiber Banana

As the name implies, this species is native to the southern Japanese islands, where the fibers of its leaves are used to produce a cloth called *bashofu*. Without much question, this is the hardiest temperate banana species, and it is the only banana species I can recommend without qualification to people in zone 6a and colder—it is almost fool-proof. Although generally listed in catalogs as root-rhizome hardy only through zone 7, people have had success with *Musa basjoo* through zone 5, and a few have reported successful overwintering of roots in even colder areas. We have grown numerous specimens for several years in Oxford, Ohio, so I can vouch for root hardiness down to at least –14°F (–26°C) with mulching. Generally reaching a height of 8–10 ft (2.4–3.0 m) during a single season, the pseudostems (perhaps 6 in [15 cm] in diameter at the base) are topped with a crown of 5- to 6-ft (1.5- to 1.8-m) long shiny green leaves with attractive reddish leaf veins (plates 70, 71). Foliage is quite frost tolerant down to about 30°F (–1°C) and even a bit lower, and pseudostems easily tolerate 25°F (–4°C). This species does fairly well in partial sun, although it does not grow as tall as in full sun. If properly overwintered, *M. basjoo* produces an erect, torpedo-shaped, yellowish orange inflorescence. The clusters of small (2 in, 5 cm) yellow bananas are inedible but attractive nonetheless. This banana suckers vigorously, so that the clump expands outward by perhaps 2 ft (0.6 m) per year. Remember that these pups can easily be transplanted to another area or given to a friend. One plant I installed in our home garden in 1998 has produced literally dozens of offspring that are now growing all over the area. With heavy mulching alone and no special consideration given to drainage virtually all of our *M. basjoo* specimens overwintered living pseudostems through the winter of 2001–2002.

Musa sikkimensis, Sikkim Banana

Sikkim banana (also known as *Musa hookeri*) has been introduced to the gardening public only recently, so its ultimate cold hardiness is not completely understood. Native to high elevations of the northeastern Himalayas, *M. sikkimensis* is the giant among temperate bananas. In its native range and under ideal conditions, it can reach 14 ft (4.2 m) in height with a pseudostem diameter of nearly 1.5 ft (0.5 m). Its leaves are equally huge and impressive. Even newly planted specimens look impressive in their first year (see figure 7), and gardeners in New York report 9-ft (2.7-m) seasonal growth. The leaves are extremely attractive—a darker and shinier green than *M. basjoo* and more prominently veined. Sikkim banana produces a magnificent tropical effect. Although officially rated (conservatively) to zone 8, based on admittedly limited experience I estimate that it is only a notch less cold hardy than *M. basjoo*, certainly root hardy through in zone 6. The foliage is slightly more tolerant of frost than *M. basjoo*; a few Sikkim bananas that I inadvertently neglected to cover in autumn survived several hours of 28°F (–2°C) exposure with only minor margin burning. In our experience, perhaps three-quarters of Sikkim banana specimens successfully overwinter here in Oxford, Ohio, although new growth sometimes does not emerge until May.

Musa paradisiaca 'Mysore'

Musa 'Dwarf Orinoco'

Musa velutina, Velvet Pink Banana

Three other outstanding temperate *Musa* species deserve mention here for their beauty and utility. Because they are relatively new to the temperate marketplace, I do not have enough overwintering data as yet to support firm root hardiness projections beyond zone 7. But in each case I think further experimentation by the gardening public will demonstrate their utility in zone 6 and perhaps colder.

In my view, one of the most beautiful of the temperate bananas is *Musa paradisiaca* 'Mysore'. Perhaps the most striking plant in our Miami University campus plots, established individuals can reach massive size. This cultivar's greatest asset, however, is the unbelievable purplish foliage with green veins and highlights (see plate 5). It is absolutely undamaged by light frosts, and leaves survive exposure to temperatures as low as 28°F (−2°C) and even a degree or two lower in sheltered sites. Two of the three specimens we installed in 2001 survived the mild winter of 2001–2002.

Musa 'Dwarf Orinoco' has been grown for many years as a potted specimen plant and is now being grown successfully through zone 7 as an in-ground perennial. Seldom reaching more than 5–6 ft (1.5–1.8 m) in height, it is a sturdy and attractive specimen or companion species to taller forms and other tropical-look plants (see plate 9).

Numerous cultivars of *Musa velutina* have also been available to the zone 7 gardener for a few years and will likely prove root hardy through zone 6. The velvet pink banana is small (5 ft, 1.5 m) with slender yellowish green to purplish green pseudostems. The oblong leaves are dark green above and pale with a red midrib below. Cultivars of this species are grown in warmer areas for their outstanding hot-pink bracts and fruits.

Musella lasiocarpa, Chinese Yellow Banana

The genus *Musella* is closely related to the genus *Musa,* and this shrub-form temperate banana makes an excellent addition to the sunny or partially sunny landscape. *Musella lasiocarpa* is becoming so popular in the southeastern United States that tissue-cultured specimens are readily available at home centers and gardening shops. Chinese yellow banana grows as a dense, short clump perhaps 4–6 ft (1.2–1.8 m) high and about the same spread, with very stiff grayish green leaves (plate 72). Because the plant is short and the leaves are stiff and leathery, this species is not at all bothered by wind. Rated as cold hardy at least through zone 7, experience indicates that it is just a bit less root hardy and foliage hardy than *Musa basjoo*. It is being grown successfully in zone 5b northeastern Ohio with excellent drainage and heavy mulching. The main ornamental use of *M. lasiocarpa* lies in its exceptional yellow flowers, which resemble huge opening artichokes. I have not been able to achieve flowering in a single growing season in Oxford, Ohio (zone 6), but none of our specimens are fully established yet. Because of the short stature of this species, I believe it would be a good candidate for overwintering inside a covered enclosure as described earlier in this chapter.

Yuccas, Cacti, and Agaves

Most people think of yuccas, cacti, and agaves as desert dwellers, and in fact these plants are well adapted to dry habitats. But a surprising number of them are native to wetter areas of the south-central and eastern United States. And, perhaps even more surprising, many species are extremely cold hardy—some cacti and yuccas grow naturally well into Canada. These plants function best as accent species in a North-by-South garden and are excellent in combination with palms, bamboos, and other exotic plants.

Size and characteristics. Most of the cold-hardy members of these three groups are relatively small shrubby plants, but some of the yuccas form trunks and can reach 10 ft (3 m) in height. All reproduce sexually via flowering, but most species sucker profusely and form colonies via vegetative reproduction. The foliage of yuccas and agaves is evergreen, and the leaves are often tipped with spines or other projections.

Cold hardiness. In this section I focus only on species and varieties that are hardy at least through zone 6.

Culture, landscaping use, and other notes. Yuccas, cacti, and agaves grow in virtually any well-drained soil, even clay. In wet-winter areas, excellent drainage is a must. To promote drainage, it is sometimes useful to grow these species in a raised bed or soil berm or in amended heavy soils with coarse sand and fine gravel. Many gardeners think of these plants as somewhat coarse, but as accents they are hard to beat, and some of the variegated varieties are surprisingly colorful. Plant yuccas, cacti, and agaves in full sun, although partial sun will also work. Many yuccas and cacti will naturalize in a woodland setting. Of course, one of the best aspects of these plants is their extreme drought and heat tolerance once established. If you have a particularly sun-scorched area with poor soils, for instance, next to a south-facing masonry wall, these might be the ideal tropical-look plants to employ.

Winter protection. As long as soils are very well drained and plants are well mulched, the species described here need little if any special winter protection. An antidesiccant spray is advisable if you are growing a species in the northern part of its hardiness range. For trunked yuccas growing in northern areas, it is usually a good idea to wrap the trunks during extreme cold spells, much as one would trunk-wrap a palm. Some people have had success establishing small mail-order specimens of agave and cacti by covering the entire plant with pine straw or another loose mulch during extreme cold spells.

Yucca aloifolia, Spanish Dagger, Aloe Yucca

Several temperate yuccas are capable of forming trunks, and this is one of the best to consider in zone 7a and warmer. Spanish dagger is native in southeastern coastal Virginia to Florida and west to Texas. Another common Southeastern yucca species, *Yucca gloriosa,* is also called Spanish dagger and strongly resembles *Y. aloifolia,* but the latter species has narrower leaves. Yuccas hybridize freely in the wild. It is entirely possible that the naturalized plants widely found in northern Tennessee and other zone 6 areas of the South are interspecific hybrids of some kind. In any case, Spanish dagger is an excellent landscape plant for warmer temperate areas. The stiff, dark green leaves taper to very sharp points at the end and are spirally borne on woody stems that can reach about 3 ft (0.9 m) in height. Stems may be branched or unbranched and sometimes bend toward the ground under the weight of the foliage. The plant suckers freely and can form a dense hedge. Numerous *Y. aloifolia* cultivars are available in the trade; 'Marginata' has green leaves with yellow margins, and 'Tricolor' features a yellow stripe along the longitudinal leaf axis.

Yucca glauca, Adam's Needle, Dwarf Soapweed

Already familiar to most temperate gardeners, *Yucca glauca* is native to zones 3–9 of North America and can be purchased containerized from virtually any gardening center. It does not form a trunk, but the 3-ft (0.9-m) rosettes of bluish green to dark green leaves and white flowers atop a 3-ft (0.9-m) flower stalk are very pleasing (plate 73). It suckers profusely to form colonies that are effective with other tropical-look species, especially cacti and agaves, or as specimens. Adam's needle grows in absolutely any soil, is amazingly drought-tolerant, and remains evergreen down to about –30°F (–34°C). Many varieties of this species exist in the trade, some of which have exceptional yellow and green variegated leaves.

Yucca gloriosa, Spanish Dagger

This species is one of the best trunked yuccas for zone 6 conditions and may succeed in zone 5 if well sited. *Yucca gloriosa* is native to the southeastern United States, where it has naturalized as far north as north-central Tennessee and southern Kentucky. The dark green, somewhat pliable leaves taper to sharp points at the end and are spirally borne on woody stems that can reach about 3 ft (0.9 m) in height, even in areas that regularly drop below 0°F (–18°C) in winter. The leaves are a bit broader (2.0–2.5 in, 5.0–6.3 cm) at the base than *Y. aloifolia*. Trunks may be branched or unbranched and sometimes bend toward the ground under the weight of the foliage. Old leaves are often persistently held on the stem, and they can be removed to reveal a beautiful, smooth, tan to dark gray trunk. Because the plant suckers freely, it rapidly forms a very impressive, picturesque, and very tropical-looking colony (plate 74). In 2000 I received some small pups from a friend who lives in zone 6b north-central Tennessee. All of these did well through our rigorous 2000–2001 winter and in summer 2002 are already forming short trunks.

Yucca rostrata, Beaked Blue Yucca

Named for the bird-beak shape of its fruits, *Yucca rostrata* is an excellent trunked yucca for zone 7 and colder—specimens are growing as far north as zone 5 portions of New York State. The powdery blue to bluish green foliage forms a spiky crown at the top of the trunk, which may be branched in older specimens (plate 75). This yucca tolerates any well-drained soil but prefers neutral to slightly alkaline pH. It provides excellent four-season interest and complements other warm-climate plants. Beaked blue yucca used to be very difficult and expensive to purchase, but is now becoming available via mail order at a reasonable cost. Personally, I think beaked blue yucca is one of the most beautiful of all the temperate yuccas, and as a specimen plant in a gravel planting bed it makes a truly unusual statement.

Yucca schottii, Schott's Yucca

This tree yucca, a native of the desert Southwest, is now becoming more common in the trade. It is cold hardy through at least zone 6 and tolerant of wet soils. *Yucca schottii* has greenish yellow leaves, but some of the more interesting varieties feature unique steel blue leaves atop a trunk that can reach 10–15 ft (3.0–4.5 m) in height. White flowers appear in autumn.

Yucca smalliana, Bear Grass, Adam's Needle

There is considerable confusion over this species and a closely related species, *Yucca glauca*, which shares a similar habit and geographic range throughout the southeastern United States. Both are small rosette forms without trunks, and both possess stiff and outwardly curving leaves. They may in fact be the same species. Taxonomy aside, *Y. smalliana* is a great plant for a tight area of your garden that needs color and strong form. This species is hardy at least through zone 6 (and I strongly suspect zone 5 or even colder based on my experience). There are several outstanding cultivars on the market. One of my favorites, 'Bright Edge', has deep green leaves bordered by a golden yellow edging (plate 76). It holds its color through the winter and looks exceptional in all seasons. Several other popular variegated forms of uncertain taxonomy are widely available and grown successfully in zone 5 and south, including 'Color Guard', which has leaves with green margins and a gold center.

Yucca thompsoniana, Thompson's Yucca

I recall that this desert species was fairly common in zone 6b/7a Stillwater, Oklahoma, as a landscape subject. A large tree-form yucca, the habit of *Yucca thompsoniana* absolutely captures the flavor of the

Southwest, with a rosette of very stiff, narrow leaves atop a thick (to more than 1 ft, 0.3 m) trunk about 3 ft (0.9 m) in height. Although this spring-flowering species is usually rated as hardy only through about zone 7, I believe this is too conservative. In any case, some varieties rated for zone 5 are now appearing on the market.

Yucca treculeana, Spanish Dagger, Palma Pita

A tree-form yucca found throughout much of Texas and northern Mexico, this is another nice possibility for the zone 6 garden. *Yucca treculeana* is very columnar in form, with a terminal rosette of stiff green leaves and a stalk with white flowers. With time, it can sucker to form large colonies. Some people growing this species in zone 6 use a plastic covering over the base of the plant in winter to keep the root zone from rotting in cold, damp weather, but Eddy Krifcher (personal communication) reports success in Pittsburgh, Pennsylvania, without extra protection.

Other Yuccas

There are literally dozens of other cold-hardy yucca species and cultivars that are common to some areas but difficult to locate in others. *Yucca rigida* is a Mexican tree-form yucca with bluish leaves that appears to be hardy through at least zone 6b. *Yucca recurvifolia* is native to the coastal South but is being used effectively though zone 6. It can be grown in sun or partial shade, has excellent bluish green to grayish green leaves, and suckers to form a multiple-trunked colony. *Yucca torreyi*, another arid-zone species and very columnar in its tree habit, is a yucca to consider if you have access to a specimen.

Opuntia, Prickly Pear Cacti

Depending on which taxonomic view you subscribe to, there are between two hundred and five hundred species of *Opuntia*, all of which originated in the Americas and are now found worldwide in arid and semi-arid regions. The taxonomy of this group is in flux and species tend to hybridize within their native range. Cholla-form members of this genus have cylindrical, knobby, jointed stems that readily attach to animals and other passers-by with long spines. Also prominent in the genus are the many species that have joints shaped like fleshy pads that are armed with vicious spines—the prickly pear cacti. It is difficult to key these plants to species, even when in flower, so I am going to take the easy way out and simply refer to them as a group.

Prickly pear cacti range from Colorado through Mexico, and isolated populations can be found as far north as the prairie provinces of Canada. They can be cultivated in wet-winter areas through the warmer parts of zone 4. Most prickly pear species tend to grow in a prostrate habit along the ground, but some grow in a tree form with a woody base. Flower color is similarly variable, from yellow to orange to red and gradations between. All prickly pear cacti have clusters of very fine barbed spines, called *glochids,* arming the pads. Don't attempt to work with these plants unless you are wearing heavy gloves—glochids are painful and very difficult to pull out of the skin. In short, this is not a plant to grow in areas where small children or pets may wander.

Prickly pear cacti are exceptionally attractive in their vegetative state and in flower and are almost impervious to cold when well-drained. Consider these plants for your succulent garden. *Opuntia humifusa* (eastern prickly pear cactus) is a good landscaping choice (plate 77). The look is especially effective when different types of prickly pear cacti are planted with yuccas and other succulents in a raised gravel bed (plate 78). There are few plants easier to install. Simply break off a pad at the joint and stick the broken end into the ground. In a few weeks, the pad will root from the joint, and new pads will begin to arise from terminal buds on the existing pad. Indeed, prickly pear cacti are so easy to root that they will often naturalize from discarded plant pieces thrown onto a compost pile or into a field or woodlot, even in zone 6.

Agave parryi, Hardy Century Plant, Mescal

Agaves are fleshy-leaved succulents that grow in a rosette form. Many subtropical species are used to produce alcoholic beverages such as tequila and pulque. The genus contains more than three hundred species, and several are cold hardy though zone 6 and even zone 5 if well sited. The taxonomy of the *Agave parryi* is confusing, and many subspecies and varieties thereof are found in the trade, varying in leaf color and size. But all members of the species are small, generally less than 2 ft (0.6 m) in height and width, with gray to bluish green foliage armed with nasty spines at the terminus (plate 79). The beautiful flower stalks with striking yellow flowers can tower up to 15 ft (4.5 m) high in summer. A related species, *Agave montana,* has a similar appearance, habit, and tolerance to cold.

Hesperaloe parviflora, Red Yucca

Despite the common name, red yucca is not a yucca at all, although like the true yuccas it is a member of the agave family (Agavaceae). Native to southwestern Texas and northern Mexico, red yucca resembles a succulent grass, with grayish green leaves that redden somewhat in full sun. The clump habit, elegant leaves, and showy salmon-colored flowers borne on 5 ft (1.5 m) flower spikes are perfect additions to any tropical-look garden. Listed as hardy through zone 7 and marginal in zone 6b, I suspect that *Hesperaloe parviflora* is hardy through all of zone 6 with minimal protection, based on experiences of Doug Cepluch, who owns Eagle Creek Nature Center, a cactus and succulent specialty nursery in zone 6a southwestern Ohio.

Dasylirion wheeleri, Blue Sotol

This is another yucca relative with powdery blue leaves that are stiff but gently twisting. Instead of having a spine on the end of the leaves, the spines are on the margins. The inflorescence spike resembles a thin bean pole. Blue sotol is considered hardy through zone 7, but will do well in zone 6 as long as the crown is kept dry during winter. One way to do this is to cover the plant with heavy-gauge landscape fabric, which is breathable but water repellent, over the winter months.

Appendix

Additional Resources

here are numerous resources available to the prospective North-by-South landscaper. You will want to build a library containing at least a few key books, and it is essential that you become familiar with the many sources of information available these days on the Internet. If you don't own a computer, your local library almost certainly has computers available for your use. Not only are most plant catalogs available online, but numerous web message boards have cropped up in the past few years. These web boards are targeted to specific areas, so you can pose questions and get answers and insights from people with similar interests—and you can get answers in real time.

As for books, no one offers more usable information about woody species than Michael Dirr, and no one else has such a wonderful way of conveying information. His *Manual of Woody Landscape Plants* (1998), now in its fifth edition, is the bible for serious horticulturists but lacks photographs of the species in the landscape. *Dirr's Hardy Trees and Shrubs* (1997) is an illustrated look at trees and shrubs that are hardy from zones 3–6, but as the author points out, most of these species also do well in warmer areas. In 2002 the much-awaited companion volume *Dirr's Trees and Shrubs for Warm Climates* was published; it covers plants for zones 7–11. Buy Dirr's books for the invaluable information; read them for enjoyment as well as the information.

The *Sunset National Garden Book* (1997) and the newer regional volumes—*Sunset Western Garden Book* (2001), *Sunset Northeastern Garden Book* (2001), and *Sunset Midwestern Landscaping Book* (2002)—are also essential books for your library. Aside from the novel use of forty-five climatic zones to classify plant hardiness, the cultural tips and general gardening information in these books are right on the money. Anyone interested in creating a tropical or subtropical look in their temperate landscape is well advised to read Robert Riffle's *The Tropical Look: An Encyclopedia of Dramatic Landscape Plants* (1998), Richard R. Iverson's *The Exotic Garden: Designing with Tropical Plants in Almost Any Climate* (1999), and Susan A. Roth and Dennis Schrader's *Hot Plants for Cool Climates: Gardening with Tropical Plants in Temperate Zones* (2000) for tips on design, maintenance, and the characteristics of plant species. All of these books are profusely illustrated and well-written. J. I. Reynolds's *Subtropical Gardening in a Temperate Climate* (1997a) has interesting historical perspectives on subtropical gardening and is especially useful for gardeners in the Pacific Northwest, his target audience.

Societies

The adventurous temperate gardener interested in growing warm-climate plants is well advised to investigate the many international and regional organizations dedicated to these fascinating species. Although several of these societies are professionally oriented and publish peer-reviewed scientific journals, membership is open to any and all interested people. Nearly everyone is on the Internet these days, and one of the best things about going to the web sites listed below is the plethora of regularly updated links to other sites.

American Bamboo Society; http://www.americanbamboo.org This society promotes the use of bamboo in a variety of garden settings, and its web site has a wealth of information and links to get you started. If you are interested in temperate bamboos, this is the society for you. The web site also has links to sites where you can share information and data with other enthusiasts.

The International Palm Society; http://www.palms.org The International Palm Society publishes the quarterly journal *Palms,* which contains a vast amount of useful information for the palm enthusiast. This society also sponsors worldwide regional chapters for more localized interest. Their web site provides an amazing array of links dealing with virtually every topic of palm cultivation, and these links are updated regularly.

Pacific Northwest Palm and Exotic Plant Society; http://www.palms.org/pacific/ Like their counterparts in the southeastern United States, the Pacific Northwest Palm and Exotic Plant Society is a regional affiliate of the International Palm Society that focuses primarily on the Canadian and U.S. Pacific Northwest. However, membership is open to anyone interested in temperate-zone cultivation of exotic plants, and their excellent quarterly journal, *Hardy Palms International,* features articles and information from all temperate areas.

The Southeastern Palm and Exotic Plant Society; http://www.speps.net This group is dedicated to growing palms and other warm-climate plants in zones 7–9 outside of Florida. Recently, their coverage has expanded to enthusiasts living in zone 6 who are also experimental gardeners. They publish an excellent quarterly newsletter, *Rhapidophyllum,* and hold regular meetings at the homes of members. The SEPEPS publishes *The Palm Reader* on their web site—a must-read for anyone attempting to grow palms outside their accepted range. There are links to plant suppliers and to the home pages of many society members.

Other Internet Sources

There are so many good web sites these days that I almost hesitate to list any for fear of leaving good ones out. Still, let me list a few that are particularly interesting to me. Of course, be advised that web site addresses change all the time. My best advice is to bookmark sites you link to and then stay current with new sites that come online. Also, the major societies listed above do an excellent job of ensuring that their links are kept updated. When in doubt, these are the first places to check for web sites that may have moved and for any new web sites that you may want to visit.

Amazing Gardens; http://www.amazinggardens.com This is a must-see site for anyone in the south-central United States. There are several linked sites that have photographs and information on palms and other warm-climate plants in zone 6 and 7 parts of Arkansas, Oklahoma, and Texas.

The Hardiest Palms and Growing Hardy Palms; http://www.hardiestpalms.com and http://surf.to/hardypalms These are two good sites to get started on, in terms of information and useful links to other sites. Both authors do a good job on updates as well. You can find plant sources, zone maps, and all sorts of accurate and fun information about palms.

Hardy Palms in Rhode Island; http://users.ids.net/~joeb/ Like many dedi-cated amateur web sites, this one is great for seeing what people in the northeastern United States are doing. It contains lots of photographs and general information as well as links.

Hardy Palm and Subtropical Board; http://members3.boardhost.com/HardyPalm This message board is excellent for gardeners in the upper South and lower Midwest. The people who frequent this listing are among the most knowledgeable and love to help people solve problems. You will make lots of Internet friends here.

Plant Sources

The first place to look for sources of plants is within your own area. It is easy to find the plants I discuss in this book in zone 7, and many nurs-eries across the United States, Canada, and Europe in zone 6 and even zone 5 are beginning to carry them as well. I listed some of these sources in the Ohio area, for example, as I discussed the bamboos (chapter 8). Also, if you are will be traveling through traditional palm country, plan to stock up on plants. In the coastal Deep South, Florida, and California palms and hardy subtropical plants are readily available and much less expensive than elsewhere. Even in relatively cooler areas of the South you can find camellias, magnolias, and dozens of the plants discussed in this book at virtually any garden center. However, you are still apt to require national mail-order firms to satisfy your needs.

I can in no way cover all of the reputable national firms here, much less those in Canada, the United Kingdom, and other countries where these plants are grown and sold. Peruse the Internet, and you'll find literally hundreds of good sources for plants in virtually every part of the world. I list here only firms that I have dealt with personally and can recommend.

Amazing Gardens, 4636 NW 10th Street, Oklahoma City, Oklahoma 73127; http://www.amazinggardens.com This is a great place to get seeds and plants that have been proven successful in zones 7a and 6b, especially some of the cold-hardy palms described in this book. Amazing Gardens employs very knowledgeable people and sells tough plants.

The Bamboo Garden, 1507 SE Alder Street, Portland, Oregon 97214; http://www.bamboogarden.com Ned Jaquith, noted authority on temperate bamboos, has a wonderful web site for browsing and purchasing, with more than two hundred species and varieties available for sale. Like many excellent sites, you can learn a great deal without ever leaving your seat.

Buckeye Bamboo Company, 10348 Wellington Road, Streetsboro, Ohio 44241; telephone (330) 274-3059 Rick Goohs does not have a web site, but he will send you a catalog if you telephone him or send him an e-mail (Arundinari@aol.com). Buckeye Bamboo Company has an extensive collection of bamboo and other warm-climate plants.

Burton's Bamboo Garden, 7352 Gheils-Carroll Road, Morrow, Ohio 45151; http://www.burtonsbamboogarden.com Jerry Burton has an extensive collection of temperate bamboo for sale and lots of information and tips. A walk around his property is like a trip to Japan.

Camellia Forest Nursery, 9701 Carrie Road, Chapel Hill, North Carolina 27516; http://www.camforest.com If you are looking for hardy camellias and many of the other difficult-to-find evergreens such as hardy orange, evergreen dogwoods, and hardy camphor trees, this is the place. Camellia Forest Nursery has a very knowledgeable staff, an excellent and well-written catalog and web site, and good-sized plants that will thrive when you plant them. The plant size issue is worth emphasizing—some mail-order plants are small, and gardeners trying to get small plants established and through their first winter at the limits of their cold-tolerance range have difficulty. The plants I have received from Camellia Forest Nursery are larger and robust.

Gerry's Jungle at the Neotropic Nursery, 730 Stallsworth Road, McDonough, Georgia 30252; http://www.neotropic.com This is not only a superb place to order virtually any kind and size of containerized cold-hardy palm, but Gerry McKiness is one of the most knowledgeable and nice people I have met in the business. Gerry is a hobbyist gone professional, and he really knows his palms. He also sells a variety of other warm-climate plants such as live oak and loquat. His catalog and web site are gold mines of information and insights, and I have found his guidance on cold-hardiness ratings for the palms he sells to be extremely accurate. Another thing I love about this man is that he doesn't patronize or otherwise put off those of us who are growing palms and other such plants in colder parts of the temperate zone. Although it is easy to order from Gerry's Jungle via mail order or the Internet, he welcomes personal visits and purchases, as long as you contact him ahead of time. An important note: As of this writing (May 2002), Gerry is in the process of moving his nursery to Florida. Consult his web site for updates and new contact information.

Glasshouse Works, P.O. Box 97, Church Street, Stewart, Ohio 45778; http://www.glasshouseworks.com Located in southeastern Ohio, Glasshouse Works has a great selection of unusual plants that are hardy in zones 6 and 5, including hardy figs, bananas, succulents, and numerous shrubs. They also have an extensive collection of books for sale.

Gossler Farms Nursery, 1200 Weaver Road, Springfield, Oregon 97478; telephone (541) 746-3922 This is another excellent source for hardy broadleaved evergreens and unusual plants. Gossler Farms provides good service and publishes a thorough catalog.

New England Bamboo Company, 5 Granite Street, Rockport, Massachusetts 01966; http://www.newengbamboo.com This company has a vast array of temperate bamboo species in many sizes, for mail order or direct pick-up. Their catalog and web site also have a great deal of practical information on how to grow bamboo that will make life a lot easier.

Plant Delights Nursery, 9241 Sauls Road, Raleigh, North Carolina 26703; http://www.plantdelights.com Located in zone 7b, this is the place to find many of the herbaceous and woody plants, including many of the cold-hardy palms and bananas, that you covet. Their catalog is informative, has wonderful pictures and insights into the plants they sell, and is humorously done. Because owner Tony Avent is an adventurous gardener of considerable note himself, Plant Delights is often the first national nursery to stock the hot new plant varieties. If you are interested in hostas, look no further: You can learn as much about this group from the Plant Delights catalog as from any book. Their web site is excellent, and ordering is easy and trouble-free. I have found their zone ratings to be accurate and, if anything, conservative. In my experience, this is one of the best mail-order firms on the planet. We've ordered thousands of dollars worth of plants and have *never* gotten a bad specimen.

Raintree Nursery, 391 Butts Road, Morton, Washington 98356; http://www.raintreenursery.com I've purchased hardy bananas, bamboo, and other plants from this nursery and have been pleased. They also sell eucalyptus, fruit trees of all kinds, and some hardy citrus. Raintree produces a very nice print catalog and web site.

YuccaDo Nursery, P.O. Box 907, Hempstead, Texas 77445; www.yuccado.com In 2002 I received my first YuccaDo catalog, which was both excellent and informative. I was pleased to note that they carried a number of plants that I'd been trying to locate for years, including *Sabal minor* 'Tamaulipas' and *Lagerstroemia fauriei* 'Townhouse'. Although this nursery specializes in arid and semi-arid plants, it has a good selection of all types of warm-climate plants. YuccaDo sells healthy, large (for mail-order) specimens, and I recommend them highly.

Bibliography

Adelman, A. H. 1995. Bamboo ground covers. *Fine Gardening* 45: 55–57.

Al-Hamdani, S., D. A. Francko, and A. Huerta. 1995. Effects of root chilling on CO_2 assimilation and stomatal conductance of wheat. *Plant Physiology (Life Science Advances)* 14: 21–25.

Arden, P. 1990. *The Hosta Book.* 2d ed. Portland, Ore.: Timber Press.

Avent, T. 2001. *2001 Spring Sales Catalog and Plant Owner's Manual.* Raleigh, N.C.: Plant Delights Nursery.

Balistrieri, C. A. 2001. Cheating your zone. *Fine Gardening* 77: 53–55.

Beaulieu, R. 1996. Managing microclimates. *Fine Gardening* 50: 39–41.

Bell, M. 2000. *The Gardener's Guide to Growing Temperate Bamboos.* Portland, Ore.: Timber Press.

Bunting, A. 2001. Evergreen hollies. *Fine Gardening* 79: 56–59.

Calloway, D. J. 1994. *The World of Magnolias.* Portland, Ore.: Timber Press.

Camellia Forest Nursery. 2000. *Fall 2000 Catalog.* Chapel Hill, N.C.: Camellia Forest Nursery.

Capon, B. 1990. *Botany for Gardeners: An Introduction and Guide.* Portland, Ore: Timber Press.

Conner, I. 2002. Bamboo that behaves. *Fine Gardening* 84: 70–73.

Dirr, M. A. 1997. *Dirr's Hardy Trees and Shrubs: An Illustrated Encyclopedia.* Portland, Ore.: Timber Press.

Dirr, M. A. 1998. *Manual of Woody Landscape Plants.* 5th ed. Champaign, Ill.: Stipes Publishing.

Dirr, M. A. 2002. *Dirr's Trees and Shrubs for Warm Climates: An Illustrated Encyclopedia.* Portland, Ore.: Timber Press.

Donov, K. 2000. Palms in Bulgaria. *Hardy Palm International* 41: 32–35.

Francko, D. A. 2000. Effect of microclimate on cultivation of cold-hardy palms in southwestern Ohio. *Palms* 44 (1): 37–46.

Francko, D. A., and S. Wilhoite. 2002. Cold-hardy palms in southwestern Ohio: Winter damage, mortality, and recovery. *Palms* 46 (1): 5–13.

Francko, D. A., and K. G. Wilson. 2001. The Miami University hardy palm project. *Rhapidophyllum* Winter: 12–15.

Gibbons, M., and T. W. Spanner. 1999. Palms in temperate climates. *Palms* 43 (2): 91–93.

Glasener, E. 2000. Luscious, long-blooming crape myrtles. *Fine Gardening* 71: 65–67

Heilenman, D. 1994. *Gardening in the Lower Midwest: A Practical Guide for the New Zones 5 and 6.* Bloomington, Ind.: Indiana University Press.

Hilley, B. 1999. Backyard reports. *Rhapidophyllum* 7 (2): 14–15.

Iverson, R. R. 1999. *The Exotic Garden: Designing with Tropical Plants in Almost Any Climate.* Newtown, Conn.: Taunton Press.

Jaquith, N. 2001. Flowering bamboo presents a challenge. Available via http://www.bamboogarden.com/when%20bamboo%20flower.htm

Jaquith, N., and R. Haubrich. 1996. When bamboo flowers. *American Bamboo Society Newsletter* 17 (1): 4–7.

Lawson-Hall, T., and B. Rothera. 1995. *Hydrangeas: A Gardener's Guide.* Portland, Ore.: Timber Press.

McClendon, T. 2000. Using palms effectively in the landscape. *Rhapidophyllum* 7 (3): 11–14.

McKiness, G. 2000. *Gerry's Jungle 2000 Sales Catalog.* McDonough, Ga.: Neotropic Nursery.

Meiser, J. 2001. Tropical attitudes in northern latitudes. *Palms* 45 (3): 115–117.

Meredith, T. J. 2001. *Bamboo for Gardens.* Portland, Ore.: Timber Press.

Mikolajski, A. 1997. *Clematis.* New York: Anness Publishing.

Nagy, E., and D. Francko. 2002. Overwintering of temperate banana species under USDA zone 6 conditions. *Southeastern Biologist* 49 (2): 124.

National Climatic Data Center. 2001. Record low temperatures for each state, including reporting station, date, temperature, covering late 1800s through 2000. Available via http://lwf.ncdc.noaa.gov

Noblick, L. R. 1998. Predicting hardiness in palms. Available via http://www.bg-map.com/Noblick.html

Putz, F. E., and M. Pinard. 1999. Saw palmettos (*Serenoa repens*): The need for patience and water uptake by the stem. *Palms* 43 (1): 35–39.

Reynolds, J. I. 1997a. *Subtropical Gardening in a Temperate Climate.* Vancouver, B.C.: Hylea Press.

Reynolds, J. I. 1997b. A palm tree shivering in Surrey shrubbery: A history of subtropical gardening. *Principes* 41 (2): 74–83.

Riffle, R. L. 1998. *The Tropical Look: An Encyclopedia of Dramatic Landscape Plants.* Portland, Ore.: Timber Press.

Riffle, R. L., and P. Craft. 2003. *An Encyclopedia of Cultivated Palms*. Portland, Ore.: Timber Press.

Roth, S. A., and D. Schrader. 2000. *Hot Plants for Cool Climates: Gardening with Tropical Plants in Temperate Zones*. Boston, Mass.: Houghton Mifflin.

Shor, B. 2001. Notes on flowering intervals. *The Magazine of the American Bamboo Society* 22 (1): 22–24.

Southeastern Palm and Exotic Plant Society. 1994. *The Palm Reader: A Manual for Growing Palms Outdoors in the Southeast*. Available via http://www.ces.uga.edu/Agriculture/horticulture/Palmreader.html

Southeastern Palm and Exotic Plant Society. 2001. Zone maps for Georgia, North Carolina, and Tennessee. Available via http://www.speps.net

Southeastern Palm and Exotic Plant Society. 2002. Palm fact sheet. Available via http://www.speps.net/palmfactsheet/html

Southern Living Plant Zone Map. 2002. Available via http://www.southernliving.com/garden/zone.asp

Sunset Books. 1997. *Sunset National Garden Book*. Menlo Park, Calif.: Sunset Books.

Sunset Books. 2001. *Sunset Western Garden Book*. K. Norris, ed. Menlo Park, Calif.: Sunset Books.

Sunset Books. 2001. *Sunset Northeastern Garden Book*. A. Halpin, ed. Menlo Park, Calif.: Sunset Books.

Sunset Books. 2002. *Sunset Midwestern Landscaping Book*. C. Bergmann, ed. Menlo Park, Calif.: Sunset Books.

Taylor, J. 1996. *Weather in the Garden*. Portland, Ore.: Timber Press.

Taylor, W. 1999. Tennessee palm godfathers. Part II. *Rhapidophyllum* 6 (3): 14–15.

Taylor, W. 2000. Tennessee, the next palmetto state. *Rhapidophyllum* 7 (4): 8.

Thomashow, M. F. 1999. Plant cold acclimation: Freezing tolerance gene and regulatory mechanisms. *Annual Review of Plant Physiology and Plant Molecular Biology* 50: 571–599.

Tollefson, D. 1999. Pot planting: Revelations and achievements as the saga continues. *Rhapidophyllum* 6 (3): 8–11.

Turner, M. 2000a. Understanding and analyzing microclimates. Part I. *Rhapidophyllum* 7 (4): 8–11.

Turner, M. 2000b. Understanding and analyzing microclimates. Part II. *Rhapidophyllum* 8 (1): 6–7.

Walters, T. J. 1998. Minimum temperatures for some cold-hardy palms. Available via http//www.hardiestpalms.com

White, L. A. 2000. Concept plan pulls it all together. *Fine Gardening* 72: 62–66.

Index

Bold page numbers indicate black-and-white photographs within the text. Color plates are in a section following page 48.

Acorus gramineus, 62
Adam's needle, see *Yucca glauca*,
   Y. smalliana
agave, 246–247
Agave montana, 246
Agave parryi, 245–246; plate 79
Albizia julibrissin, 199–200; plate 55
   'E. H. Wilson', 200
aloe yucca, see *Yucca aloifolia*
American holly, see *Ilex opaca*
Araucaria araucana, 180; plate 42
Araucaria imbricata, see *Araucaria*
   araucana
Arundinaria gigantea, 214, 225;
   plate 63
Arundo donax, 60
Aspidistra elatior, 62, **63**
Aucuba japonica, 161–162; plates
   13, 31
   'Rozannie', 162
   'Variegata', 161
Australian pittosporum, see
   Pittosporum undulatum

bald cypress, see *Taxodium*
   distichum

bamboo
   clump, 216–218, 222–224
   running, 216–221, 224–231
Bambusa multiplex, 222–223;
   plate 3
   'Alphonse Karr', 223
bananas, temperate, 231–240
beaked blue yucca, see *Yucca*
   rostrata
bear grass, see *Yucca smalliana*
beautiful bamboo, see
   Phyllostachys decora
Bergenia cordifolia, 62
Bermuda sabal palm, see *Sabal*
   bermudana
bigleaf hydrangea, see *Hydrangea*
   macrophylla
big leaf magnolia, see *Magnolia*
   macrophylla
bird of paradise, see *Strelitzia*
   reginae
black bamboo, see *Phyllostachys*
   nigra
blue bamboo, see *Phyllostachys*
   nigra 'Henon'
'Blue Boy' holly, see *Ilex* ×*meserveae*

bluebush palmetto, see *Sabal minor*

blue fountain bamboo, see *Fargesia nitida* 'Nymphenburg'

'Blue Girl' holly, see *Ilex* ×*meserveae*

blue hesper palm, see *Brahea armata*

blue needle palm, see *Trithrinax campestris*

blue passionflower, see *Passiflora caerulea*

'Blue Prince' holly, see *Ilex* ×*meserveae*

'Blue Princess' holly, see *Ilex* ×*meserveae*

blue sotol, see *Dasylirion wheeleri*

bluestem palmetto, see *Sabal minor*

Bougainvillea, 206

Brahea armata, 143

Brazoria palm, see *Sabal* ×*texensis*

Buddleja davidii, 62–63

bull bay magnolia, see *Magnolia grandiflora*

Burford holly, see *Ilex cornuta* 'Burfordii'

Buriti palm, see *Trithrinax acanthocoma*

Butia capitata, 135, 137–140, **138**

Butia eriospatha, 138

Butia × *Jubea*, 137

Butia yatay, 137–138

butterfly bush, see *Buddleja davidii*

cabbage palm, see *Sabal palmetto*

cabbage palmetto, see *Sabal palmetto*

cacti, 240, 244–245

Caladium bicolor, 66

calamondin orange, 174

California fan palm, see *Washingtonia filifera*

Camellia japonica, 162–163
    'April Blush', 163
    'April Dawn', 163
    April Series, 163
    'Berenice Boddy', 163
    'Red Jade', 163

Camellia oleifera, 163–164

Camellia sasanqua, 164

Camellia sasanqua × *oleifera*, 164
    'Carolina Moonmist', 164
    'Mason Farm', 164
    'Survivor', 164
    'Winter's Beauty', 164
    'Winter's Charm', 164; plate 32
    'Winter's Star', 164

Camellia sinensis var. *sinensis*, 164

canebrake bamboo, see *Arundinaria gigantea*

Canna, 66
    'Pretoria', 66; plate 8

cape jasmine, see *Gardenia jasminoides*

Carolina cherrylaurel, see *Prunus caroliniana*

Carolina jessamine, see *Gelsemium sempervirens*

cast-iron plant, see *Aspidistra elatior*

castor bean, see *Ricinus communis*

Cercidiphyllum japonicum, 200; plate 56

Chamaedorea elegans, 104, 120

Chamaedorea microspandix, 121

Chamaedorea radicalis, 120–121; plate 17

Chamaerops excelsa, see *Trachycarpus fortunei*

Chamaerops humilis, 142–143 var. *cerifera*, 142

chameleon plant, see *Houttuynia cordata*

Chilean wine palm, see *Jubea chilensis*

Chinese cycad, see *Cycas panzhihuaensis*

Chinese evergreen dogwood, see *Cornus angustata*

Chinese fan palm, see *Livistona chinensis*

Chinese holly, see *Ilex cornuta*

Chinese windmill palm, see *Trachycarpus fortunei*

Chinese yellow banana, see *Musella lasiocarpa*

Christmas fern, see *Polystichum acrostichoides*

Christmas rose, see *Helleborus niger*

Chusan palm, see *Trachycarpus fortunei*

cider gum, see *Eucalyptus gunnii*

Cinnamomum camphora, 181

Cinnamomum checkiangensis, 181

citrange, see *Citrus* 'Morton', 'US-119'

Citrus ichangensis, 175

Citrus ichangensis × *reticulata*, 175–176

Citrus 'Morton', 176

Citrus 'Thomasville', 176

Citrus 'US-119', 176

Citrus 'Yuza', 175–176

Clematis, 63

Cleyera japonica, see *Ternstroemia gymnanthera*

Colocasia esculenta, 66, **67**

common fig, see *Ficus carica*

common passionflower, see *Passiflora caerulea*

companion plants, 59–67

Cornus angustata, 181

Cornus kousa, 181

crape myrtle, see *Lagerstroemia*

Cycas panzhihuaensis, 119–120

Cycas revoluta, 119–120

Cycas taitungensis, 119, **120**

Cyrtomium falcatum, 181

Dahoon holly, see *Ilex cassine*

Daphniphyllum macropodum, 181; plate 43

Dasylirion wheeleri, 246

David Bissett bamboo, see *Phyllostachys bissettii*

dawn redwood, see *Metasequoia glyptostroboides*

Drepanostachyum falcatum, 223
dwarf bamboo palm, see
   Chamaedoria radicalis
dwarf Burford holly, see *Ilex*
   cornuta 'Burfordii'
dwarf Orinoco banana, see *Musa*
   'Dwarf Orinoco'
dwarf palmetto, see *Sabal minor*
dwarf soapweed, see *Yucca glauca*
dwarf variegated bamboo, see
   Pleioblastus variegatus

eastern prickly pear cactus, see
   Opuntia humifusa
elephant's ear, see *Colocasia*
   esculenta
emperor sago, see *Cycas*
   taitungensis
empress tree, see *Paulownia*
   tomentosa
English holly, see *Ilex aquifolium*
English laurel, see *Prunus*
   laurocerasus
Erica carnea, 165
Eriobotrya japonica, 165–166
Eucalyptus gunnii, 166
Eucalyptus niphohila, 166
Eucalyptus neglecta, 166
European fan palm, see
   Chamaerops humilis
evergreen giant liriope, see *Liriope*
   gigantea, Ophiopogon jaburan

fancy-leaf caladium, see *Caladium*
   bicolor
Fargesia dracocephala, 223

Fargesia murielae, 223–224
   'Humbolt', 224
   'Mary', 224
   'Picturum', 224
   'Simba', 224
Fargesia nitida, 224
   'Ems River', 224; plate 62
   'Nymphenburg', 224
Fatsia japonica, 166–167
Ficus carica, 200–201
   'Brown Turkey', 201
   'Celeste', 201
   'Desert King', 201
fishpole bamboo, see *Phyllostachys*
   aurea
Florida anise tree, see *Illicium*
   floridanum
Florida coontie palm, see *Zamia*
   pumila
Fortune's holly fern, see
   Cyrtomium falcatum
Fortune's palm, see *Trachycarpus*
   fortunei
Foster's hybrid hollies, see *Ilex*
   ×*attenuata*
fountain bamboo, see *Fargesia*
   nitida
Franklinia alatamaha, 168, 201
Franklin tree, see *Franklinia*
   alatamaha
Fraser photinia, see *Photinia*
   ×*fraseri*

gardenia, see *Gardenia jasminoides*
Gardenia jasminoides, 167
   'August Moon', 167

'Chuck Hayes', 167
'Kleim's Hardy', 167; plate 33
Gelsemium sempervirens, 167–168
giant reed, see *Arundo donax*
giant timber bamboo, see
    Phyllostachys bambusoides
gold dust plant, see *Aucuba*
    japonica
golden bamboo, see *Phyllostachys*
    aurea
Gordonia lasianthus, 168
Gunnera tinctoria, 63–64

Hakonechloa macra, 60
hardy camphor tree, see
    Cinnamomum checkiangensis
hardy century plant, see *Agave*
    parryi
hardy citrus, 174–176
hardy dragon bamboo, see
    Fargesia dracocephala
hardy orange, see *Poncircus*
    trifoliata
hardy sugar cane, see *Saccharum*
    arundinaceum
heartleaf bergenia, see *Bergenia*
    cordifolia
heavenly bamboo, see *Nandina*
    domestica
hedge bamboo, see *Bambusa*
    multiplex
hellebore, 64
Helleborus niger, 64
Helleborus orientalis, 64
Hesperaloe parviflora, 246
hibiscus, hardy hybrid, 64; plate 6

Hibiscus moscheutos, 64
Himalayan windmill palm, see
    Trachycarpus takil
holly, see *Ilex*
Hosta, 65; plate 3
Houttuynia cordata, 65; plate 7
Hydrangea macrophylla, 202–204;
    plate 57
Hydrangea quercifolia, 202–204,
    203
    'Snowflake', 204
    'Snow Queen', 204

Ilex aquifolium, 159
Ilex ×attenuata, 156–158
    'East Palatka', 158
    'Foster's #2', **157**; plate 26
    'Foster's #4', 157
Ilex cassine, 156
Ilex cornuta, 158–159
    'Burfordii', 158; plate 27
    'Carissa', 158–159; plate 29
    'Dwarf Burford', 158; plate 28
    'Needlepoint', 159
Ilex ×meserveae, 156
    'Blue Boy', 156
    'Blue Girl', 156
    'Blue Prince', 156
    'Blue Princess', 156
Ilex 'Nellie R. Stevens', **159**, 160
Ilex opaca, 156, 160–161; plate 30
Ilex vomitoria, 161
    'Nana', 161
    'Pride of Houston', 161
Illicium floridanum, 168
Illicium lanceolatum, 168

ichangdarin, see *Citrus* 'Yuza'

Ichang lemon, see *Citrus ichangensis*

India hawthorn, see *Rhaphiolepis indica*

Indocalamus tessellatus, 225; plate 64

Japanese camellia, see *Camellia japonica*

Japanese cleyera, see *Ternstroemia gymnanthera*

Japanese fatsia, see *Fatsia japonica*

Japanese fiber banana, see *Musa basjoo*

Japanese forest grass, see *Hakonechloa macra*

Japanese holly fern, see *Cyrtomium falcatum*

Japanese maple, 184

Japanese palm bamboo, see *Semiarundinaria fastuosa*

Japanese skimmia, see *Skimmia japonica*

Japanese spurge, see *Pachysandra terminalis*

Japanese ternstroemia, see *Ternstroemia gymnanthera*

Japanese timber bamboo, see *Phyllostachys bambusoides*

Japanese tobira, see *Pittosporum tobira*

Japanese umbrella pine, see *Sciadopitys verticillata*

Jasminum nudiflorum, 168–169; plates 34, 35

jelly palm, see *Butia capitata*

Jubea chilensis, 143

katsuratree, see *Cercidiphyllum japonica*

Kumaon palm, see *Trachycarpus takil*

kumquat, 176

Lagerstroemia fauriei, 185, 198
  'Fantasy', 198
  'Kiowa', 198
  'Townhouse', 198, 253

Lagerstroemia indica, 184–193
  'Carolina Beauty', 192; plate 46
  'Centennial', 192
  'Centennial Spirit', 192
  Chica Series, 197
  'Dallas Red', 192–193; plate 47
  Dixie Series, 197
  'Glendora White', 193
  'Peppermint Lace', 193
  Petite Series, 197
  Pixie Series, 197
  'Prairie Lace', 193
  'Twilight', 193
  'Victor', 193; plate 48

Lagerstroemia indica × *fauriei*
  'Acoma', 194; plate 49
  'Hopi', 187, 194–195; plates 50, 51
  'Muskogee', 195; plate 52
  'Natchez', 195–196; plate 53
  'Pecos', 196
  'Tonto', 196–197; plate 54

'Zuni', 197

lance-leaf anise tree, see *Illicium lanceolatum*

Lantana montevidensis, 66–67

laurel oak, see *Quercus hemisphaerica*

leatherleaf mahonia, see *Mahonia bealei*

lenten rose, see *Helleborus orientalis*

lily turf, see *Liriope muscari*

Liriope gigantea, see *Ophiopogon jaburan*

Liriope muscari, 60

live oak, see *Quercus virginiana*

Livistona chinensis, 113, 119; plates 15, 16

loblolly bay, see *Gordonia lasianthus*

loquat, see *Eriobotrya japonica*

Louisiana dwarf palmetto, see *Sabal* 'Louisiana'

Magnolia 'Freeman', 155

Magnolia grandiflora, 145–153; plate 22

'Bracken's Brown Beauty', **149**; plate 23

'Claudia Wannamaker', 151

'D. D. Blanchard', 150

'Edith Bogue', 148–149

'Little Gem', 150, **151**; plate 24

'Opal Haws', 153

'Poconos', 152

'Saint George', 153

'Samuel Sommer', 150

'Tulsa', **152**

'24 Below', 152

'Victoria', 150

'Winchester', see 'Tulsa'

Magnolia grandiflora × *virginiana*, 155

Magnolia 'Griffin', 155

Magnolia macrophylla, 204; plate 58

Magnolia 'Maryland', 155

Magnolia virginiana, **153**, 153–155; plate 25

var. *australis* 'Henry Hicks', 154, **155**

var. *australis* 'Satellite', 154

'Northern Lights', 155

Mahonia aquifolium, 169, **170**

Mahonia bealei, 169; plate 36

maiden grass, see *Miscanthus sinensis*

Mandarin orange, 174, 175

maypop, see *Passiflora incarnata*

Mazari palm, see *Nannorrhops ritchiana*

Mediterranean fan palm, see *Chamaerops humilis*

Mediterranean heather, see *Erica carnea*

Merserve hybrid hollies, see *Ilex* ×*meserveae*

mescal, see *Agave parryi*

Metasequoia glyptostroboides, 204–205

Mexican fan palm, see *Washingtonia robusta*

mimosa, see *Albizzia julibrissin*

miniature Chusan palm, see
  Trachycarpus wagnerianus
Miscanthus sinensis, 60, **61**
mondo grass, see *Ophiopogon
  japonicus*
monkey puzzle tree, see *Araucaria
  araucana*
Moroccan silver palm, see
  Chamaerops humilis var.
  cerifera
Musa acuminata 'Rajapuri', 235,
  236–237; plate 69
Musa basjoo, 86–87, 236, 237–238;
  plates 70, 71
Musa 'Dwarf Orinoco', 239;
  plate 9
Musa hookeri, see *Musa sikkimensis*
Musa paradisiaca 'Mysore', 239;
  plate 5
Musa sikkimensis, **115**, 238
Musa velutina, 239
Musella lasiocarpa, 231, 239–240;
  plate 72
Myrica cerifera, 205–206
  'Hiwassee', 206
Myrica pensylvanica, **205**, 206

Nandina domestica, 170–172, **171**;
  plate 37
  'Fire Power', 172
  'Harbour Dwarf', 172
Nannorrhops ritchiana, 117
Narihira bamboo, see
  Semiarundinaria fastuosa
needle palm, see *Rhapidophyllum
  hystrix*

Nepal windmill palm, see
  Trachycarpus martianus
Nerium oleander, 172
  'Hardy Double Yellow', 172;
  plate 38
  'Hardy Pink', 172
northern bayberry, see *Myrica
  pensylvanica*

oakleaf hydrangea, see *Hydrangea
  quercifolia*
oleander, see *Nerium oleander*
omeo gum, see *Eucalyptus neglecta*
Ophiopogon jaburan, 60, **61**
Ophiopogon japonicus, 60; plate 4
Opuntia, 244–245; plate 78
Opuntia humifusa, 245; plate 77
Oregon grapeholly, see *Mahonia
  aquifolium*

Pachysandra terminalis, 65
palma pita, see *Yucca treculeana*
palms
  arborescent, 103, 121–143
  clump, 103, 104–121
Passiflora caerulea, 206–207
Passiflora incarnata, 206–207
Paulownia tomentosa, 207, **208**;
  plate 59
Phoenix roebelinii, 120
Photinia ×*fraseri*, 172–173; plate 39
Phyllostachys aurea, 226
Phyllostachys aureosulcata,
  226–227; plate 65
  f. *aureocaulis*, 227
  f. *spectabilis*, 227

Phyllostachys bambusoides, 217, 227
  'Castillon', 217
Phyllostachys bissettii, 227
Phyllostachys decora, 227
Phyllostachys dulcis, 228
Phyllostachys nigra, 228; plate 13
  'Henon', 228
Phyllostachys nuda, **229**
Phyllostachys rubromarginata, 229;
    plate 66
pindo palm, see *Butia capitata*
Pittosporum tobira, 173–174;
    plate 40
Pittosporum undulatum, 173–174
Pleioblastus variegatus, 230;
    plate 67
Polystichum acrostichoides, 65
Poncirus trifoliata, **175**
  'Flying Dragon', 175
pond baldcypress, see *Taxodium
    ascendens*
prickly pear cactus, see *Opuntia*
Prunus caroliniana, 176–178, **177**
Prunus laurocerasus, 176–178
  'Otto Luyken', 177
  'Schipkaensis', 177
pygmy date palm, see *Phoenix
    roebelinii*

queen palm, 30, 31
Quercus hemisphaerica, 208–211
Quercus laurifolia, see *Quercus
    hemisphaerica*
Quercus nigra, 179, 208–211
Quercus phellos, 208–211, **210**;
    plate 60

Quercus virginiana, **178**, 178–180
  var. *fusiformis*, 179

red tip, see *Photinia* ×*fraseri*
red yucca, see *Hesperaloe parviflora*
Rhaphiolepis indica, 180; plate 41
Rhapidophyllum hystrix, 27, **89**,
    104–110, 113; plates 11, 12
Ricinus communis, 67; plate 9
rose mallow, see *Hibiscus
    moscheutos*
royal paulownia, see *Paulownia
    tomentosa*

Sabal bermudana, 113, 137
Sabal 'Birmingham', 137; plate 19
Sabal 'Louisiana', 110–114; plates
    10, 13
Sabal mexicana, 136
Sabal minor, 84, 102, 110–114,
    111, 132, 136; plates 4, 12,
    14
  'McCurtain County', 112
  'Tamaulipas', 111, 113, 253
sabal palm, see *Sabal palmetto*
Sabal palmetto, 104, 113, 132–136,
    133, 137; plate 18
Sabal texana, see *Sabal mexicana*
Sabal ×*texensis*, 136
Saccharum arundinaceum, 62;
    plate 5
sago palm, see *Cycas revoluta*
Sasa senanensis, 230
saw palmetto, see *Serenoa repens*
Schipka laurel, see *Prunus
    laurocerasus* 'Schipkaensis'

Schott's yucca, see *Yucca schottii*
Sciadopitys verticillata, 181–182;
    plate 44
Semiarundinaria fastuosa, 230
Semiarundinaria okuboi, 231;
    plate 68
Serenoa repens, 110, 113–117, **115**
    green form, 116
    silver form, 116
shrub verbena, see *Lantana*
    montevidensis
Sikkim banana, see *Musa*
    sikkimensis
silk tree, see *Albizzia julibrissin*
Skimmia japonica, 182
small-leaf tea, see *Camellia*
    sinensis
snow gum, see *Eucalyptus*
    niphohila
southern live oak, see *Quercus*
    virginiana
southern magnolia, see *Magnolia*
    grandiflora
Spanish dagger, see *Yucca aloifolia*,
    Y. gloriosa, *Y. treculeana*
Strelitzia reginae, 59
sweet bay magnolia, see *Magnolia*
    virginiana
sweet flag, see *Acorus gramineus*
sweet shoot bamboo, see
    Phyllostachys dulcis

Taxodium ascendens, 212
Taxodium distichum, 211–212;
    plate 61

tea-oil camellia, see *Camellia*
    oleifera
Ternstroemia gymnanthera, 182;
    plate 45
Texas palmetto, see *Sabal texana*
Thompson's yucca, see *Yucca*
    thompsoniana
Trachycarpus fortunei, 21, 113,
    121–130, **123**, **126**, **130**,
    142; plate 10
    'British Columbia', 127
    'Bulgaria', 127
    'Charlotte', 127
    'Greensboro', 127
    'Taylor Form', 127
Trachycarpus latisectus, 131
Trachycarpus martianus, 131
Trachycarpus takil, 113, 131–132
Trachycarpus wagnerianus, 131
trifoliate orange, see *Poncirus*
    trifoliata
Trithrinax acanthocoma, 143
Trithrinax campestris, 117–118

umbrella bamboo, see *Fargesia*
    murielae

velvet pink banana, see *Musa*
    velutina

Washingtonia ×*filibusta*, 142
Washingtonia filifera, 140–142;
    plate 20
Washingtonia robusta, 140–142;
    plate 21

water oak, see *Quercus nigra*

waxmyrtle, see *Myrica cerifera*

willow oak, see *Quercus phellos*

Windemere palm, see
    Trachycarpus latisectus

windmill palm, see *Trachycarpus*

winter jasmine, see *Jasminum*
    nudiflorum

woolly butia, see *Butia eriospatha*

Yaupon holly, see *Ilex vomitoria*

yellow-groove bamboo, see
    Phyllostachys aureosulcata

Yucca aloifolia, 241
    'Marginata', 241
    'Tricolor', 241

Yucca glauca, 242, plate 73

Yucca gloriosa, 242; plate 74

Yucca recurvifolia, 244

Yucca rigida, 244

Yucca rostrata, 242–243; plate 75

Yucca schottii, 243

Yucca smalliana, 243
    'Bright Edge', 243; plate 76
    'Color Guard', 243

Yucca thompsoniana, 243–244

Yucca torreyi, 244

Yucca treculeana, 244

Zamia pumila, 117–118